Praise for *Overdressed*

"Elizabeth Cline is the Michael Pollan of fashion. . . . Hysterical levels of sartorial consumption are terrible for the environment, for workers, and even, ironically, for the way we look."
— Michelle Goldberg, senior writer, *Newsweek/The Daily Beast*

"How did Americans end up with closets crammed with flimsy, ridiculously cheap garments? Elizabeth Cline travels the world to trace the rise of fast fashion and its cost in human misery, environmental damage, and common sense." — Katha Pollitt, columnist, *The Nation*

"*Overdressed* is eye-opening and definitely turns retailing on its head. Cline's insightful book reveals the serious problems facing our industry today. The tremendous values and advantages of domestic production are often ignored in favor of a price point that makes clothing disposable." — Erica Wolf, executive director, Save the Garment Center

"The good news for shoppers, notes Brooklyn journalist Cline in her engagingly pointed, earnestly researched study, is that cheap knockoffs of designer clothing can be found in discount stores almost instantly. The bad news is that "fast fashion" has killed America's garment industry and wreaked havoc on wages and the environment." — *Publishers Weekly*

"The wastefulness encouraged by buying cheap and chasing the trends is obvious, but the hidden costs are even more galling. Cline contends that 'disposable clothing' is damaging the environment, the economy, and even our souls, and she presents a dense and sobering skein of data to support her thesis. When Cline writes that 'people crave connections to their stuff,' she prompts another question: Have we somehow become disconnected from ourselves? If we don't stop to consider this, we may end up perpetually rushing out to buy more 'stuff.' never realizing what we truly need, ge̶̶̶̶̶̶̶̶̶̶ l to waste."
nes

"One of the most appealing aspects of *Overdressed*, Ms. Cline's fretful and mildly censorious account of the effects of cheap clothing on America's culture, is that she fully admits to her own weaknesses for low-cost clothing. But then, *Overdressed* isn't a book about policy. Rather, it's an attempt to analyze what exactly makes a designer dress cost so much and an H&M dress cost so little—and what the end result of our attitudes toward clothing will be. She believes it leads not only to workers being unfairly treated abroad, but also diminishes our sense of craftsmanship and care about what we wear."

—*The Wall Street Journal*

"*Overdressed* is the fashion world's answer to consumer-activist bestsellers like Michael Pollan's *The Omnivore's Dilemma*. Self-deprecating about her own lack of style—she has a thing for fleece-lined sweatshirts—Cline writes with the zeal of a reformed shopaholic. Like Pollan, she traveled extensively to follow her subject along the whole chain of production. She visited factories in China, gaining entry by masquerading as a clothier; learned sewing from Dominican seamstresses; and went shopping in Manhattan with 'haulers,' fast-fashion addicts who brag about their purchases in YouTube videos. Haulers are Cline's antiheroes."

—*Businessweek*

"Elizabeth L. Cline goes for the jugular straight away in this exploration of the consumer love affair with cheap clothing. Cline's target is, therefore, broader than her book's title implies. She is almost as skeptical of designer fashion as she is of affordable fashion—criticizing the whole industry for its over-accelerated trends and lack of individuality. The most urgent, engaging chapters are about the factories in which cheap clothes are made in places such as Bangladesh, China and, yes, Los Angeles."

—*Los Angeles Times*

PORTFOLIO / PENGUIN

OVERDRESSED

Elizabeth Cline is a Brooklyn-based writer and editor. She holds a degree in political philosophy from Syracuse University and has written for *The Nation*, *New York*, *The New Republic*, *The Daily Beast*, *GOOD*, *The Village Voice*, and *The Etsy Blog*, among others.

Visit overdressedthebook.com.

Overdressed

The Shockingly High Cost of Cheap Fashion

ELIZABETH L. CLINE

PORTFOLIO / PENGUIN

PORTFOLIO / PENGUIN
Published by the Penguin Group
Penguin Group (USA), 375 Hudson Street,
New York, New York 10014, USA

USA | Canada | UK | Ireland | Australia | New Zealand | India | South Africa | China
Penguin Books Ltd, Registered Offices: 80 Strand, London WC2R 0RL, England
For more information about the Penguin Group visit penguin.com

First published in the United States of America by Portfolio/Penguin,
a member of Penguin Group (USA), 2012
This paperback edition with a new afterword published 2013

THE LIBRARY OF CONGRESS HAS CATALOGED THE HARDCOVER EDITION AS FOLLOWS:
Cline, Elizabeth L.
Overdressed : the shockingly high cost of cheap fashion / Elizabeth L. Cline.
p. cm.
Includes bibliographical references and index.
ISBN 978-1-59184-461-7 (hc.)
ISBN 978-1-59184-654-3 (pbk.)
1. Clothing trade—Social aspects. 2. Clothing trade—Environmental aspects. 3. Fashion—Social
aspects. 4. Fashion—Environmental aspects. 5. Shopping—Environmental aspects. 6. Consumption
(Economics)—Social aspects. I. Title.
HD9940.A2C54 2012
338.4'774692—dc23
2012004525

Printed in the United States of America
5 7 9 10 8 6

Set in Stempel Garamond LT Std
Designed by Alissa Amell

To my grandmothers, Routh and Margarett

Contents

Introduction Seven Pairs of $7 Shoes 1

1 "I Have Enough Clothing to Open a Store" 11

2 How America Lost Its Shirts 36

3 High and Low Fashion Make Friends 62

4 Fast Fashion 95

5 The Afterlife of Cheap Clothes 119

6 Sewing Is a Good Job, a Great Job 138

7 China and the End of Cheap Fashion 161

8 Make, Alter, and Mend 187

9 The Future of Fashion 207

Afterword to the Paperback Edition 223

Acknowledgments 235

Notes 237

Index 251

Overdressed

Introduction

Seven Pairs of $7 Shoes

In the summer of 2009, I found myself standing in front of a rack of shoes at Kmart in Astor Place in Manhattan. This particular location is inside the former Wanamaker's, one of those regal midcentury department stores that sold fine goods of all varieties, including high-end fashions direct from Paris. Today, Wanamaker's is gone. Today, Wanamaker's is a Kmart.

The rack itself stretched above my head, and the shoes—canvas slip-ons made of nothing more than a rubber sole glued to a sheath of cotton—hung like fruit from a tree. In my mind, these shoes might as well have grown there on that metal tree. They had no origin, no story. They just magically appeared. And to my unbelievable fortune, they had been marked down from $15 to $7 a pair. My synapses started firing, my pulse quickened, and before my thinking brain could kick in, I was standing at the cash register with my bright red plastic shopping basket brimming with seven pairs of plucked slip-ons. I cleared the store out of my size.

My arms ached as I carried my haul in two parachute-size bags to the subway. Those shoes looked like a cross-section of the earth's crust within a few weeks—the thin rubber soles cleaving and separating from the flimsy canvas tops. Before I could wear them all out, I got tired of them and they were no longer in style, so I've got two pairs left taking up space in my closet.

The average price of clothing has plummeted in recent decades. And cheap clothes have undergone a total image overhaul, where they no longer imply some inherent compromise in style and quality. Budget fashion is seen as chic, practical, and democratic, and our conversations are dotted with wow-inducing stories of clothing "steals." At a birthday party last year, a college friend thrust a ruffled, canary yellow pleather bag in my face. "Five dollars!" she boasted. Another friend messaged me online recently to exclaim: "I just paid ten dollars for a fifty-dollar dress! Thirty dollars for a sixty-dollar one!" Fashion magazines, tabloids, and morning talk shows now routinely run stories on how to land fashion deals.

For a decade, I *only* bought cheap fashion, and the vast majority of it was from four budget-fashion retailers that seemed to appear out of nowhere about ten years ago: H&M, Old Navy, Forever 21, and Target. I owned a few items from off-price stores Ross and T.J. Maxx, as well as from the buzzy basics chain UNIQLO and the Spanish retailer Zara. H&M, Zara, and Forever 21, known as fast-fashion retailers, are experts in constantly stocking new trends and know exactly how to hook consumers into shopping more regularly. But these aren't the only retailers moving away from the seasonal cycle of selling and toward luring shoppers into their stores on a continual basis.

There are some regional differences in the cheap fashion available to people. Maybe your preference is for discounted name brands at the outlet mall or T.J. Maxx or regional fast-fashion stores like Cato, Charlotte Russe, Rainbow, and rue21. Maybe you shop at department store chains like Kohl's, or at pure discounters like Walmart or even Dollar General. But these retailers are all running on the same high-volume, low-priced fashion formula that has squeezed the life out of the rest of the industry, forcing independent department stores to consolidate, middle-market manufacturers to shutter, and independent retailers either to go high-end or go home. Budget fashion has now remade the entire apparel industry in its image. And it has profoundly changed the way we think about clothing.

We tell ourselves we can't afford higher prices. We're in a recession. Health-care costs are out of control. And have you seen gas prices? But many consumers are just hooked on a cheap fashion treadmill—we've grown accustomed to paying less and getting more. My sister will pay $400 a month to drive a nice car, but don't try to charge her or me more than $40 for a dress. I've seen guys in my local coffee shop working on $1,800 Apple laptops and wearing $10 Walmart shoes. Americans spend more money on eating out in restaurants every year than they do on clothes. It's not that we can't pay more money for fashion; we just don't see any reason to.

As any economist will tell you, cheaper prices stimulate consumption, and the current low rate of fashion has spurred a shopping free-for-all, where we are buying and hoarding roughly 20 billion garments *per year* as a nation.[1] We're running out of oil and water. Icebergs are melting. We've permanently altered our climate. China, where most of our clothes are now produced and where the population is gaining a taste for fashion, is in environmental crisis and on track to gobble up more fiber and fashion-related resources than we do. The problems created by the fashion industry in the West are quickly being matched and multiplied in other parts of the world. Buying so much clothing, and treating it as if it is disposable, is putting a huge added weight on the environment and is simply unsustainable.

Here's an incredible fact—I paid less than $30 per item on average for each piece of clothing in my closet. Most of my shoes cost less than $15 a pop. That clothes can be had for so little money is historically unprecedented. Clothes have almost always been expensive, hard to come by, and highly valued; they have been used as alternate currency in many societies. Well into the twentieth century, clothes were pricey and precious enough that they were mended and cared for and reimagined countless times, and most people had a few outfits that they wore until they wore them out. How things have changed. We've gone from making good use of the clothes we own to buying things we'll never or barely wear. We are caught in a cycle of consumption and waste that is unsettling at best and unsatisfying at its core.

When I started writing this book, I got all my clothes out of storage and piled them in my living room. I cleaned out the closets in my bedroom and hall, pulled out the bins from underneath my bed, and dragged three trash bags and two oversize plastic containers up from my basement. I made a mountain of it, and then sorted it all, making lists of the brand name or designer, the country of origin, the fabric, and, if I could remember, the year I bought it and how much I paid. It took me almost a week to go through it all. My roommate helped me bring the clothes up from the basement and commented dryly, "I find owning so much clothing overwhelming." It was such a simple statement, but she said it as if I'd done it on purpose. Each of those purchases seemed almost inconsequential in the moment, a deal here, a deal there. But just as a few extra calories here and there result in an expanding waistline, my closet and my life were consumed with cheap fashion.

Here's the damage: I owned 61 tops, 60 T-shirts, 34 tank tops, 21 skirts, 24 dresses, 20 pairs of shoes, 20 sweaters, 18 belts, 15 cardigans and hooded sweatshirts, 14 pairs of shorts, 14 jackets, 13 pairs of jeans, 12 bras, 11 pairs of tights, five blazers, four long-sleeved shirts, three pairs of workout pants, two pairs of dress pants, two pairs of pajama pants, and one vest. Socks and underwear notwithstanding, I owned

354 pieces of clothing. Americans buy an average of 64 items of clothing a year, a little more than one piece of clothing per week.[2] It might not seem that extreme, until you see it all piled up in your living room. My wardrobe is what the average American produces in a little more than five years, precisely the amount of time I lived in my apartment. My 300-piece clothing collection made me almost exactly an average American consumer.

Another humbling fact about my wardrobe: I owned more clothing than I did *anything else* and probably knew the least about it of anything I bought. I checked the labels on my eggs, but not on my T-shirts. I didn't know the significance of fibers like polyester, nylon, or elastane, of which so much of our clothing is now made. I knew nothing about garment construction, nor could I recognize quality. And I was certainly no fashionista with an encyclopedic knowledge of the designers where all these trends were coming from, although I sometimes wish I looked as put together as those girls. I have friends who were surprised I was writing a book about clothes. "You?" they'd say, scanning my outfit for some missing sign of great style. But one need not have the sharpest fashion acumen or know a single thing about clothes to accumulate massive amounts of them.

I always hear in the news that we're going to shop our way out of the current recession. It's hard to believe when you consider what's happened to the domestic garment and textile industries, once an important segment of America's manufacturing base. The United States now makes 2 percent of the clothing its consumers purchase, down from about 50 percent in 1990. We have chosen low-priced clothes made in other countries, and the loss of our garment trade has contributed to a decline in domestic wages, the loss of the middle class, and the problem of unemployment, especially for those at the bottom of the economic ladder. It would now take tremendous investment and training to get our garment industry back in shape to compete with other countries, particularly China, where a staggering 41 percent of our clothes are now made. I traveled to factories there and was astonished at not only the sophistication of the factories but by how the American consumer lifestyle is spreading there as well.

Many books about fashion begin with an argument for why we should take fashion seriously. I'm going to take a different approach and say that fashion largely deserves its bad reputation. It's now a powerful, trillion-dollar global industry that has too much influence over our pocketbooks, self-image, and storage spaces. It behaves with embarrassingly little regard for the environment or human rights. It changes the rules of what we're supposed to wear constantly, and we seem to have lost our sense of self along with changing trends. We oscillate through countless colors, prints, and silhouettes each year. Most of the time we are buying the same basic item of clothing—tank tops and sweaters in the latest color, simple blouses with some added embellishment, jeans in a new fit—over and over again, just tweaked slightly with the season's latest must-have feature.

Designer or brand-name clothing has become a proxy for quality and style. We travel 60 miles round-trip on average and pay the attendant gas and tolls to get deep discounts on brand names at outlet malls.[3] Some of us stand in line at Target, H&M, or Macy's—overnight in some cases—to be the first to grab shoddy facsimiles of clothing by luxury fashion designers such as Versace and Missoni. We've completely lost our gauge of whether or not the material garment we're buying is worth our money. The fashion industry has largely been split into ultra high-end and low-end clothing; consumers have been divided into warring camps of deal hunters and prestige shoppers, with little in between. And with "good" clothes now outrageously priced, shopping cheap is more of a nonchoice than we recognize.

Fashion should be flexible and responsive. Instead, global chains are trying to take the risk out of fashion by selling the same carefully orchestrated trends, which are repeated on the racks of virtually every retailer, making our store-bought looks feel homogenous and generic. A half century of competition based on low price has also forced the fashion industry to cut corners on quality, construction, and detail, leaving most of us wearing painfully simple designs that are crudely slapped together. Just two decades ago, the garment industry wasn't nearly so consolidated. Our choices weren't nearly so narrow and controlled and focused on the bottom line.

Fashion is obsolescence. Fashion *is* change. The fact that thousands of affordable variations on the hot, new look can go from design concept to a store rack in a matter of weeks or a couple of months is, if nothing else, a modern marvel—as designs have to be drawn and transmitted, fabric has to be ordered, and the garment has to be sewn by human beings before being shipped around the world to retail outlets. It could be argued that the fashion industry has mastered what it is designed to do—sell affordable versions of new styles.

Because of low prices, chasing trends is now a mass activity, accessible to anyone with a few bucks to spare. Trends are quickly exhausted, giving the fashion industry yet another opportunity to come up with something else for us to buy and wear. This cycle is speeding up, and more trends than ever now exist at any given moment. In Brooklyn I watch them spread before my eyes. One week I spotted a handful of people wearing sailor-inspired blue-and-white striped shirts. Two months later virtually one in every five people seemed to be wearing the fad. In recent months I've seen the same thing happen with high-waisted shorts, jumpsuits, midriffs, combat boots, and floral-print dresses.

Fashion is publicly expressed. Everyone can see who's out of step.

And keeping up with the latest styles now demands that we shop constantly. T.J. Maxx recently ran a commercial featuring a fashion student named Lindsay, who chirps, "I never wear the same thing twice." T.J. Maxx would have us believe cash-strapped college students should buy a new piece of clothing *for every single day of the year*. Similarly, many celebrities are never photographed wearing the same thing twice. Today's trendsetters seem to be the people who change their outfits the most often.

Here we are, having arrived in a so-called fashion democracy, where everyone can afford to be stylish and follow trends. How does it feel? I started writing this book because chasing trends with one eye on the price tag didn't get me any closer to liking my clothes. My wardrobe ultimately left me feeling slavish and passive. I definitely wasn't any closer to being well dressed. I was devoting too much time and way too much space in my house to a habit I knew shamefully little about. Why would someone who knows nothing about clothes own so much clothing?

People crave connections to their stuff, and I was missing that connection. Our fashion choices *do* have social outcomes and meanings, and I had to dig deep to find them. Supply chains are spread all over the world, few of them in the United States. We're completely in the dark about what fashion has cost the environment and American jobs. These costs certainly aren't on price tags, which are dropping lower and lower every year. I went in search of the rest of the story of our clothes.

Most of our lives are spent in clothing. It's a basic need, but more than that, clothing and style are a huge and integral part of our everyday lives. Clothes are an essential part of the economy and easily the second largest consumer sector, behind food.[4] Dressing sharp, dressing up, and caring about what we wear existed long before the fashion industry, and these values can exist outside it as well. Surely our closets can be defined by something other than price-gouging designers, discounted brand names, or the cheap trends that follow them both.

Clothes could have more meaning and longevity if we think less about owning the latest or cheapest thing and develop more of a relationship with the things we wear. Building a wardrobe over time, saving up and investing in well-made pieces, obsessing over the perfect hem, luxuriating in fabrics, and patching and altering our clothes are old-fashioned habits. But they're also deeply satisfying antidotes to the empty uniformity of cheapness. If more of us picked up the lost art of sewing or reconnected with the seamstresses and tailors in our communities, we could all be our own fashion designers and constantly reinvent, personalize, and perfect the things we own.

I haven't just looked to the past for clues on how to dress going forward. Thanks to advancing technology, more progressive garment production models, and the development of environmentally friendly textiles, it's now entirely possible to design clothing responsibly without sacrificing style. In fact, I found that ethical designers, without the pressures of having to satisfy corporate shareholders or consistently dazzle with high-profile runway shows, are not only working with some of the most interesting and amazing-feeling fabrics on the market, they are also some of the most innovative designers in the industry right now.

In the days after I lugged those bags of slip-ons down Second Avenue, shamefaced, I started thinking about how I shopped growing up. It was the midnineties, not so long ago, and the global clothing giants had taken their hold. But clothes were still expensive enough that buying them was a semiannual treat. In middle school my friends and I would share new clothes to make our wardrobes seem bigger. But more often I shopped in thrift stores because they were affordable and full of unexpected treasures. I loved scrounging through the Salvation Army looking for T-shirts that I could cut up or pants that I could shred and restyle. My mom also had a sewing machine when I was little, and a few times I remember going to a seamstress to have our clothes taken in or let out.

I didn't have much to go on, other than these little hints that clothing used to foster relationships and stay with us throughout life. We were once stewards of the clothes we owned. The promise of a different way of doing things, of actually liking and understanding clothes, and the embarrassment of lugging those bags of shoes on the subway were enough to set me on a journey. In the process, I found out how exactly cheap fashion took over, met the people who have escaped the tyranny of trends, and ultimately curbed my own dead-end cravings for low-cost clothes.

1

"I Have Enough Clothing to Open a Store"

"I know it's not something that I need. I have other blazers that look like it. But if it was $45, I would take it right now." Lee Councell was standing in a crowded H&M store in New York City's SoHo, holding court with her pretty, clothes-crazy girlfriends over whether or not she should buy *yet another* blazer. "I love blazers. I put them over dresses. I wear them in the summertime and wintertime, all year long," she went on, toeing the line between excusing a habit and reciting the many practical uses of the boyish jacket. The 23-year-old, doe-eyed, curvy Kim Kardashian look-alike owns 16 or 17 blazers, she told me, and at least one in the same ivory color as the H&M prospect. But there is no such thing as too many blazers or too much clothing in Councell's world. "My friends say I have enough clothing to open a store."

Councell had, hawklike, caught sight of the blazer on a mannequin the moment we walked through the door. "I feel if I spot it, it's meant to be," she told me earnestly. After a five-minute hunt, the full stock was located hanging near the window. It was priced much higher than the average garment found in H&M, the Swedish cheap-fashion chain that now has more than 200 stores in the United States. Councell rubbed the fabric between two fingers. "It's good quality," she said confidently. I checked the tag: 100 percent polyester. There was no lining. The buttons were plastic. But I knew what she meant. When buying trendy, cheap fashion, quality has a relative meaning. It is best measured in washes. As in, how many times can you wash it before the fabric pills or stains, the garment loses its shape, a button falls off, or a seam busts open. "How thick is it? How durable is it?" Councell clarified. "There are certain things that I buy that after one wash, they'll fall apart." In the age of cheap fashion, you just need it to last until the next trend comes along.

Councell had already made up her mind about the H&M blazer. She wasn't buying it. The deciding factor, the thing standing between this girl and that blazer, was the price. It was $59.95. "I won't spend over $45 on a blazer," she said firmly, leaving it hanging on the rack. In fact, she's paid far less than that. Among the blazers in Councell's collection, which can be viewed in her YouTube video "♥ My Blazer Collection ♥," is a Miley Cyrus Max Azria blazer from Walmart, just $8. She also shows off a corset-style black blazer and a fitted gray number, both from Forever 21, where the price for blazers rarely inches past the $30 mark. Another item in her collection, a pinstriped blazer, is from Kmart, which at the time of this writing has five blazers for less than $15 apiece on its Web site.

For the last 15 years, Americans have enjoyed an almost unabated and unprecedented free fall in the average price of clothing. We pay less for clothes, when measured as a share of our income, than ever in history. In 2009 American consumers dedicated less than 3 percent of their annual household budget to apparel.[1] We've really never had it so good. The price of just about everything in America has climbed in recent decades—housing, gas, education, health care, and movie tickets. Meanwhile, clothing is a better bargain than ever.

The deals are everywhere. You've got your stories, I've got mine. Here is the outfit I'm wearing as I write this, from head to toe: The hooded sweatshirt from Forever 21 cost $12.95. I got the faux leather jacket from T.J. Maxx for $28. The red Urban Outfitters T-shirt was $16, the black knit miniskirt was $5 at H&M, and the tights were $14 at American Apparel. Nothing more than $30; definitely nothing more than $45. My personal spending limit for a blazer? I don't have a firm price ceiling like Councell, but the $8 one from Walmart is more my speed.

Councell's shopping ethos is simple: "If it's under $20, honestly I don't mind spending it," she told me. It sounds familiar. It sounds like my shopping ethos and probably yours. The retailers with the lowest prices are the ones that have earned Americans' loyalty. As the nation has experienced unemployment, stagnant wages, and mounting debt, we have become far more cautious shoppers. Does this mean we're looking for high-quality investment pieces? Not at all. We just shifted more of our shopping to chains such as Walmart, fast-fashion stores such as H&M, and outlet malls.

According to Standard & Poor's Industry Surveys, the three retailers with the highest brand value (meaning a store's ability to generate excitement and demand) during the recession are H&M, Walmart, and Zara. Forever 21 would probably be on the list if it weren't a privately held company. Councell's favorite store is the homegrown Forever 21, which, according to *Women's Wear Daily*, has an average price of $15.34 as of September 2010. Her second favorite store is H&M, but she also frequents Macy's during sales, which happen constantly, and discounters such as Walmart and Kmart, whose cut-rate clothing deals have gotten much more fashionable in recent years.

After a day of shopping, Councell keeps her new duds tucked away in their shopping bags. "I know if I put stuff away, I won't put it all in the video," she explained. Councell is a YouTube personality who videotapes DIY consumer reviews of her newest fashion buys and posts them online. These videos are known as "shopping hauls," and they were one of the fastest-growing categories on the Internet video site in 2010.[2] The most successful haulers can rack up a million hits per video and are courted by fashion brands and retailers, who offer them free products in hopes their stuff will appear in a haul.

All of Councell's shopping buddies do hauls—that's how they met—but Councell, a glitzy and business-savvy young woman with all the makings of an It girl, is the most successful of the bunch. Her YouTube channel, mamichula8153, has 50,000 thousand subscribers as of January 2013 and is openly sponsored by dozens of beauty and fashion brands, including a trendy Miami label that gives Councell free clothes in exchange for coverage in her haul videos.

Haulers are not without their critics. "A lot of people look at haul videos as a way of showing off how much money you spent," Councell told me. If she posts more than one haul a month, the comments section of her channel fills up with hateful feedback. But these critics have certainly missed the point. A sweater in one of Councell's most viewed "Rainy Outfit of the Day" videos is from H&M and costs a *mere $10*, less than a meal at most restaurants. Even the most cash-strapped high schooler could afford such a wardrobe addition.

In the video, Councell stands up to get the full length of her sweater on camera: "It is a white sweater and it has a big bow right across here," she says, making a circular motion across her chest. Haulers are not exactly experts. A lot of them don't even try on the clothes, opting instead to hold them up, while ticking off the obvious—color, noting whether the item is a dress or a shirt or pair of earrings, and pointing out whatever detail drove them to buy it. The popularity and appeal of hauls lies elsewhere: in their familiarity. They are a way to share and strategize about what has become a popular pastime in our culture: buying a lot of clothes for very little money.

———————

It's hard to imagine the haul phenomenon without cheap fashion. It's virtually impossible to imagine shopping hauls existing 20 years ago, before YouTube and stores like Forever 21. But let's just pretend for a moment that they did and that they were made, as they are now, by young women of regular means. They'd come out seasonally and feature just a handful of new purchases at a time, as that's how the average American shopped. Hauls would be pretty boring.

Low price and, of course, the Internet are the scaffolding upon which hauls are built. Forever 21, which often has $2 denim sales on its Web site, is featured in more haul videos than any other retailer—more than 100,000. H&M, Walmart, and Target, where prices on fashion almost dip to pocket change, also crop up in tens of thousands of hauls. Councell and her friends agree that the affordability of the products in hauls is key to their appeal. "It's not like we're shopping at, like, Guess? or higher-end stores like Dolce & Gabbana, spending seven hundred dollars on one item," says Councell's friend Melyssa, a pint-size, assertive 23-year-old. "One of the things that I feel like people like about these haul videos is that we do sort of show cheap clothes. A lot of these girls that are watching these videos don't have very much money." Haulers, perhaps unsurprisingly, are typically teens and women under age 25, a demographic that has always shopped more than others and on a tighter budget.

After abandoning the blazer at H&M, upon my suggestion the haulers and I scoured deals up the block at Forever 21. I felt drab in last year's boots and a black hooded sweatshirt next to the petite pack of trend-hunters. "Are you a secret shopaholic?" Councell asked me playfully as we fought the crowds on Broadway. I am. That must be the worst kind, I thought, shopping all the time and still not having good style to show for it.

Inside, Forever 21's colorful, girly clothes popped against shimmering black-and-white tile floors. Cheap jewelry was scattered across tables; floral-print dresses and nautical-striped tops, two of the season's biggest trends, were hanging drunkenly off their hangers. It looked like the aftermath of a fire sale, but the bright yellow placards advertised even better prices than H&M. When Forever 21 marks their clothes down, you can get a fully formed party dress for $3.

Before I knew it, I had wandered away from Councell and her friends and lost myself in the cutesy bargains. Forever 21 is known for youthful, glitzy clothes that are the antithesis of classic fashion—selling items like six-inch leopard-print platform stilettos or a clutch festooned from top to bottom in bows and gemstones. They're dazzlingly tempting products that draw you in, but they often aren't very wearable, especially if you're not a teenager. I spotted a sheer black sleeveless dress with a 1980s brushstroke print. It was lined with a stretchy black material, which gave the dress a nice weight. The price was a reasonable $19.80, giving it acceptable "quality" when measured in number of washes. Even if it didn't last past a single spin cycle, this dress was a steal.

Another of Councell's friends, Caryn, was in line in front of me buying a navy and white canvas tote for $20.80. "It'll be good for the beach," she reasoned. I showed her the dress. "Yeah, it's cute," she said approvingly. The conversation was idle chitchat. We weren't really looking for a good reason to buy. *If it's under $20, honestly I don't mind spending it.*

Jonathan Van Meter wrote a prescient article for *Vogue* called "Fast Fashion: Americans Want Clothing That Is Quick and Easy" that hinted at this scene. The year was 1990, and Van Meter was talking, oddly enough, about Gap, the clothing chain better associated with snoozeworthy basics these days. Twenty years ago Gap was the hottest brand the country had ever known.

In Van Meter's view, Americans had "previously been denied well-designed, well-made classic clothing for reasons either financial or geographic." This was a distortion of history at best. Compared to popular high-end designers of the day, like Ralph Lauren and Calvin Klein, who also traded in classic clothing, Gap *was* quite affordable. In 1990 dollars, a plain black Gap T-shirt was $11, their jeans were around $30, and a mock turtleneck was $23. But Gap also convinced us, through advertising in upscale magazines, celebrity branding, and ubiquitous placement of its stores, that buying generic T-shirts and jeans was our key to the fashion castle. Gap marketed Americans away from fashion.

Gap was also one of the earliest retailers to get us hooked on shopping frequently. Ilse Metchek, the president of the California Fashion Association, worked for a manufacturer that produced for Gap in the '90s, and recalls, "Every month, Gap had a new color that went into the window. It may have been the same sweater, but every month the color theme changed." Suddenly a dizzying number of people across the country were splurging on the latest Gap turtleneck in a new hue. "Gap was ordering hundreds of thousands of units," recalls Metcheck. "And it was constant. They moved not only jeans but new sweaters and jackets and new knickknacks and jewelries to support their basic commodity, jeans."

Gap started out as a Levi's and vinyl store in the late 1960s. But there were too many players in the denim game, and by the '80s Gap had to rethink its corporate vision. They hired a new CEO, Mickey Drexler, who has since moved on to J.Crew, and an in-house design team, which was an uncommon strategy for a retailer at the time. Lisa Schultz, then head of women's design, said: "There are designers that have their own stores; well, we're retailers that have our own designers."

Being a designer for one of the huge clothing brands like Gap was not necessarily a dream job, as the task involved churning out very ordinary clothes that did not evolve much from year to year. A former designer for Tommy Hilfiger described working for the clothier to me this way: "I was a sketch artist for generic crap." But these so-called private label retailers or chain boutiques are enormously profitable. By cutting out the middleman, they can offer a product similar to their competitors' at the same or better price. As *Adweek* noted in 1986, store-brand apparel equals "fat margins, guarantees a retailer exclusivity on an item and helps build a unique identity for a store."[3] Stores that design and market their own brands are common in the retail industry today, from Walmart, Old Navy, and H&M to Abercrombie & Fitch and Express.

By 1991, just a few short years after its transformation into a brand, Gap was doing almost $2 billion a year in sales.[4] By the end of the decade, they were famously opening at least one store a *day*—570 stores in 1999 alone.[5] Other retailers quickly followed in Gap's footsteps, and the country was blanketed with bland clothing giants such as Eddie Bauer, American Eagle Outfitters, and The Limited.

Gap grew to almost have a monopoly effect on the way Americans dressed. I have the high school photos of kids in unflattering, tapered Gap denim to prove it. Charity shops are filled to the brim with Gap T-shirts and sweaters now deemed uncool, the remnants of the casual-prep zeitgeist. Gap's control over the fashion winds had much to do with the sheer number of stores it owned, as well as its advertising budget. The company could run a commercial commanding, "Everybody in cords," and almost every American had a local Gap where they could do the company's bidding. "Americans could," noted Van Meter, "now simply pop into the neighborhood Gap as they do the 7-Eleven and, without much commitment or thought, come out looking as if they were *born* with good taste."

The Gap revolution culminated in Sharon Stone's making fashion history by wearing a charcoal Gap turtleneck with a Valentino skirt to the Oscars in 1996. The media celebrated Stone's outfit as groundbreaking for pairing relatively low-cost clothing with designer duds. Metchek agrees that it was a historic moment, signaling that low-priced fashion was being accepted across all class lines. "That statement rippled throughout the fashion community," says Metchek. "We didn't know it, but that was the beginning of fast fashion becoming acceptable."

Two decades later the full vision of Jonathan Van Meter's "Fast Fashion" has been realized. But it's not Gap leading the charge. Gap is still one of the world's largest retailers, with more than $14 billion in revenue in 2010 and with more than 1,000 stores in the United States alone, but it is being deftly knocked off its perch by vastly cheaper and faster ways of selling fashion.

Today, celebrities combine their designer wardrobes with much cheaper fashion from stores such as H&M and Target. When Target opened in West Hollywood in Los Angeles, actors Charlie Sheen and Hilary Duff were in attendance. Sandra Bernhard emceed. Michelle Obama has been photographed several times in a Merona print dress from Target, a brand usually priced below $40, and she created quite the buzz when she wore a $34.95 H&M number on the *Today* show. In *Michelle Obama: First Lady of Fashion and Style, More* magazine editor Susan Swimmer applauds Mrs. Obama for being "savvy enough

to embrace the new, stylish discounters such as H&M." She claims
that Michelle Obama's style is "uniquely American" because her
clothing choices are both "aspirational and accessible at the same
time."

———

American style for hundreds of years was handmade or made by
a dressmaker or tailor. Pilgrim women wore handwoven dresses,
waistcoats, and two layers of petticoats dyed from plant and animal
sources.[6] When factory-made, store-bought clothes became increasingly available around 1900, clothing became less rarified, but buying
the latest fashions was out of the reach of most Americans. According
to *100 Years of U.S. Consumer Spending*, a 2006 study by the U.S.
Department of Labor, the average American family in 1901 had an
income of $750 and spent over 14 percent of their earnings, or $108 a
year, on clothing.

Jan Whitaker, consumer historian and author of *Service and Style:
How the American Department Store Fashioned the Middle Class*, has
collated prices of clothing from this early period. She found that wom-
en's ready-to-wear suits were the most popular store-bought clothing
item at the turn of the twentieth century, as they were somewhat affordable, at $15 apiece (about $380 today). In 1906 a budget ready-to-
wear suit bought in the bargain basement of a department store would
have still been around $8, or $200 today.

After World War I, the price of dresses came down, with a midprice
frock selling for about $16.95, or less than $200 today.[7] Annual expenditures on clothes were $238, close to 17 percent of annual income.
The drop in price paired with fattening paychecks allowed more
women of modest means to keep up with fashion trends, but in a very
limited way. By one account, in 1929 the average middle-class man

owned six work outfits and the average middle-class woman nine.[8] My grandmother, born in 1931 in the midst of the Great Depression, remembers having no more than five dresses as a child, at least a few of them made from cloth flour sacks. The boys in the neighborhood wore the same pair of patched-up overalls for a week straight. "You didn't throw away anything, *ever*," she says. "It was unheard of."

It wasn't until after World War II that the average American really started to gain wealth, and our expenditures on clothing and everything else grew alongside our paychecks. Middle-class life and consumer society had arrived. By 1950 incomes had spiked to $4,237 a year, with $437 of it spent on clothes. Americans started to accumulate far more clothing than they could regularly wear and to follow fashion in ways that hinted at what was to come. But there were still limits to how much clothing was owned, including physical space: The average home in 1950 was 983 square feet, compared to the 2004 average of 2,349 square feet.[9] My mother, born in 1949, guesses she owned about three pairs of shoes and one outfit for each day of the week as a teenager, plus a few church dresses and extra styles for special events.

Depending on how a person shopped in midcentury America— either buying the hottest fashions from the downtown department store, last year's clearance items in the bargain basements, or from mail-order catalogs such as Sears or Montgomery Ward—that $437 could either go a little or a long way. And husbands and kids had to be clothed on that budget as well. For the bargain shopper, there was the 1955 Sears catalog, which had large economies of scale that kept prices down. Sears sold a 100 percent nylon ballerina gown for $15.98 ($130 today). A rayon blouse was $1.89 and their advertised "lowest priced" dresses were $2.49, which is in line with today's budget fashion chains' $20-or-less mantra, when adjusted for inflation. Middle-market juniors' brand Jonathan Logan was lauded for their "junior"-size prices by *Time* magazine in 1963, but Logan didn't sell many dresses for less than $14.98, which is more than $100 today.

According to annual statistics compiled by the U.S. Bureau of Economic Analysis, individual spending on clothing is now just less than $1,100 a year. Families spend about $1,700 a year on clothes.[10] Though it's the smallest percentage of our incomes ever dedicated to clothes, our money has never gone further. Nowadays, an annual budget of $1,700 can buy a staggering surfeit of clothing, including 485 "Fab Scoopneck" tops from Forever 21 or 340 pairs of ladies' sandals from Family Dollar or 163 pairs of seersucker capri pants from Goody's or 56 pairs of Mossimo "Skinny Utility" cargo pants from Target or 47 pairs of glitter platform wedges from Charlotte Russe or 11 men's Dockers suits from JCPenney or nine Lauren by Ralph Lauren sequin evening gowns from Macy's.

Clothing has seen such dramatic declines in price that it's gone from a budget-buster and a defining purchase for the American household to discretionary spending. I often see women on the subway in New York holding a yellow Forever 21 bag alongside a small Duane Reade drugstore purchase and a bite to eat. A recent *Vogue* article asked, in light of a $4.95 dress for sale at H&M: "Do I Get a Coffee? A Snack? Or Something to Wear?" Indeed, clothes are so cheap today that buying them often feels inconsequential.

In the early days of the American garment industry, clothing manufacturing was run by independent, almost mom-and-pop businesses that sold through numerous independent department stores. Jan Whitaker says, "For decades in the U.S., the fashion industry wasn't characterized by any big producers. Really anybody could start up anytime and there were just many small garment makers." As late as 1990, there were 65 publicly traded apparel companies, compared with more than 12,000 independent clothing manufacturers.[11] In the 1960s juniors' brands Jonathan Logan and Bobbie Brooks were among the first fashion companies to go public. Brand marketing began to influence what consumers were buying in a much greater way. Whitaker says these "bigger corporate entities" started taking out full-page ads in such national magazines as *Mademoiselle* and *Seventeen*, which had an enormous influence on what was considered fashionable in post–World War II America. "Who's winning consumer loyalty now?" asks Whitaker, who says that previously consumers were mostly exposed to department store advertising, which amounted to sketches of new styles in the local newspaper. Whitaker says, "If consumers are going into the stores and asking for Bobbie Brooks, then Bobbie Brooks has the upper hand now."

Still, Jonathan Logan and Bobbie Brooks had little in common with today's clothing behemoths. In 1962 Logan achieved $80 million in sales and Brooks $44 million; the American garment trade *as a whole* was a $12 billion enterprise.[12] Many of the retailers we shop at today are singularly larger than the entire 1962 American clothing industry. The Gap, Inc.'s sales for 2010, which includes sales for Old Navy and Banana Republic, were more than $14 billion; H&M achieved almost $4 billion in that same year.

The quantity of clothing being produced today is also in another stratosphere compared to the post–World War II industry. A huge order used to be maybe 2,000 or 3,000 pieces of a single style. It's now business as usual for mass-market clothiers such as Gap, Tommy Hilfiger, Nike, Walmart, and Target to order tens of thousands, hundreds of thousands, or even millions of one style. One Chinese factory manager I spoke to, who's been in the garment industry for 34 years, was producing for the youth retailer Aéropostale around the time they began selling private-label goods in the late 1990s. He recalls, "At first they were buying maybe two thousand pieces per style. And now they do easily one hundred thousand pieces or half a million pieces." A former designer for Tommy Hilfiger likewise saw the brand place orders in the hundreds of thousands. She says, "They'd make tank tops with the little flag and sell it in every store around the world."

Today, discounters Walmart and Target probably place the largest orders. As designer Isaac Mizrahi boasted of his partnership with Target in 2003: "I have always wanted to make a pointed sneaker, and I couldn't get it done when I was on my own. No one will make you a mold for under fifty thousand pairs. But when I signed up with Target, it was like the first thing I did. It's really setting me free!" [13] Mizrahi was a famed runway designer in the 1990s whose high-end career burned bright for a decade and then fizzled out. While many people applaud the quirky and charismatic designer's resurrection in the mass market, I can only imagine where those 50,000 pairs of shoes or those two million pairs of Gap jeans or Tommy Hilfiger tank tops are now. Collecting dust in closets? Rejected by the African secondhand market, which doesn't have a taste for pointed sneakers? Releasing toxins in a landfill?

Retailers have one of two ways of earning their profits: They can either sell fewer goods with a higher markup or more goods with a lower markup. A local boutique or an independent department store is a good example of the markup strategy, and Walmart is the ultimate example of the volume strategy. Most consumers view the volume strategy pioneered by discounters and chain stores as the fair one. Penn State marketing professor Lisa Bolton explains that consumers don't want to pay a higher markup simply because a store has less inventory. "Consumers don't see that alone as a good reason to pay a higher price," she says. This preference pushes everyone in the industry toward selling higher and higher volumes of stuff.

―――――――――

R ecently my father and I went shopping at a Belk department store in Georgia. I hadn't been in a department store in a decade. I found it achingly unchanged: the racetrack walkways, the difficult-to-find cashier posts absent cashiers, generic ties and watches stacked on tables in the middle of the aisles. To be fair, this particular location hadn't been renovated in decades, but as I picked through the racks, I couldn't help but think that I could get better prices and better styles at a place like H&M. The prices—$60 for a basic shirt—and the incoherent jumble of fashion were jarring to my cheap-fashion-adjusted brain.

But this wasn't a department store, at least not as my father knew them growing up. From the 1900s into the post–World War II years, department stores at their best were retail institutions that anchored civic and economic life and balanced the relationship between seller, manufacturer, and consumer. They often took up entire city blocks in prime downtown areas throughout America. When my dad was a kid, he and my grandparents would get dressed up on Saturdays and either drive half an hour north to Loveman's in Chattanooga, Tennessee, or, for a special treat, two hours down to Rich's in Atlanta, Georgia. My father has strong memories of the thrill of riding the escalators and oohing and aahing over all of the fashionable wares at Rich's, which had five stories and a basement. He says, "It was like Dorothy going to Oz. The opulence was mind-boggling."

Every city in the country had its famous department store, sometimes a number of them. Cincinnati was known for Shillito's; Dallas for Neiman Marcus; Philadelphia for Strawbridge & Clothier and

Wanamaker's; New York for Bloomingdale's, Macy's, and Best & Co.; and Chicago for its beloved Marshall Field's. The stores catered to a local or regional clientele, and according to Metchek, even department store chains that had locations around the country hired individual buyers for each store, meaning a big manufacturer like Jonathon Logan had to adjust its styles to cater to each.

After World War II, Americans started to move out of the city centers and malls became the meeting places. Suburbanization hurt the department stores because of the loss of downtown shopping. And a new kind of department store—the chain—also started to gain power and lure in consumers. JCPenney had locations in all 50 states by 1966. Then the discount chains, such as Bradlees, Mammoth Mart, Zayre, JCPenney-owned The Treasury, and E.J. Korvette started to take market share. Department store historian Michael Lisicky told me via e-mail: "E.J. Korvette put the fear of God in America's department stores. Korvette's offered free parking, late hours, and discounts on hard goods. No department store could come close to matching them."

Moving into the 1970s, a shopping-mall boom swept the country and Americans started to embrace the discounters and the deals offered by the mall chain stores. My father remembers buying cheap imported polyester shirts for the first time from Kmart during this period. Shopping cheaper wasn't just a change in culture or preference, says Lisicky; it had to do with changing demographics. "The middle class was disappearing and stores needed to find their customers," he told me. "The suburban housewife of the nineteen seventies embraced the prices that discount stores offered, especially as they tried to spend as little as possible on clothing for growing children. Eventually these middle-class American families were either afforded the opportunity to trade up or were forced to trade lower." Two decades later, the discounter Walmart would be selling more apparel than all department stores combined. [14]

By 1983, *The New York Times* was reporting "A Revolution in American Shopping," noting the explosive growth of off-price apparel stores such as Plums, Mandy's, and T.J. Maxx, where brand-name clothing could be had for a fraction of the department stores' prices. Where unique products could once be found at department stores, similar or identical goods were now available at a variety of retailers. The story cited a number of strategies that traditional retailers—who depended on higher markups—could deploy to compete with these cheaper upstarts, including improved service, private label goods, and price cuts of their own. [15]

Throughout the decade, department stores engaged in vicious markdown wars and continuous sales. They had turned solely to the final strategy mentioned in the *Times* piece: "Keep offering sales and cut-priced goods to stimulate store traffic and help increase sales of their regularly priced goods." But this only trained consumers to wait for the sales and to distrust the department stores' prices. Metchek says department stores for a very long time have operated on the principle that the only way to bring in consumers is with a sale. She says, "This is why the only clothing ads you see in newspapers now are sales ads. You rarely see style ads." Department stores now put merchandise on sale and clear it out every ten weeks. And big brands that sell through department stores now agree to pay "markdown dollars," which are essentially the difference between what was expected to sell at full price versus what actually sold at full price. As of 2005, consumers were buying more than 60 percent of department store merchandise on sale. [16]

Department stores rapidly consolidated to compete for market share and cheapening consumers—the average shopper was both get-

ting poorer *and* expecting better and better deals. Many of them, like
Philadelphia's Lit Brothers and Snellenburg's, tried to expand into
suburban malls, but failed and closed anyway. According to Teri
Agins, author of *The End of Fashion: How Marketing Changed the
Clothing Business Forever*, department stores started "streamlining
their operations and filling their floors with more affordable merchandise." Their new modus operandi was to be cheaper and more predict-
able. Better-made clothing was put out to pasture, and higher-end
lines were cut in many stores. In the 1990s, Federated department
stores yanked Ellen Tracy, Anne Klein, and DKNY—bridge lines all
priced to be more affordable than top-tier designer goods—from all
but 45 of their 420 stores. And Isaac Mizrahi's bridge line called
"Isaac" that sold $150 dresses and $300 jackets was forced out of business in 1997. [17]

Department stores are generic chain stores now, bearing little re-
semblance to their progenitors. In 2005, Federated Department Stores,
which owned Bloomingdale's, Macy's, and several other department
store chains, brokered an $11 billion deal to purchase their rival, May
Department Stores. The deal created the nation's second-largest department store company, behind the Sears Holdings Corporation
(which owns Kmart as of 2004), with more than 950 department stores
under the same umbrella and selling similar assortments of national
brands in all of them.

After the deal went through, Federated changed its company name
to Macy's, Inc., and started converting its purchases into Macy's
stores. The name change affected a dizzying number of long-standing
regional department-store chains, including The Bon Marché, Bur-
dines, Famous-Barr, Foley's, Hecht's, Goldsmith's, Kaufmann's,
Lazarus, L.S. Ayres, Meier & Frank, Rich's, and Robinsons-May.
Other purchases were simply shuttered. The most publicized closings

were the famed Kaufmann's flagship in downtown Pittsburgh and Chicago's Marshall Field's. A group of Chicagoans have been boycotting the store and hold a protest every year on the anniversary of the name change. Filene's, the 1912 department store in Boston's Downtown Crossing, was closed because there was already another Macy's across the street. Consolidation gave the remaining department stores better buying power, but it made them less competitive: They are too rigid and their product assortment is as generic as the big-box retailers they compete against. Their prices are often higher than the local Gap and much higher than H&M or Forever 21.

With the same or similar products available at so many different stores, we presume whoever offers us the lowest price is being fair and we give them our business. Lisa Bolton says consumers not only interpret a lower price as the fair price, but we believe that if one retailer can produce a perfectly attractive $30 dress or shirt, then another retailer charging $100 for an only slightly better version must be cheating us, even if the store might have smaller inventory, better service, and more overhead costs. This constant cost comparison puts pressure on all retailers to lower prices however possible.

Department store mergers and the growth of branded clothing chains such as Gap cost countless clothing manufacturers their distribution as well. They went out of business, opened their own retail stores and became importers, or got bought up themselves. Bobbie Brooks is no longer a manufacturer but a Dollar General brand that includes a line of jeans and tops that retails for less than $16. Jonathan Logan is gone.

The places we shop for clothes today are the survivors of three decades of ruthless competition based largely on price. The fashion industry has become so homogenous that most consumers now shop at retailers who give us the lowest price first and do so year-round. We shop loyally at discounters like Walmart, Kohl's, and Target. We look to outlet malls for marked-down brand names. We rove through off-price stores such as Burlington Coat Factory, Century 21, Loehmann's, Marshall's, Ross, Tuesday Morning, and the übersuccessful T.J. Maxx, where we can find overproduced clothing from department stores for 20 percent to 80 percent off the retail price. Even high-end and designer clothes can now be had for cut-rate prices on Web sites such as Bluefly, Gilt Groupe, and Ideeli.

I trace my own induction into budget fashion to Old Navy. Gap's budget chain debuted in 1994, my freshman year of high school. As a *New York Times* article noted that year, Old Navy was shaking up the retail world by offering an alternative to the "bland, poorly made and often carelessly displayed offerings" of cheap clothing of the time. But Old Navy was also a discounter now selling to the former department store consumer, while offering them shoddier products with "more synthetics and less detailed stitching and workmanship than traditional Gap merchandise."[18]

Old Navy leveraged its parent company's in-house marketing muscle to help boost the image of its downgraded duds. Not long after the chain got on its feet, it was spending a staggering $20 to $30 million per year on advertising, and brought in fashion industry celebrities, including models Marcus Schenkenberg and Jerry Hall as well as former *Vogue* editor and tastemaker Carrie Donovan, for the inaugural campaigns.[19] They also stepped up the in-store experience of a discounter, shrink-wrapping T-shirts and sweatshirts and stacking them in fake freezer cases. The neon signs, grinning clusters of mannequins, and retro-infused signage ("Wholey moley! 40 percent off the whole store!") are still staples of the whimsical Old Navy shopping experience.

At the same time, Target was edging into the cheap fashion game and quickly established itself as an "upscale discounter" and a fashionable alternative to Kmart and Walmart. Target dedicates more of its floor space to clothing than its competitors and was using focus groups to help its buyers choose on-trend cheap fashion as early as 1991.[20] Target's success is widely cited as a reason for Kmart's bankruptcy filing in 2002 and for Walmart's identity crisis. Walmart took out an eight-page spread in the 2005 September issue of *Vogue* magazine in an attempt to rebrand itself as fashion-forward.

Target also used massive marketing budgets and those omnipresent bull's-eye ads with the bull terrier dog to convince the taste-conscious and a new generation of celebrities that cheap clothes, not to mention a big-box discount store, can be stylish and chic. As Rhonda Richford noted in a July 28, 2006, article for *Variety*, "Fashion snobs—and the occasional Nicole Kidman or Al Pacino—mingle in the aisles [of Target] with suburban moms." Target gained such a culty following that some communities actually petitioned to get a location built in their neighborhoods. Between 1991 and 2011, the company pulled off Gap-like growth, expanding to 1,763 stores in the United States.

Cheap fashion and off-price chains have come to occupy a significant part of the retail market. Their dominance, paired with the majority of department store clothing now being sold on sale, has fully reset our expectations about how much clothes should cost and what they are worth. This constant chipping away of the price of apparel has shifted the concept of what is "affordable," with once-reasonable prices now seeming expensive to us. My own deal hunting led to a certain point where I started to feel indignant if I saw a price tag on a top that was more than $30.

Retailers today are now forced to sell exactly the same product for less than they did 15 years ago. In 2008 *The New York Times* tracked the price deflation in fashion and found that the price of Liz & Co. capri pants had fallen by a third and a Lacoste polo shirt by almost a quarter. A pair of Levi's 501 jeans sells for $46 today, about $4 less than it was in the late 1990s, when adjusted for inflation. Of nine items that declined in price, the *Times* found that those that dropped the most were basics like underwear and T-shirts, by as much as 60 percent. [21]

When Dianna Baros, 31, started her cheap fashion blog, *The Budget Babe*, in 2007, it didn't surprise anyone who knew her. Growing up, Baros was always frugal when it came to fashion, hitting the clearance racks at department stores and scouring sales. Then, Baros, a writer at Oprah.com, became that girl around the office known as "the bargain hunter," who always managed to put together great outfits for a pittance. "My salary was on the low end, just like most writers and editors and producers," she says. "But I still wanted to look good, so I would shop at Forever 21 and Target."

Baros remembers vacating department stores for Forever 21 somewhere in the late 1990s. She says the retailer opened up a whole new world of possibilities. "You felt like a kid in a candy store," she recalls. "You could just walk right in and anything you liked you could just buy it. And I think that was really exciting for people who always felt like they were relegated to the sales rack. You could load up, and you felt like a princess."

Baros's story conjured my own memories of shopping at H&M for the first time. It was 2001, around the same year as Baros's first Forever 21 experience. I remember coming down the escalator in the Carousel Mall in Syracuse, New York, my pulse quickening at the thought of going through the doors and being able to buy whatever I wanted.

H&M is alluring because it doesn't *seem* cheap. Where discounters of decades past were fluorescent-lit and disorganized, H&M stores are all gleaming white walls and polished ash wood floors. There are few price signs and no garishly advertised deals. Clothes are organized by trend, department, and color scheme. But I was also drawn to H&M because it was unique; I was in one of the first locations in the United States and at the time I had no reason to believe the entire country would flock to buy $10 dresses.

Target and Old Navy initially needed marketing to redefine cheap fashion as chic, but today cheap fashion needs no endorsement. Whether we're buying from off-price stores, department store sales, or from pure discounters, landing clothing deals in the realm of $30, or often much less, is ingrained in our culture. It's simply the way most of us shop. The cheap-fashion chains do their part to seem motivated by some socialistic aims. H&M's people like to say they're "for everyone, not just the elite."[22] Cheap basics company UNIQLO runs subway ads with one revolutionary-tinged line: "Made for all." And Isaac Mizrahi launched his Target collection under the tagline "Luxury for Every Woman Everywhere."

Even the wealthy supplement their wardrobes with cheap fashion, and hold it up as a symbol of our consumer democracy. Sarah Jessica Parker, the very person who led many American women to buy overpriced designer garb through her character Carrie Bradshaw on *Sex and the City,* produced a clothing line in 2008 for the now-bankrupt fast-fashion retailer Steve & Barry's. Among the pieces were an $8.98 flowery sundress and a T-shirt that read FASHION IS NOT A LUXURY. "What has changed," Parker told the *New York Times,* "is that now people have bragging rights about what they paid. I admired a woman's pair of pants at a party recently and she said, 'Fourteen dollars! H&M!' It really is, among the people I know, part of what they do now."[23]

Even *Vogue* surprised not a few people in 2009 when they introduced a "Steal of the Month" column and a "100 under $100" fea-
ture. Many mainstream women's fashion magazines were already
running similar columns: In "Splurge vs. Steal," *Marie Claire* editors offer a more sensible H&M dress in place of a $500 designer
dress.

Cheap-fashion blogs such as the *The Budget Babe, Frugal-
Fashionista,* and *The Recessionista* have proliferated in recent years.
The Budget Fashionista blog founder Kathryn Finney has appeared on
NBC's *Today* show, CNN's *Headline News, E! News,* and ABC's
Good Morning America to dole out budget fashion advice. And Baros
says she's seen her own blog go from the margins to the mainstream.
"When this blog was born four years ago," she writes on the site,
"budget fashion was still taboo in the industry. Now, fashion bloggers
sit front row at Marc Jacobs and Missoni is collaborating with Target.
Le cheap, *c'est chic* has never been truer."

In one of her "Rainy Outfit of the Day" videos, Lee Councell cap-
tures her delight in discovering H&M's astonishing prices for the very
first time. Councell thought H&M was one of *those stores,* "Where,
you know, you can't find a shirt for under $40." Though cheap fashion
feels like a choice, it has become such a huge part of the apparel market
that it is impossible to ignore. Its sheer ubiquity has made it acceptable. Cheap doesn't just stay in its corner and play nicely by itself. It
aggressively chases and kills off anything priced near it.

If you'd asked me ten years ago if I thought I'd still be shopping
in H&M as an adult, I'd probably have said no. I assumed I'd eventually graduate from cheap fashion to stores that sell clothing made
of good fabric with amazing draping, whatever that is. My aversion
to paying good money for clothing eventually ran too deep. But
more than that, if I wanted to buy well-made, fashionable, moder-

ately priced clothing, I wasn't sure where to look. Where my father's generation could shop in their downtown department store for unique and well-made clothes, we're now faced with a cookie-cutter fashion landscape that offers many great deals, but not much in the way of actual choice.

2

How America Lost Its Shirts

No one was picking up the phone at the Garment Industry Development Corporation. It was just ringing and ringing. A few days passed, and I finally got a response via e-mail and an invitation to the GIDC's headquarters in the heart of Manhattan's Garment Center. I exited the subway at West Thirty-fourth Street and passed a trendy hole-in-the-wall boutique with a banner hanging over the entrance that read, "Price is king." I crossed over to gritty Seventh Avenue, Fashion Avenue as it's known, and passed Joey, a discount wholesaler where I once bought 50 T-shirts for $1 apiece to silk-screen and sell. Months later, a friend who had bought one of the shirts wanted me to know that hers had unraveled at the seams and could she have a new one?

As I turned down West Thirty-eighth Street, I finally saw signs of life. I passed fabric and trim shops hidden behind scaffolding and a truck unloading finished dresses wrapped in plastic. I took the elevator up to the fifth floor of a turn-of-the century building and knocked on an unmarked door. A very tall, striking man in jeans and a fitted dress shirt answered and showed me to a chair in the middle of a small room, furnished with little more than two empty desks and a dozen racks of clothing. We were alone. Andy Ward sat down across from me. "We have downsized," he said, his eyebrows raised into sarcastic arcs. I didn't see a phone anywhere. And there was no one to answer it other than this one man. This is not how I pictured the Garment Industry Development Corporation.

Apparel manufacturing was named one of the fastest-dying industries in America of the past decade, topped only by newspapers, wired telecommunications, and textile mills, which can hardly be counted separately.[1] We lost almost 650,000 apparel jobs in the ten-year period ending in 2007.[2] Wondering what, if anything, this has to do with cheap fashion, I went in search of garment factories in New York City to find out.

The GIDC is a nonprofit, as it turns out. The group was created in the late '80s as the ombudsmen of Manhattan's Garment Center, a slice of the West Side between Thirty-fourth and Forty-second streets where the garment trade has grown and waned organically for more than a century. The GIDC's official purpose is to make sure that law offices and the like don't move into Garment Center buildings, zoned since 1987 for fashion-related business, by seducing landlords with promises of higher rent. It's a tall order. There are now nowhere near enough garment manufacturers left in New York to fill the allotted space. Of the nine million square feet zoned for garment production in the Garment Center, Ward says less than a fifth of it is being used to make apparel.

These days, the GIDC mostly focuses on pairing independent fashion designers with the remaining factories best suited to handle their order. "If someone wants to do evening wear, we'll find them a factory," explains Ward. "We fine-tune their sourcing." The GIDC once had a full staff and a larger office with a proper showroom, but they fell behind on rent and had to move out. Their woes are due partly to mismanagement by former executives. But funding from the city and the state of New York has also dried up. All of the paid employees have been let go except for one, Andy Ward, who actually has not been paid in a while. Now he is running the whole show on a budget of zero. "I'm the GIDC, which is not a good place to be," Ward said. "We might just be on death's door." The same could be said for the entire domestic garment industry.

Now home to Mercedes-Benz Fashion Week and the headquarters of more than 800 fashion companies, New York is an undisputed fashion design hub.[3] But it used to be the capital of garment production as well. The garment industry was New York City's largest employer as early as 1900. A majority of the dresses and fashionable women's wear worn in the United States were made there for the better part of the twentieth century. A smaller but still sizeable men's wear industry thrived as well. For decades, the sidewalks of the Garment Center were impassable from the trolleys of cut fabric and racks of finished garments. The storefronts below Andy Ward's offices were once almost exclusively lined with ancillary businesses such as fabric, button, and notion shops. Today, that ecosystem still exists, but on a much smaller scale.

The Garment Center was once a way for immigrants and those without college degrees to work their way up. The industry had a place for many more blue-collar and middle-class positions, including brokers, wholesalers, salesmen, printmakers, pattern makers, cutters, and of course a veritable army of sewing-machine operators. The few hundred remaining union garment workers in New York today still eke out a decent living, making between $35,000 and $100,000 a year plus benefits, depending on their skill level and experience.[4]

After visiting several factories in New York over the course of a year, the Garment Center became familiar to me. What used to look like a sad and run-down part of the city looked familiar in a different way: It was a place where things got made instead of bought. There was no reason for it to be polished and inviting. The designers and factories that still toil here depend on the buttonhole makers and the little unassuming storefronts that sell linings, fusibles, thread, needles, and snaps.

Dalma Dress Manufacturing is one New York City factory that has managed to weather more than three decades of change and stay competitive in an industry that now overwhelmingly favors imports. The company has operated in the Garment Center since the late 1970s, first occupying a two-floor factory on West Thirty-ninth Street that employed 200 workers. Dalma Dress started off by producing good quality but still popularly priced women's clothing for large and once-legendary dress manufacturers such as Abe Schrader and Malcolm Starr. Ralph Lauren and Bill Blass were two of their biggest clients. Dalma's owners had no idea they'd opened their factory doors at almost the precise moment when everything would change. "It happened fast. We're talking about the late seventies. It maxed out over here," says factory manager Michael DiPalma, whose father Armand opened Dalma Dress.

Dalma Dress has a sort of unreformed appeal to it. Rolls of fabric, documents outlining the technical specifications of each garment (called "tech packs"), and dress forms are strewn haphazardly around the small workshop. While DiPalma and I talked in his office, one of his seamstresses popped in. "This was done by machine," she explained, holding a gold beaded gown that would retail for several thousand dollars. "I don't care," DiPalma barked, "I want it done right." The zipper on the dress had been finished on a sewing machine, but DiPalma was sure it would rip under the weight of the dress unless the closure on the zipper was sewn by hand. DiPalma is a high-strung guy who spews garment industry jargon like a second language. He also spends a lot of time out on the floor with everyone else, helping to get dresses made right in order to keep the factory going. He says, "Nobody just sits and does nothing here."

In the early years, Dalma Dress produced 1,000 blouses in a typical order for a client like Ralph Lauren. "That was great. That was 'found money,' we call it. That's the first thing that went over," DiPalma said, pointing to a hat rack in his office that became our stand-in for Asia. Today, the factory has shrunk to one floor and about 40 employees and makes high-end designer evening wear and bridal wear for two very famous American fashion designers. At one time Dalma Dress, and most factories in New York, would have turned away the small batches of labor-intensive garments that are now the Garment Center's means of survival. "The high end was always here," says DiPalma. "But you never sought it out. You just want to go home and relax and know you're going to get another five hundred out by the end of the week. The very difficult stuff always existed, but nobody looked for it."

Garment factories prefer higher-volume, less-complex work for a number of reasons—setting up an order and training workers takes time and money, so higher numbers mean spreading costs out, and simpler styles mean the order moves faster and does not require advanced sewing skills and specialized machines. Whether an order is big or small, a factory has the same up-front costs, including procuring fabric and thread, setting up machines, making and shipping samples, and buying things like shrink-wrap packaging and hangtags.

Ashraful "Jewel" Kabir, a Dhaka, Bangladesh–based factory owner who makes clothes for Echo, Universal Studios, and Umbro (a subsidiary of Nike), told me that he prefers the large orders from these huge companies because it allows him to recoup his investment and make a nice profit. "Whether we're producing five hundred or five thousand pieces, I have to maintain the same things," says Jewel. "Big quantities are much better. Definitely better. It's quantity based. That's how these companies make their money too."

Jewel's factory, Direct Sportswear Limited, employs roughly 200 people and churns out more than 400,000 basic garments like T-shirts and track pants per month. He is able to reduce his fees dramatically once a client starts ordering thousands upon thousands of the same garment. If Jewel can offer a client a price of $10 per piece for a 1,000-piece order, the price comes down dramatically as the numbers go up. "If they go up to ten thousand, I can come down to five dollars," explains Jewel—half the cost. At some point the economies of scale do balance and the price cannot be lowered. The exact point where a factory is turning a decent profit and offering the customer the lowest possible price? At Direct Sportswear Limited, Jewel says it's a startling 25,000 pieces of clothing. "That is the optimum level," he told me.

The fashion industry started to chase lower wages and cheaper prices into surrounding states, out to the West Coast and down into the South as early as the 1930s and 1940s. But the jaw-droppingly low prices were found overseas. Andy Ward, whose grandfather owned a woolens factory in Maine and whose father once owned a large men's wear brand called New York Sportswear Exchange, says that the move overseas made domestic manufacturing almost instantaneously uncompetitive. "When everybody went offshore to the Orient, we opened Pandora's box," he says. "After that, you couldn't manufacture clothing without being in Asia. You can never shut that box and say we can go back to where we were. It's open. It's done. It's finished."

As early as the 1950s, the United States started to import cotton clothing from Japan. A decade later, clothing from Hong Kong, Pakistan, and India started to flow in, but the numbers were comparatively tiny. In 1965 imports were less than 5 percent of all clothing sold in the United States. DiPalma says more simple and basic garments were the first to be produced overseas if for no other reason than it was easier to communicate their specifications in an era before cell phones, fax machines, or the Internet. "A blouse. What is it? It's two fronts. And a back. Two sleeves. A collar. A pocket. Put the buttons on," he says. "I just described the whole shirt in less than a minute. I can do that on the phone." However, the quality of imports was still very difficult to control in the early years.

To understand why fashion is so beguiled by overseas production, consider that even after outsourcing almost our entire clothing industry to low-wage countries, labor is still a huge part of the cost of garment production. According to recent estimates, raw materials account for 25 to 50 percent of the cost of producing an item of clothing, while labor ranges from 20 to 40 percent.[5] "Fashion is a labor-intense industry, not a technology-intense industry. You need someone to sit at a sewing machine," DiPalma says. Clothing, even when produced in a factory, is really a handmade good broken down into assembly-line steps. The sewing machine is more a tool than a machine, as it really just facilitates and speeds up manual work. The uniquely labor-intensive nature of clothing is why sewing is one of the most common professions in the world and the most common profession in the fashion industry.

That clothes are essentially handmade might seem obvious, but this simple fact has a profound effect on the prices we pay for our clothes. The wages paid to sewing machine operators and the money paid to garment factories enormously affects the prices we pay for fashion. To make a cheaper car, cheaper parts are necessary. Cheap fashion does rely on cheaper materials, but DiPalma told me that the difference in fabric prices between two countries, for example Japan and China, might be 50 cents, not enough to really impact price tags. "That means nothing," claims DiPalma. "That's not where my savings are. It's labor. Over here, there are labor laws. And I can't pay less than the minimum wage." To make cheap clothes, you really need cheap labor.

Labor rates within the United States vary. Andy Ward told me that a higher-skilled garment worker in New York might be paid $12 to $15 an hour, while a good pattern maker could probably earn $17 or $18 an hour. According to government statistics, the average wage of sewing-machine operators in the United States is much lower, now $9 an hour, or about $1,660 a month. But compare that to the minimum wage in the Dominican Republic, where it is 4,900 pesos a month within the free trade zones, which amounts to less than $150. China, where wages have spiked in recent years, still has minimum wages in the coastal provinces ranging from $117 to $147 a month.[6] Bangladesh, which raised its minimum wage in November 2010, only requires factories to pay their sewing-machine operators $43 a month. Garment workers in the United States today, although poorly paid by American standards, make more than four times as much as Chinese garment workers, 11 times Dominican garment workers, and 38 times Bangladeshi garment workers.

Here's just a few examples how these vast differences in wages might impact the price of clothes: Jeff Rudes, the executive of J. Brand, a premium jeans label, told the *Wall Street Journal* that his $300 jeans could sell for $40 if he manufactured them in China.[7] I asked DiPalma what his factory would charge me to make a lined and shirred black polyester miniskirt, which I bought at Urban Outfitters on sale for around $30 and brought with me to his factory. Before I could finish the sentence, DiPalma fired back, "$30." His price did not include the cost of fabric. I had the same skirt priced at four factories in China. I was given three quotes for less than $5 and one at a higher-end factory for $12, *fabric included*. In Bangladesh the price at one factory was also less than $5 a skirt. Another Chinese factory offered to ship my skirts for less than $1.50 apiece, making my total costs well less than half of what Dalma Dress, a factory in my own city, could make it for.

Of course, many factories in the United States do pay less than the minimum wage and have used their low wages to compete in an industry obsessed with cost cutting. America's association with sweatshops is as old as the Industrial Revolution and the antisweatshop movement in the garment industry dates back to at least 1911, when an infamous fire at the Triangle garment factory in New York killed 146 of its employees. The owners had locked the workers inside to prevent theft. About a third were killed by jumping from the windows or falling off the ramshackle fire escape.

Business in New York has also long been attracted to illegally run factories in Manhattan's Chinatown. Sally Reid, a garment production and quality control expert with more than 30 years in the New York industry, remembers when the factories were booming in the downtown neighborhood in the 1990s. At the time, she was working for an Italian-owned and unionized factory on Fifteenth Street. The factory specialized in lined blazers that cost between $42 and $48 apiece. A Chinatown factory came along and offered to make a lined blazer for $28, which put her client out of business but also made it uncompetitive to make this kind of garment in New York City under legal conditions.

Where were such dramatic savings coming from? An identical jacket made for $48 in one factory and for half the price in another? "They were not paying their workers minimum wage. I'm sure of that," Reid recalls. "And in the same factory that gave the twenty-eight-dollar price, you have cockroaches living everywhere, you have rats, and there are no toilets." Many of the Chinatown factories at the time were in condemned buildings, and Reid remembers seeing holes in the ground where the owners did not bother to install proper bathroom facilities.

Today, most of the factories in Chinatown, which established itself
for decades as a resource for high-volume, mass-market garment production, are gone. Chinatown was never zoned for clothing factories
and as developers have moved in and pushed the rents up, the factories
there have been wiped out more deftly than in the Garment Center.
Ward estimates there were 250 mass-market shops in Chinatown as
late as 2003. "Now there are twenty," he says. A huge Chinatown factory that could make 40,000 skirts in a weekend and was known for
quality sewing was the latest victim.

A lower-wage garment industry sprang up in Los Angeles as early
as the 1950s and grew as New York's industry receded. In the late
1990s L.A. had almost 120,000 people working in its garment factories
and even today has the biggest garment industry in the United States.[8]
The West Coast fashion industry has always been much different from
New York's, and the coasts weren't necessarily in direct competition.
The East Coast specialized in more formal and tailored garments, like
the dresses and men's suits portrayed in the 1960s-set television show
Mad Men. Even today, New York is the best place in the United States
to produce a tailored men's jacket or high-end evening wear.

L.A. is the birthplace of the more laid-back California style known
as sportswear. Not a reference to jogging shorts and yoga pants,
sportswear is industry lingo for the looser, lighter, and far less formal
clothing that most Americans spend their lives in today. California
Fashion Association president Ilse Metchek has worked in the state's
garment trade since sportswear started to boom on the West Coast in
the 1960s. She remembers when women started to abandon the New
York look of dresses worn with girdles and big crinolines for the simpler styles of the Golden State. "We saw a sudden schism between the
New York chic and the California look," Metchek recalls. More recently, Los Angeles has also built a formidable premium denim indus-

try, a category of high-end jeans that typically retail for more than $150 a pair.

I visited a Los Angeles garment factory building in August 2010 to see how imports have affected the industry there. With me were a college student translator named Michelle and Lupe Hernandez, a Mexico City native who has sewn clothes in L.A. for almost two decades. Hernandez helped spearhead a campaign against Forever 21 a decade ago, when it came out that the people sewing its clothes in downtown L.A. factories were being paid far below the minimum wage.[9] Hernandez was one of those workers. Forever 21 has since shifted to sourcing more of its products from overseas, but some of its more fashion-sensitive goods that need to get into stores fast are still made in Los Angeles.

Hernandez, a 37-year-old five-foot-tall dynamo wearing a black spaghetti-strap tank top, a gold crucifix, bright red lipstick, and drawn-on eyebrows, took us to a factory building on West Eighth and South Broadway in downtown Los Angeles, where Forever 21 and its subsidiary brand Reference still sew some of its clothes. There are about six factories to a floor. They are small and plain, each employing roughly two dozen middle-aged Hispanic women and a handful of men, who I saw positioning fabric under the needles of their sewing machines and hanging finished garments on racks.

Virtually all of L.A.'s garment workers are paid per finished garment (known as piecework). For example, a worker like Hernandez might make four or five cents for trimming a shirt, which involves cutting loose threads. Employers are technically required to pay the minimum wage regardless of the number of pieces a worker completes. Experienced sewers who are faster can in theory earn more. Metchek says, "The law is that even if you don't sew enough to make the minimum wage, the boss still has to pay you the minimum wage." But this contradicts the experience of many L.A. factory workers, or at least implies that they must fulfill hefty weekly quotas.

Hernandez told me that most of the garment workers in Los Angeles she knows put in ten-hour days and work six days a week making countless garments just so they can drag their earnings up to minimum wage. I asked Hernandez how she could be so sure of what the workers were making. Didn't wages vary from factory to factory? "The wages are pretty much the same since the time I got here eighteen years ago," she said, exasperatedly. "The workers have to work more now because the cost of living has actually gone up. We work more now in order to get by."

At the time, Hernandez was working for American Apparel, the trendy youth brand that has built its name around racy ads and its all-L.A. production. A federal investigation led the company to fire around 1,800 allegedly undocumented workers in October 2009, at a time when unemployment was the highest it had been in a quarter century. Many of the pink-slipped workers had been at the company for a decade or more. The government placed Lupe, who was unemployed herself, in the suddenly understaffed factory. Metchek told me that the controversial anti-immigration program meant the loss of some of Los Angeles' most experienced garment workers. Hernandez agrees, saying, "Because unemployment rates are so high, a lot of people are being sent to work for American Apparel, but they don't even know how to do the jobs. They're just taking up space."

American Apparel, aside from owning its own factories and using domestic labor, is an industry exception in other ways: It offers its employees health benefits, stock options, and the occasional free on-site massage. Yet according to Hernandez, it still isn't enough to truly give garment workers a leg up in the American economy. Hernandez can't afford the retailer's clothes, she told me. They sell a polyester

button-up shirt for $58, a reasonable enough price, but not if you're
living on today's garment worker wages. I asked Hernandez if she
likes her job at the retailer. "Workers stay at American Apparel because the minimum wage is guaranteed," she said, as are breaks and
overtime. But Hernandez wouldn't go as far as saying her job was a
good one: The daily quotas are huge she says (2,300 pieces a day) and
the pressure to complete them intense. Hernandez says, "American
Apparel is just less worse than the other ones," meaning factories.

At first L.A.'s lower wages kept the industry more competitive in
the global economy, but conditions have eroded to the point where
low pay, bad working environments, and a total lack of job security
have become the norm. According to Katie Quan, the associate chair
of the UC Berkeley Center for Labor Research, it's almost impossible
to unionize the city's garment workers to improve their situation.
"The industry is really globalized at this point," says Quan. "So, it's
hard for the union to come up with a strategy that would actually be
effective at retaining the work in the United States and raising wages
over time." Even American Apparel, held up as a labor leader in the
industry, is not unionized. The union UNITE HERE tried to orga-
nize the company in 2003 to gain paid time off, more affordable health
care, improved production methods, and better treatment by supervisors.[10] The attempt failed—with the company claiming the workers
didn't want the union and the union claiming the workers were bul-
lied by management. Quan says, "We used to say just casually that
wages and working conditions were so bad in L.A. that it was practically like having Mexico in California."

A few weeks before I went to L.A., I took a seven-hour drive
through the Smoky Mountains, over the Georgia–South Carolina
border, finally arriving in Greenville, South Carolina. This is the heart
of the country's dying textile mecca, which once stretched along I-85

from Greenville to Greensboro. I was there to visit Olean Kiker, a childhood friend of my dad's who worked in textiles for more than 40 years. Kiker, a thoughtful and impassioned man who lives in a pair of wraparound sunglasses and sports sandals, drove me a few miles outside of Greenville along I-85 before exiting into the very small town of Inman, South Carolina, where it was obvious that nothing new had opened there, save a Hardee's and a McDonald's, in a very long time. We came to a green sign marked Inman Business District. There was nothing there. At the corner, a white plantation-style home sat on top of a hill. "That was probably the mill president's house," Kiker told me, and turned down a narrow residential road sandwiched on both sides with very neat little box homes with yards. These were built as millworker houses.

At the end of the road, we arrived at a looming, four-story brick factory right out of a picture book on the Industrial Revolution, complete with a tapered smokestack saluting the sky. I got out of the car and walked around the side to a guardhouse overgrown with weeds. The windows, many with no panes, were empty. I saw the clear, blue Carolina sky straight through them. This was Inman Mills, a yarn-making plant that was once home to some of the most coveted jobs in South Carolina. In an e-mail, current Inman Mills CEO Norman Chapman told me that the company built a baseball field, a church, a school, a community swimming pool, and a bowling alley for their employees, and sponsored athletic leagues.

Though Inman still has a handful of mills running, the original mill closed in 2001, in part because it was a 100-year-old dinosaur in what has become a very high-tech industry. Textile factories are very different from sewing factories. They are highly automated today, employing an array of sophisticated machines that weave, dye, print, finish, and dry fabric, with very little labor. Modern textile firms are able to churn out thousands of square yards every hour with as few as ten or 20 employees.[11] Chapman told me that garment factories "can move quickly, require little energy and far less training" when compared to textiles. Yet even they have buckled under foreign competition. In 1996 the American textile industry employed 624,000 workers. Today, that number has fallen to less than 120,000.[12] I asked Chapman what closed the mill down. "No business," he wrote back in an e-mail, adding that textiles from Asia "flooded into our market at unbelievable prices."

Kiker and I spent the rest of the afternoon peering through chain-link fences guarding shuttered textile mills along I-85. I missed the end of the textile boom in the American South by about 30 years. Many factories I saw had already been converted into condos for the rich. But that doesn't mean the job loss hasn't been felt. As of July 2011, South Carolina has one of the highest unemployment rates in the country, at 10.9 percent.

Kiker started out as a low-level manager in a yarn-spinning plant in 1968 making $1.25 an hour. "You couldn't see your own hand in front of your face," he recalls speaking of the pollution in the mills back then. Over time he saw wages and environmental conditions improve enormously in the textile industry. Today, an American textile worker makes from $11 to $13 an hour and is protected by strict health and environmental regulations. Eventually Kiker worked his way up to plant manager of TNS Mills, overseeing three yarn-spinning plants headquartered in northern Georgia that produced one million pounds of yarn a week. For years, one of their biggest customers was Levi's.

In order to compete in the globalized economy, TNS automated as much of their production as possible, but the company wasn't getting enough orders and their customers were going out of business as well. Six of the company's 20 mills were closed in 2002. Kiker was moved to VP of manufacturing over the remaining plants the following year, but they still couldn't survive in the face of increasing imports. The company sold the two remaining plants in 2009, and Kiker left with the closings, ending his career in the textile industry.

As Kiker climbed the textile-industry ladder in the late 1970s, three-fourths of our clothes were still made in the United States. But the threat of cheaper-made imports was palpable. The International Ladies Garment Workers Union reacted by appealing to patriotism with the famed "Look for the union label" television campaign. In a 1981 TV spot, a feather-haired woman holds up a maroon cowl neck blouse and makes the following plea: "This is no import. We made this blouse . . . We have sewn our union label right in here. It tells you we're able to do what every American wants to do: have a job doing honest work at decent wages. When you see our union label, think of us making a living making your clothes right here in America." You can still find the ILGWU Union label affixed to the side seams of a lot of clothing made before 1990.

The owners of American textile mills and garment factories also fought imports by creating formidable political alliances and lobbies and by establishing limits and quotas on clothing from other countries. In 1962 the United States had exactly one export restraint agreement on clothing, and it was leveraged against Japan. The number of restraints mushroomed over the decades, extending to 40 countries by 1994, when restraints governed about half of U.S. clothing imports.[13]

A single worldwide quota system, the Multi Fibre Arrangement (MFA), was eventually established in 1974 to bring together all of the restrictions. The MFA limited the number of clothing exports from developing countries into industrialized ones, but only when the number of imports climbed high enough to pose a threat. The result was a convoluted system of quotas that limited the import numbers of

more than 100 categories of clothing, like cotton knit shirts or blue
denim, on a country-by-country basis.

The Multi Fibre Arrangement shaped the garment industry worldwide from 1974 until 2005, and its effects are still felt. In order for a
country to keep their quotas, the quotas had to be fulfilled every
year, which led to shady new professions in quota brokering. More
significantly, the MFA also resulted in quota gobbling garment factories overseas with huge workforces. Very big overseas factories employing thousands of people became the norm, particularly in China
in more recent decades. Andy Ward says these factories were so big
they would refuse order sizes in the hundreds or even low thousands.
"The quotas kept factories at two thousand or three thousand people," he says. "They had no interest in doing a hundred-piece order.
They wanted to work with JCPenney and do a hundred thousand dress
shirts." This drove domestic retailers who could afford to move overseas to produce in higher volumes. Overseas factories are still largely
set up to handle gargantuan orders, having employed large numbers
of people and invested in costly machinery, huge facilities, and workers' dorms.

Huge and capable foreign factories were such a potential cash-cow
that clothing chains figured out ways to get around the quotas: They
simply spread their supply chains all over the world, taking advantage
of cost savings in every country they could. By 2003 Gap Inc., which
also owns Banana Republic and Old Navy, was ordering its clothes
from more than 1,200 different factories in 42 countries, and Liz Claiborne, which owns Mexx and Juicy Couture among others, was using
factories in 40 different countries.[14] The MFA did little to prevent imports from coming into the United States. If anything, it grew garment industries in other countries like Bangladesh, where factories
opened to take advantage of more lenient quotas.

Offshore outsourcing also gave rise to a new kind of clothing company: one that only designed and marketed clothes rather than making them. Cheap labor enabled such brands as Nike and such monolithic retailers as Gap, the clothiers that we began to worship moving into the 1980s and '90s and that heavily contracted out production. By selling private-label products, these companies were already at a huge cost advantage. But it was imports that gave them an unbeatable edge. In 1995, at a time when half of our clothing was still made at home, Gap was already making 65 percent of its products in foreign factories.[15] The GIDC has discussed having Gap do some test-run garment production in the United States, but Ward says even today they won't consider it. "Why not do a couple hundred dozen garments here, see if it works, and then bring the bulk in from offshore?" he asks. "But they don't have the time or the patience to do that." Nike shoes were *never* made in the United States. In fact, as former sweatshop monitor T. A. Frank pointed out in the April 2008 issue of *Washington Monthly*, Nike "based its business on the premise that the company would not manufacture shoes—it would only design and market them." Even in the early years, Nike, the all-American sneaker, was made in Japan and Taiwan.[16]

It's no coincidence that early adopters of imports—Gap, JCPenney, Sears, and Nike among them—are the ones whose goods we are still purchasing today. The 1990 Standard & Poor's Industry Survey for apparel noted that the retail markup on private-label goods made overseas usually started at 65 percent and went as high as 75 percent at the time. By contrast, brands that were made domestically were only taking a 50 to 60 percent markup. Wages in the global south at this time were so low (56 cents an hour in El Salvador in 1995, for example), apparel importers were often able to get their labor costs down to less than 1 percent of the retail price of their clothes.[17]

Importers could offer the same or better level of quality and style while still hugely undercutting their domestic rivals. Any company making clothing in the United States couldn't compete. They either had to shut down or move on to importing. As Richard P. Appelbaum and Edna Bonacich note in their 2000 book *Behind the Label: Inequality in the Los Angeles Apparel Industry*, clothing companies that do take advantage of lower labor costs inevitably "put pressure on those that do not, driving all to move toward this cost-cutting approach."[18] Guess? Inc., a California brand that once sourced all of its clothes in Los Angeles–based factories, dropped 40 percent of its domestic production in one six-month period in the late 1990s.[19] Levi's was one of the last major garment manufacturers to give in and source from overseas, closing its last factory (in San Antonio, Texas) in 2004.

Like a massive engine grinding to a halt and then slowly turning in the opposite direction, import barriers on clothing to the United States began to be deftly wiped out in the midnineties. Job loss in the clothing production trades was heaviest during these years of aggressive trade liberalization and quota removal.[20] The first big hit to the L.A. garment industry came in the form of the North American Free Trade Agreement, ratified in 1993, which removed duties on exports to Mexico. The effect of NAFTA was that many American companies moved cut-and-sew operations just over the Mexican border to *maquiladoras*, where garments could be slapped together for much lower minimum wages. Metchek recalls, "Whole factories, machines and everything, moved to Mexico." This cost the Los Angeles industry tens of thousands of jobs in the year following NAFTA and pushed down wages for workers in Los Angeles.

The following year, the World Trade Organization ruled that the quotas established by the Multi Fibre Arrangement were an unfair trade advantage for developed countries. The MFA entered into a decade-long phasing out. Metchek bristles at the mere mention of the MFA's expiration. "Don't even get me started on that," she exclaims. "I have been pounding the table on that one and have been for years. The Chinese were shipping in jeans, T-shirts, sweatshirts, junk by the tonnage. The tonnage!" Chinese imports increased exponentially as the MFA began its decline. In 2005, when the MFA fully expired, Chinese cotton trousers exported to the United States leapt by an unreal 1,500 percent and shipments of cotton knit shirts were up 1,350 percent; meanwhile 16,000 U.S. textile jobs were lost and at least 18 factories closed that year.[21]

In 2000 the Caribbean Basin Trade Partnership Act and African Growth and Opportunity Act granted those countries numerous breaks on footwear and apparel, followed by the Trade Act of 2002, which bestowed duty-free access to most apparel and virtually all footwear from Bolivia, Columbia, Ecuador, and Peru. But with China in the picture, these countries had a hard time gaining a significant share of U.S. clothing production.

After the quotas were lifted, employment in the L.A. factories "dropped precipitously," says Quan, who surveyed the city's garment workers after the MFA expired. Paychecks, already dismally low, took another hit. "We found that wages dropped nine percent in the year after the end of the MFA and that employment was harder to find," Quan says. She also found that the out-of-work garment workers, most of them non–English speaking immigrants, were pushed into even lower-paying jobs like child care, home health care, and "other small odd jobs" in the informal economy.

In March 2011 *The New York Times* reporter Nadia Sussman documented the lives of New York City garment workers in a video segment called "Struggling to Stitch." Sussman interviewed Hispanic day laborers lined up in the early morning hours on Eighth Avenue at West Thirty-eighth Street in the Garment Center, vying for scarce jobs sewing, packing, ironing, or cutting loose threads. She found a situation strikingly similar to Los Angeles, where garment workers were turning to lower-paying jobs, like housecleaning and babysitting, and some were moving back to their home countries. The garment industry today is offering fewer immigrants a lifeline into the American economy. Nor is there a comparable job market replacing it.

Low wages don't just affect immigrants and garment workers. According to a report by the Economic Policy Institute, "Heavy competition and cheap labor from abroad has pushed down wages for U.S. workers and reduced their bargaining power." In 2006 a full-time median-wage earner lost $1,400 due to globalization, according to the report.[22] Long before the recession began, jobs were becoming increasingly polarized in the United States, with *The New York Times* reporting in 2010 on a number of economic studies that showed high-paid occupations that demand higher education and advanced skills growing alongside low-wage, entry-level, service, and retail jobs. This trend is intimately related to the loss of manufacturing in the United States. Skilled middle-income jobs, those once populated mostly by factory workers, are the ones that have disappeared, and they have evaporated even faster since the start of the current recession.[23]

There are also just fewer jobs in general. "The lion's share of our unemployment is from manufacturing," says DiPalma. "What are we going to do with these people? People come from all over the world to the U.S. with a skill. People come here because they want to work and they know the more they work, the more they get ahead. More people are going to come and now we have no jobs. We're not a lazy country. There's just not any work."

Dynotex is a Greenpoint, Brooklyn–based garment factory that opened in 1999, at a time when most were shuttering fast in the face of foreign competition. The Hong Kong–born Alan Ng worked in the Chinese garment industry for 20 years before moving to New York and, even though the odds were stacked against him, deciding to get into the garment industry in the United States. Ng opened Dynotex and then decided to move his factory out of the Garment Center and into Brooklyn, where rents are lower.

Dynotex started out with one client, J. McLaughlin, a private label retailer that now has more than 50 locations. As the retailer increased in size, it moved some of its production overseas, and Dynotex has had to refocus its business. It now caters more to higher-end designers with smaller orders, much like what Dalma Dress has done.

When a fashion designer is just getting started, using foreign manufacturing isn't an option. Most don't have the travel budget or big enough order sizes to make it possible. For small orders, the import costs can make overseas production as expensive as domestic, and most overseas factories refuse small orders anyway. Ng says his factory will take runs as few as 40 pieces, but the average order is 400 pieces of a single style. It sounds like a lot, but Ng says, "That's a quantity that import countries don't want to touch. They want at least a thousand."

Dynotex also offers higher-skilled sewing and additional services such as pattern making and sampling to stay competitive. "We sell mainly good quality and good workmanship. We take care of a lot of details of style and construction," says Ng. He says there are only two ways his factory can survive: "One is we can make a high-end product, and the other one is to promote that we're made in New York."

Ng told me unapologetically that his factory charges some of the highest prices in the city, roughly $20 on average per garment.

Nanette Lepore is a respected women's wear designer who still produces 85 percent of her clothing domestically, around 20,000 to 30,000 pieces per month. Erica Wolf, Lepore's executive assistant, says that Lepore prefers New York City production precisely because she can take advantage of specialized skills that still exist there (like expert pattern makers or seamstresses capable of advanced hand stitching and high-end finishes) to make a better-constructed product. "The Garment Center doesn't make one-offs like an H&M does," says Wolf. "It doesn't make something that follows a trend and will only last you three weeks." Keeping production local also allows the designer unbeatable control to make last-minute adjustments and to monitor quality. Wolf says, "Nanette thinks it's amazing for turnaround time, incredible production control, and incredible quality control."

Because of intense competition, Ng says the cost of producing clothing in New York has actually risen very little over time. The city has always been known for better-made, higher-end garments and local production inherently gives designers tighter reins over their creations. What's changed is consumers' price expectations and their wardrobes. As Wolf points out, neither Nanette Lepore's prices nor Dynotex's client's prices are H&M or Target cheap; the products produced in New York are rarely trendy and disposable. Still, factories in the United States can and do produce moderately priced garments. A blouse made at Ng's factory might retail for $125, a pair of pants for $150, and a jacket for $200, he says. Most of Nanette Lepore's dresses retail for between $240 and $400.

Even though these prices were quite common a generation ago and still only amount to a portion of an American's annual wardrobe budget, they're now considered expensive. Retail analysts now define moderately priced clothes as about $29 to $69 for a top or between $49 to $110 for a skirt or a pair of pants.[24] The widespread availability of ultracheap clothing compels the domestic industry to brand itself as high-end, when often it is producing and selling what was historically a midpriced garment.

Ng says that when he first moved to the United States from Hong Kong, he was shocked by Americans' disposable attitude toward clothes. "The most general consumer would rather buy the cheap stuff because they don't want their clothes the next season," he says disapprovingly. "They will spend twenty dollars [on a garment], so they can buy sixty or one hundred pieces, but they will not spend one hundred and fifty dollars [on one garment and buy fewer pieces]. It's very wasteful." If consumers weren't so focused on quantity over quality and trends over innovative design, the price of domestic production might not seem so exorbitant.

The low prices Americans now expect to pay for clothing are built around the cost of production in *other* countries. Ng gets all kinds of interesting business propositions, all based around prices capable only in low-wage countries. One company came to Dynotex wanting to make a baby bib that would sell in stores for $5, less than what it would cost the factory to make it. Another client asked if the factory could make 50 pairs of leg warmers that would sell in stores for $7.99 per pair. Ng says, "[The retail price] is not even enough for me to start talking to them and analyze all the details of the project, not to mention to pay the workers to sew it." He was also approached by Babies"R"Us about producing a line of T-shirts. Ng offered the company a price of $2 or $3 per shirt, but it turned out the big-box store wanted to sell a half-dozen shirts for that price.

The expectation of cheap also hurts clothing designers. A drama unfolded in the spring of 2011 on the Web site Well Spent, a site devoted to handcrafted and locally made products that "don't cost an arm and a leg." Independent men's wear company UNIS, owned by New York–based designer Eunice Lee, was criticized on the Web site's message boards for the price of her men's khakis, which retail for $228. A commenter named Jason wrote: "Ordinary khakis that look no better than Dockers (frankly it looks like they wrinkle easily) retail here for $228. They don't even appear to be organic! I understand they are hand sewn in NY, but if we can't find a way to be fashionable and ethical for less than $228 per pant, there's no future to this endeavor."

Lee took the time to break down her costs in a full-length article for the site, which is an effort I hope more designers and clothing companies make going forward. She explained that UNIS is a small company that produces relatively small batches of clothing, which means they do not have the economies of scale of a company like Dockers. There's also a quality difference. The khaki is made from Italian double-weave cotton, the pants have a tailored construction, and the buttons are made from a corozo nut. Also, UNIS is produced domestically, where factory resources are now narrow and finding a competitive price is difficult. In a comment back to Jason, Lee writes impassionedly: "YOU, the consumer has chosen. You have chosen to buy cheaper, and companies have listened! They moved their production off shore."

Eliza Starbuck, a fashion designer who produces her own sustainable line called Bright Young Things, was delighted to have the line picked up by Urban Outfitters in the spring of 2011, until she had to figure out how to produce it under cost. Urban Outfitters, a chain store that targets the college market, sells most of its clothing for well under $200. Starbuck did not want to compromise on fabric—most of her pieces are made from a blend of environmentally friendly rayon called Tencel that feels like silky cotton. She contracted out the work to a factory in Chinatown, as she didn't have the volume to produce overseas and also because local production is important to her. The factory was facing huge gaps in its production schedule, Starbuck says, and offered her a price far lower than what they normally would. "Really, it was too low," she confessed. "I wouldn't be in Urban Outfitters if it wasn't for this factory. They probably charged me half of what it was worth." A Bright Young Things halter sold for $89, a cream wrap dress for $179, a khaki dress that doubles as a jacket for $240, and a pair of adjustable pants for $188.

Consumers might think that at these prices either the store or the designer made a huge profit, yet according to Starbuck both she and Urban Outfitters took the lowest markups they could, knowing that if the price climbed any higher, shoppers (especially cash-strapped college students) would balk. Americans are so convinced that cheap fashion deals are fair that we often view with suspicion designers who make a well-made product that isn't cheap. Yet once Starbuck described the costs and financial investment involved in making a relatively basic, four-piece clothing line in the United States, it was clothing sold for anything less than what she charges that became suspicious to me.

Yes, low prices like a $13 halter on sale at Forever 21 or a $15 wrap dress at H&M have always flabbergasted me, but watching a designer struggle to break even while selling clothes for ten times more made those low prices incomprehensible. The demand for cheaper and cheaper garments has all but wiped out the American garment industry; it's also made it very difficult for small designers and independent companies to find proper and affordable factory resources here, and to charge prices that generate fair profits and pay decent wages.

3

High and Low Fashion Make Friends

Kimberly Couzens is a six-foot-tall, twentysomething blonde and my shopping opposite. She's bought a $2,500 Valentino handbag, a $700 Louis Vuitton purse, and a pair of $300 purple flats by Miu Miu. Most of her wardrobe is by high-end contemporary American designers such as Marc Jacobs and Diane von Furstenberg, purchased almost exclusively at luxury department stores Saks Fifth Avenue and Bergdorf Goodman in Manhattan. The salespeople know her so well they call her when new stock arrives and immediately set aside items in her size. "I go shopping at least four times a week on my break from work," Couzens explained, as I trailed her around Saks one rainy afternoon. "But mostly just window-shopping."

Couzens has a very dedicated method of shopping, one that I don't have the patience or self-control for—not to mention the bank account. Couzens was working as a financial news editor making $42,000 a year when I met her, a good salary for a recent college grad, but hardly enough to maintain a full-priced high-end wardrobe. If there's a designer item she just *has* to have, Couzens will wait for it to go on sale or hunt it down on eBay, where she also auctions off most of what she buys to fund her next purchase. But every now and then, her self-restraint caves and she pays full price. "These are the most expensive shoes I have," she told me, pointing to her $300 purple Miu Mius, Prada's more popularly priced line. "They were a very stupid purchase because they're purple and they don't go with anything." Couzens told me she wished she'd purchased more neutral black flats by Chanel instead, which she imagined she'd get more use out of. Classic Chanel flats start around $500.

I found Couzens through her Web site, Elite Gossip Girl Style, a blog dedicated to the posh wardrobes worn on the popular teen TV drama *Gossip Girl*. The characters are extravagantly fashionable—and privileged—Upper East Side prep school kids who regularly carry $600 handbags and wear $2,000 designer coats. On her blog, Couzens—who is refreshingly down-to-earth, despite buying clothes out of her price range—meticulously identifies the designers behind every item in each character's outfit, of which there are dozens per episode, and provides links that point to where to buy the pieces online.

The site got 50,000 page views a month at its peak in 2009, and most of the traffic is from young women similar to Couzens who love designer clothing but can't really afford it. This doesn't always stop them from buying it. Couzens's Valentino handbag, an amethyst-colored confection that has earned her plenty of compliments, was a piece worn by actress Taylor Momsen on *Gossip Girl*. The show was shooting an episode near Couzens's office one afternoon, and, incredibly, she got the chance to talk to Momsen and show her the bag. It turns out Momsen had less in common with her well-off character than Couzens imagined. "She told me she loved the bag too, but couldn't afford it!" Couzens said incredulously, wondering if something was not quite right about the high-end world in which she shopped.

Today, who doesn't know an out and proud high-fashion fanatic?

She's the yin to a cheapskate's yang. For every budget fashion shopper paying impossibly low prices for everything she wears, there seems to be someone else laying down a house payment for an exotic-sounding designer frock. As the price of most apparel has plummeted in recent decades, top-tier clothing has become significantly more expensive. The price of high-end women's dresses climbed an average of 250 percent between 1998 and 2010, with the top 10 percent of dresses sold leaping from an average price of around $200 to upward of $600.[1] Relatively unknown contemporary designers now pump their prices up to several hundred dollars, with some price tags topping out at more than $1,000.

Sex and the City first captured but also fueled this new type of consumer, the girl of average means who pursued clothing that was dangerously and irrationally expensive. The show premiered on HBO in 1998, around the time I started buying three-for-$20 paper-thin tank tops at Old Navy. Sarah Jessica Parker's character Carrie Bradshaw famously loves $500 Manolo Blahniks. Kim Cattrall's Samantha covets a $4,000 Hermès Birkin bag. By the time *Sex and the City* went off the air in 2004, the designer footwear and handbags Bradshaw and her friends adored had skyrocketed in the real world. Blahniks go for close to $800 a pair today; Birkins start around $9,000, with no corresponding upgrade in materials or craftsmanship. And an entire generation of women had been hooked on overpriced designer clothes.

When Alexandra Isenberg left for Europe in the late '90s to study at London's famous Central Saint Martins College of Art and Design, popular knowledge of high fashion was still relatively limited. "Ten years ago, who could name an editor of *Vogue*?" she recalls. "Now Anna Wintour is a household name. Marc Jacobs, Chanel, and Hermès—those were brands that were unknown to the world unless you were superwealthy. And now they're brands that people aspire to own."

Today, most of us have an acute sense of fashion designers. Just by watching the red-carpet procession at the Academy Awards or flipping through a fashion magazine or tabloid, we become familiar with Marc Jacobs, Chanel, and Hermès. TV shows such as *Sex and the City*, *Gossip Girl*, and *Project Runway* have all boosted designer exposure, as has the Internet. Nowadays, consumers are just as likely to get their fashion news from blogs as they are from *Vogue*. Whereas Isenberg spent $100 on a *Collezioni* magazine with the runway collections inside as a student, because she didn't want to wait six months until the collections hit stores, access to runway shows is now immediate, thanks to the Internet. When I worked at *New York* magazine, I burned the midnight oil a few times helping to build online photo slide shows of all the catwalk collections from New York's fall Fashion Week as they were happening. This is common practice across the Internet today.

Isenberg, who now runs the fashion news blog *Searching for Style*, says that celebrities are a key reason fashion designers have become such well-known personalities. Giorgio Armani was early to harness Hollywood's commercial potential by dressing Richard Gere head to toe in Armani for *American Gigolo* in 1980. But it was around the time that Isenberg left for Europe that celebrity obsession really took hold. "Suddenly celebrities were being photographed at fashion parties and fashion shows," she remembers.

Much of the content on *The Budget Babe* blog is dedicated to knocking off high-end celebrity wardrobes. Editor Dianna Baros told me she isn't even really interested in celebrities. "I quickly found that a huge part of fashion today is paparazzi stalking celebrities and brands sending free products to them," she told me, and she's found herself tailoring her blog's content to this reality. After *The Budget Babe* gained popularity, Baros started receiving dozens of press releases a day from clothing brands, stylists, and PR companies alerting her to what certain celebrities were wearing. "I'll get a press release saying Gwyneth Paltrow was spotted wearing our Maxi Dress. It's three hundred dollars. You can get it here." Instead of directing her readers to the designer version, Baros will show them how to create a similar look by shopping at cheap fashion chains.

Designer worship is confounding when you consider that fashion designers toiled in relative obscurity for so long. Parisian couturiers of the early twentieth century were known among certain circles, but American women would often buy copies of Parisian dresses at department stores with no knowledge of the particular designer who inspired the dress. Until the '60s, department store clothing typically carried the store or a manufacturer's label. Michael DiPalma recalls, "In those days, you bought an Abe Schrader dress by Joey G. or an Abe Schrader by Morton Myles or whatever. These guys never touched a pencil to design anything. They were businessmen." Designers were a part of the manufacturer's team, not their shining stars. DiPalma says the designer's power was often limited to showing sketches to the manufacturer, and if their lines sold, they'd keep their jobs.

Ready-to-wear designers started to crop up and venture out on their own in the 1960s, but the game was much different and much more small-time. According to journalist Teri Agins, Ralph Lauren and Calvin Klein needed only around $10,000 to start their businesses in the late '60s, compared with the $1 million entry fee required to start a prestigious label by the 1990s.[2] High fashion is now a slick, glitzy, heavily marketed and largely corporate industry. Runway shows have become million-dollar affairs, with *Forbes* reporting that jeans designer Rock & Republic spent $2.5 million on its 2007 New York show and Yves Saint Laurent had laid down more than $1 million just on the perfect tent location behind the Musée Rodin in Paris.[3] Hollywood actors are now paid to wear designers' clothing on the red carpet and to attend runway shows. Though many in the industry deny it, celebrities can earn as much as $50,000 per show to sit in the front row, wear a designer's clothes, and say positive things about them in interviews.[4]

High fashion also sold out to Wall Street, forcing designers to go big or go home, says Agins. Forty fashion companies went public between 1995 and 1997, including more popularly priced brands like Tommy Hilfiger, Polo Ralph Lauren, Jones Apparel Group, Guess?, and Donna Karan. A brand such as Polo, which sells a classic and consistent product, can better survive the growth pressures required of a public company, but a more fashionable designer like Donna Karan quickly realized what going public meant: "It's not about luxury and cashmere and fabric and color. It's the bottom line."[5]

Countless couture houses and ready-to-wear designer labels have also merged into conglomerates in recent decades. French tycoon Bernard Arnault acquired Christian Dior in 1987, and thus the luxury goods conglomerate Moët Hennessy–Louis Vuitton (LVMH) was born. In the years since, as Dana Thomas explains in her book, *Deluxe: How Luxury Lost Its Luster*, almost the entire luxury market has sold its small-family-owned flavor for global expansion funded by shareholder dollars. Today, LVMH owns around 60 fashion, spirits, and accessories brands, including fashion labels Fendi, Givenchy, and Marc Jacobs. A second major luxury conglomerate, PPR, owns Bottega Veneta, Gucci, Yves Saint Laurent, Balenciaga, Boucheron, Sergio Rossi, and half of Alexander McQueen and Stella McCartney.

Tom Ford, who served as creative director of Gucci from 1994 to 2004, is generally credited with the new-era luxury profit formula, which is essentially selling marked-up accessories and handbags to the masses. Open the pages of any fashion magazine today and you'll find they're front-loaded with ads for handbags, shoes, watches, sunglasses, and perfume. This is where these companies take their big margins. Luxury handbags are one of the biggest scams in the retail world, and Thomas found they are marked up as much as ten to 12 times over the cost of production.[6] Alexandra Isenberg, a former junior designer for French luxury fashion label Sonia Rykiel, says that designer shoes are also overpriced. "Back in the day you could get an amazing pair of shoes for like three hundred and fifty dollars," she recalls. "But now they're like eight hundred dollars. I don't know what happened there, but those products do have higher margins."

The tinted fortresses of the luxury brands Armani, Bottega Veneta, Escada, Fendi, Gucci, Louis Vuitton, Prada, Pucci, and Sergio Rossi are all lined up near Central Park on Manhattan's Fifth Avenue. These companies put on a good show of being Old World and exclusive, yet they're clearly marketing to every Jane Doe from Idaho to Georgia who walks that stretch of sidewalk. They all have similar layouts. The first floor is the most welcoming, well lit, and staffed. This floor is dedicated to scarves, jewelry, and other small accessories, but mostly handbags. In a day of luxury window-shopping, the only store where I encountered a crowd was Louis Vuitton, where hordes of college-age girls swarmed a discounted rack of purses festooned with the interlocking L-V logo. On the higher floors, the environs get far more exclusive. This is where the clothes are.

Now that much of high fashion has become big business, the clothes sit in limbo, occupying a precarious place on profit and loss spreadsheets. Marc Jacobs's ready-to-wear collection for Louis Vuitton is often credited for setting the tone for the entire fashion industry each season, yet it constitutes a meager 5 percent of Vuitton sales.[7] A representative from luxury branding firm BETC Luxe told Thomas that clothing is understood to be an actual loss for most luxury brands.[8] But holding runway shows and putting actresses in designer dresses on red carpets is about branding, sometimes even more than it is about selling the actual clothes. The fashion serves to raise the profile of the designer in question, creating lust for their name and then driving sales to marked-up handbags, shoes, and profitable knickknacks.

But designer clothing also has the surprising and perhaps unintended consequence of driving demand for cheap fashion. Our general awareness of exorbitantly priced dresses makes the prices at stores like H&M, Target, and Forever 21 seem that much more irresistible. For more deal-oriented consumers like me, we see cheap fashion as a badge of honor, as proof that we are not one of *those people* who would ever pay too much for a designer name. According to C. W. Park, the editor of the *Journal of Consumer Psychology* and a marketing professor at USC Marshall School of Business, "What these luxury fashion goods really do is open up the growth possibility of low-end products, because they serve as reference prices when people buy inexpensive products." For other consumers, the in-your-face advertising of designer fashion has done something else entirely—it has created huge unfulfilled demand for affordable clothing by famous designers. And it's cheap-fashion chains that are satisfying those manufactured yearnings as well.

On September 13, 2011, a collection of knitwear shut down Target's Web site. The line was by Italian luxury fashion house Missoni, whose bold, multicolored zigzag and striped-pattern knits often retail for well over $1,000. That day my Facebook feed filled with mentions of failed attempts to log on to the Target Web site and a photo of a gargantuan Missoni puppet in a mall in Minneapolis. I was amazed at the number of people I knew who were aware of an Italian luxury label. CNN called the event unprecedented, citing bigger sales volumes than Black Friday. [9] The Missoni for Target collection clearly tapped into some widespread longing for designer clothes.

Though Target dabbled with designer collaborations as early as 2003 with Isaac Mizrahi, it was actually H&M that achieved "international notoriety" by convincing some of the brightest stars in fashion to produce limited collections for the company.[10] In 2004 Karl Lagerfeld, the shades-sporting, white-ponytailed designer of Chanel and the artistic director of Fendi, was the first to partner with H&M. At the time Lagerfeld claimed to have never set foot in an H&M. He told *The Independent* that his first encounter with the retailer was coming across a well-dressed girl at Chanel. Lagerfeld complimented her. " 'It's H&M,' she responded, 'because I'm not paid enough to be able to afford Chanel.' "[11]

The H&M in Herald Square was mobbed when Lagerfeld debuted his 30-piece line in its store. Prices ranged from $34.90 for a silk dress and $49.90 for a tuxedo shirt to $129 for a wool blazer, a premium compared to most of H&M's prices. The Lagerfeld collection sold out within days of hitting the floors. In Paris it sold out in minutes. And the collaboration boosted H&M's sales by 24 percent that month.[12]

Every season another mass-fashion retailer announces a buzzy new partnership with a famed designer, hoping to create the Lagerfeld effect, growing sales by drawing hysterical early morning queues and stampedes that clean out stores in the blink of an eye. H&M has rolled out budget lines from a succession of pedigreed fashion designers, including Lanvin, Comme des Garçons, and Versace. UNIQLO, Walmart, and Gap have all collaborated with well-known designers, as has Forever 21. Target has partnered with more than a dozen now, including Rodarte, Thakoon, and Proenza Schouler.

A Missoni for Target dress has little in common with a real Missoni, which is made of blends of virgin wool, viscose, alpaca, and other high-end fibers knitted in the company's own factories outside of Milan.[13] Blog reports noted the Target Missoni knits were made of acrylic in China.[14] No matter; consumers were just after the name, "a Missoni." CBS writer Ysolt Usigan posted to the *Tech Talk* blog the day the line went on sale that she was able to land $200 of "Missoni stuff" from Target.com, including a blouse, a sweater dress, a sweater skirt, and a jumpsuit. "I don't know what they look and feel like in person," Usigan writes. "I don't know if they'll fit. I'll worry about that next week when my shipment finally arrives." Where girls once would have paid at least some attention to the craftsmanship of the product, or even might have sat behind a sewing machine and created their own Missoni-inspired or Karl Lagerfeld look-alike, they can now line up passively to buy disposable versions of it.

To get a sense of what designer clothing fetches these days, I made several trips to the storied New York City department store Bergdorf Goodman. Since 1928 women's wear has been housed there in a Beaux Arts mansion that sits across from the southern entrance to Central Park and stretches the length of the block. It has been a destination for the leisure class ever since. Today, the fabulously wealthy may have their hair styled in the penthouse John Barrett Salon, acquire the services of a personal shopper, or take in prime park views and hobnob with ladies who lunch in the posh BG Restaurant. And Bergdorf Goodman sells some of the finest clothing money can buy, including couture and very established ready-to-wear lines by Oscar de la Renta, Chanel, and Yves Saint Laurent. They also carry contemporary designers such as Jason Wu, Norma Kamali, and Michael Kors.

I looked at the tags and labels on several hundred items of clothing at Bergdorf Goodman, trying to make sense of the huge price variations. There were clothing lines where the handiwork and fabric seemingly justified the price. Gowns by American designer Ralph Rucci can run thousands upon thousands of dollars, but are also complex, hand-finished constructions that are veritable works of art. Some of Oscar de la Renta's gowns are equally opulent.

There *are* those high-end clothing designers who achieve their exclusionary prices by using exquisite or lavish materials such as angora, exotic animal skins, cashmere, or lamb's wool. Tomas Maier, the German designer who heads the Italian luxury brand Bottega Veneta, is known for fine fabrics, like a Japanese viscose so fine it must be cut with a laser.[15] In the absolute top tiers of the fashion world—where the $17,000 furs and $10,000 gowns reside—the idea is not to make sensible clothing. The extravagance is all part of the point, the spectacle, and ultimately the price. According to Park, "What these companies do is only sell their products to those who can afford to pay that much." In other words, luxury designers engineer clothing with the knowledge of what their wealthy clients can afford, and add luxurious details.

Dalma Dress sews designer gowns that would sell in Bergdorf Goodman for thousands of dollars, and DiPalma says that the price is justified by the craftsmanship and labor involved. I asked DiPalma if the dresses were overpriced. "Labor is labor," he replied, defending the high-end garments his factory now makes. With a bit more pressing, he went on to explain that if his expert sewers must attach strings of beads and encrusted jewels onto a gown by needle and thread or hand-sew lace onto the train of a wedding dress, the production costs are going to be very high. "These are the designer's signature pieces," DiPalma said, meaning the creations for which no expense is spared. "This is the stuff you see in *Vogue* and on the runways."

DiPalma is only privy to the labor and material costs that go into *sewing* a dress. But he could still explain how one made of extraordinary materials could potentially retail for more than a grand. "Here, I'll do the math," he said, extending his finger over the keys of a calculator that he keeps ready and waiting by his phone. He asked me to imagine a very high-end designer using $500 worth of imported embroidery to make a dress. "If it's five hundred dollars for embroidery and then I charge one hundred dollars for labor," DiPalma said, *click, clack, clicking* on his calculator. "And I charge twenty-five dollars in lining, three dollars for pads, and a zipper." *Click, clack, click.* "A hanger, a bag, and a hangtag are another five dollars. So far, that's six hundred and thirty-three dollars in cost," he stated, like the proud winner of a school debate.

Our imaginary dress would not be sold in stores for $633 however. If it cost $633 for materials and labor to make the dress, the price would then be doubled for the wholesale price (this is the price we pay for sale items). If the dress is sold through a store, the store marks it up 2.25 times over the wholesale price, at the very least, which would land the new dress on the rack at $2,848.50. Eliza Starbuck, the fashion designer who produced a line for Urban Outfitters, told me that for something plainer, the costs would be lower. "Let's say you make a dress in Italy in silk; it might actually cost you two hundred dollars to make it," she says. After the wholesale and retail markups, it would land on racks at just under a grand.

Sonia Rykiel is a seminal French fashion designer who was once called the Queen of Knits and shook things up by putting seams on the outside of garments. Owning a Sonia Rykiel will set you back hundreds and even thousands of dollars. Isenberg says that some top-notch designers overcharge but many others do not, including Rykiel. Isenberg started out as an intern in the production department at Rykiel, where she was privy to the production costs as well as the final retail costs. "When you're getting something made in France, you're getting Italian fabrics, and you're not just paying people decent wages, but good wages—the markups on the clothes are not incredibly high," she says.

But alongside the finely crafted pieces in Bergdorf Goodman that do much to earn their shocking price tags, there are just as many if not more garments that are as trendy and ordinary as what's sold on the rack down the block at H&M. These garments, such as a thin, plain, cream-colored cotton dress by a popular American fashion designer priced at $994 are clearly overpriced. The $994 dress is no doubt produced in very small quantities (buyers for Bergdorf for example often only order one dress in each standard size), and the cotton is presumably finer than anything I'd buy at a cheap fashion chain. The famous designer and her team of people are no doubt handsomely paid.

But I also found a translucent made in China tag hidden behind the designer's label. These Chinese-made ghost labels are increasingly common in the world of extraordinarily expensive clothing. Country of origin does not necessarily impact quality, but it enormously impacts production costs. Such costs for a $994 cotton dress, which includes the price of a couple of yards of knit fabric and Chinese labor (which is still around a dollar an hour), fall dramatically short of this price tag. There's clearly more to the story behind that shocking number, one that has little to do with the actual dress and the costs associated with making it.

Robert Riley, the head of the design lab at the Fashion Institute of Technology throughout the 1960s and '70s, started out at Lord & Taylor in the 1940s, when France was occupied. The store helped fill the fashion void left by Europe by launching sportswear and the American Look pioneered by designers such as Claire McCardell. By the end of his twenty-five-year tenure with FIT, Riley saw the writing on the wall, where fashion designer's names were being held above the beauty and craftsmanship of clothing. "Look at almost any well-known designer today," he told *The New York Times* upon stepping down from his post in 1981. "Why is he well-known? Because he actually makes exceptional clothes or because he has the right publicity? Then take a look at a volume line like Bobbie Brooks and you'll see more quality there than you will in a thousand-dollar ball gown even if there is no design inventiveness. From my vantage I think we are entering parlous times. Quality and creativeness are being sacrificed for money and big business."[16] There used to be more of a direct connection between high-end clothing and quality. Now a designer name is no guarantee of craftsmanship. As early as 1994, *Consumer Reports* was finding that designer clothing at Barneys, in the case of a rayon chenille sweater, often offered no better quality than Kmart.[17]

I found myself back at Bergdorf Goodman a few months after my price-comparison trip on a different mission. What seemed to be absent in the prestige versus low-price wars was the actual tangible clothing itself. Beyond the designer label or the outrageous deals, is there any remaining clothing that is just plain beautiful and made well? Of course there is. A close friend of mine recently dropped $550 on a wool silk-lined Helmut Lang blazer, and she had to pry me out of it. The difference in quality between this jacket and anything I owned was visceral and obvious. This jacket felt amazing. It looked amazing on.

I conscripted wardrobe consultant Joan Reilly to go on my quality-finding mission. She and I walked all over Bergdorf, where she once worked, running our hands over ethereal fabrics, lifting up seams to study the stitching, and asking salespeople to explain different grades of cashmere and the like. "It's all about detail and the garment construction," Reilly explained, as we stuck our faces next to an exquisite hand-stiched $4,400 gown by Ralph Rucci. We walked past Swiss designer Andrew Gn's collection, and I reached out and touched a pair of pants and exclaimed, "Wow. This feels amazing." Reilly, impressed I'd developed a hand feel in such a short period of time, told me, "You've graduated!" Again, the difference was so visceral and obvious I didn't feel I deserved any credit.

We then moved on to another collection where the saleswoman wouldn't even indulge my questions about quality. She walked over to a bright orange cotton shirt with an embroidered neckline and pulled it off the rack. "Seven hundred dollars for a freaking tunic?" she said in a thick Long Island accent. "I don't think so." This Bergdorf saleswoman told me directly that quality was not at all that was motivating her consumer. It was prestige. They were after the designer's name. Reilly agreed that many consumers and even her own clients are more name obsessed and status motivated than anything. One client asked for help in planning an outfit around a pair of Jimmy Choo heels, having never shown her the shoes. "There wasn't even a description of the shoe," Reilly recalled. "I said, 'How is that going to help me help you pick out an outfit?'"

This takes us back to the $994 dress. Park explains that while some luxury clothing designers do engineer a luxuriously made product, others simply add hefty markups to draw in the ideal consumers and to make their product *seem* more prestigious. "The high price sends a market signal that that product is only for a very exclusive set of people," he says. The problem with this type of marketing strategy is that the "exclusive set" of people is getting more exclusive by the year. *Sex and the City* types and people such as Kimberly Couzens who shop beyond their means aren't, it turns out, the typical high-end clothing consumer. According to *Time* magazine, the wealthy now dominate sales at top-tier stores and are also the largest buyers of all clothing.[18]

In the United States, the chasm between the rich and poor narrowed throughout the early twentieth century. By the 1950s income was remarkably equal and upward mobility achievable for many. But in recent decades, the haves and the have-nots have been returning to their respective corners and, embarrassingly, the United States is one of the only developed countries that has experienced growing income inequality. Now the top 1 percent of American households takes almost a quarter of all household income, a share not seen since 1929.[19] We're now wearing this yawning income gap on our bodies.

What happens when the primary consumers of "good" clothing have such deep pockets is that prices are driven up for everyone else. It's not unlike when rich people move into a neighborhood and rents skyrocket. Take nice jeans: According to *Women's Wear Daily*, when retailers and clothing designers saw that some people would pay $100, then $200 or more for a pair of high-end cotton pants, producers of other types of high-end garments realized they could raise their prices too.[20] There was clearly a customer out there willing to shell out despite such high prices. So up went the prices on designer dresses, tops, and everything else.

One would think that as stores like H&M, Forever 21, and Target offer increasingly sophisticated designs that consumers would demand lower prices at the higher end of the clothing market as well. Cheap fashion seems to have had the opposite effect on upmarket clothing buyers. *Women's Wear Daily* also reported that cheap-fashion prices are not pulling down designer price tags but driving them up: Consumers are shopping at the high-end specifically to "max out their Visas."[21] They are using clothes as a type of competitive consumption.

In economics, there is a principal known as "Veblen goods." These are the products we desire more the *higher* their prices go because we hope this will show other people that we have wealth and status. Clothing is very sensitive to this effect since it deals directly with personal expression and ego. We see it as an extension of ourselves, and it is the most visible way we can strut our stuff. "Fashion is the most unique product in this sense because it deals with presenting yourself to the outside world," says Park. "That is the reason why we pay so much attention to clothing, and that is the reason why some people are willing to pay so much for it." There is no other consumer category for which such huge price extremes are driven by our ceaseless pursuit to look good and prove ourselves to others.

When I first met Kimberly Couzens, I was drawn in by her method of shopping. She's very selective about what she buys and is rarely impulsive. She loves fashion to a degree that I find inspiring. "I don't identify with the lifestyle of wealthy people on the whole," she says. "I'm a middle-class girl. I just really appreciate fashion as an art form, and that aspect of the lifestyle drew me in." I initially reached out to Couzens because I thought buying designer fashion was the antidote to buying cheap. I quickly came hard up against the fact that I couldn't afford most of it.

One afternoon I went shopping at the Fendi flagship. I was ushered into the store by security guards wearing earpieces and climbed the stairs to find a deathly quiet carpeted and deserted salon where a slim selection of garments hung against the wall. Ample couches and side tables took up most of the space. I had the feeling I'd stumbled uninvited into someone's dressing room. Eventually a young salesman emerged like a specter and looked utterly surprised to see me, or anyone. "I love your hat," he chirped. I was wearing a knit toboggan from Target with a ridiculous pom-pom on top. It cost $12. I appreciated the gesture. But I wasn't supposed to be here. There was nothing I could afford. A pair of fur-trimmed gloves on this floor was $700.

Couzens's designer habit finally caught up with her, costing her an office worker's annual salary in credit-card debt, which she only hinted at the first time I met her. Two years later Couzens was in a much different place in her life and that's when she confessed to me that her expensive tastes had gotten her into extreme financial trouble. "I had to drastically change my lifestyle," she explained with the zeal of a convert, having just passed her one-year anniversary of being in a debt management program, the tradeoff for avoiding bank-ruptcy at age 25. "I don't have any disposable income," she says. "I don't go out much, I don't travel, I don't really shop, I spend maybe fifty dollars a month on entertainment." She'd also mostly stopped watching *Gossip Girl*, after having to cancel her cable subscription. "The show's moment has also sort of passed anyway," Couzens told me sheepishly.

The hardest part of Couzens's transformation was having to sell almost every single piece of designer clothing she owned to help pay down her debt. She has since switched to wearing a lot of basics from chain stores such as Express, Gap, and American Eagle Outfitters. The designer maven now wears a winter coat from Kmart, of all places, and a pair of Steve Madden shoes from the discount footwear chain DSW. She says her Express clothes are decently made for the price, but they're not particularly fashionable. Couzens says she is content to blend in until she gets her life back on track.

I asked Couzens how she feels about high-end designers now. She said she still feels confident that many of the pieces were good invest-ments. "All of the designer pieces I bought had resale value," says Couzens. "I was never disappointed in the quality I got for my money and the fit." She says if she had it to do over again, she'd try not to spend more than she can afford and would try to buy more classic items that don't date as quickly. Couzens had kept one single designer purchase, the $700 Louis Vuitton purse, with this thought in mind: "It's actually the most worthwhile purchase I've ever made," she told me. "I've worn it almost every day for four years, and it's still kicking."

This isn't the first time the fashion industry has been divided along the lines of the haves and the have-nots. In the early twentieth century, most people were either very rich or very poor, and the American fashion industry looked almost exclusively to Parisian couturiers to set styles. According to Whitaker's *Service and Style,* early department stores operated on a high-low model that produced cheap imitations of the Parisian designs for lower-end consumers and expensive licensed copies for the wealthy.[22] Around 1902, when lingerie-style dresses came into vogue, Whitaker found that knockoffs were available at Marshall Field's for $25 ($621 in today's dollars) to $75 ($1,864), far out of the reach of most consumers. Buying a real couture dress, the inspiration for early mass-manufactured women's wear, was also out of the question for anyone other than the rich. Even today, couture gowns often start at $25,000.[23]

Any comparisons between the high-low industry of 1902 and today likely end there because women knew how to sew. Gabrielle Chanel and Jeanne Lanvin, for example, weren't the heads of luxury conglomerates hawking branded perfume and sunglasses. They were two professional home dressmakers who were eventually recruited by couture houses to make the exquisite made-to-order, hand-finished garments of the trade.[24] Valerie Steele, the director of the Museum at the Fashion Institute of Technology and a respected fashion historian, explains that the early fashion industry was distinctly different from today, as it rotated around custom dressmaking. "The average woman would not have been able to afford couture," says Steele, "but you certainly would have been able to hire a little dressmaker to make a custom copy of a couture dress. Or you could have made it yourself."

Many women were such talented seamstresses that price couldn't exclude them from the fashion game. During the Christmas shopping season of 1902, Whitaker notes that department stores sold enormous volumes of lace and embroidery, as women opted to just make their own versions of the lingerie style.[25] Department stores of the day had bigger fabric departments than ready-to-wear sections, and affordable patterns, some inspired by couturiers, were available in publications like the *Vogue Pattern Book*. Women who could afford it took illustrations clipped from newspapers or fashion magazines along with bolts of fabric to a dressmaker.

As income distribution started to even out after the Great Depression, upwardly mobile Americans started to flex their buying power. Store-bought clothing was widely embraced; early problems with sizing and uneven quality had been corrected. But there was little virtue in buying cheap. As Whitaker explains in her book, the middle class looked to department stores as places where they could buy better-quality goods that allowed them to show off their newfound economic status. And department stores marketed to consumers' increasingly highbrow tastes. "As the whole institution of the department store evolved, they set themselves up as a bulwark of standards," Whitaker says.

Even Sears, the catalog and chain store known for its cheap goods, had quality standards. In the back of the 1955 Sears catalog, a picture taken inside its apparel-testing laboratory is accompanied by a guide to "buying wisely," which lays out the differences between reprocessed and virgin wool, sunfast versus sun-resistant fabrics, and so on, as well as a glossary of every man-made fiber used at the time. Regular department store consumers could find a range of clothing that varied from conservative to quality-conscious to fashion-forward. And it was all decently made. Even discount stores had to aim higher during this period to lure in the middle class.[26]

Clothing of this era was produced by small-scale, independent manufacturers, and the garment trade was highly competitive, which often resulted in more stylish, more detailed, and better-constructed clothing than we find in stores today. As the 1955 Standard & Poor's industry survey noted, "To compete with the great number of small concerns operating in the industry, most of the larger apparel companies concentrate their production on quality, trade-marked products, distributed on a national scale through independent retailers."[27]

At 67, Jan Whitaker remembers when most store-bought duds were of a different caliber, often finished with a blind hem, a labor-intensive and subtle type of stitch that's almost invisible. Women often resewed hems to make a garment look more expensive. "You *never* saw clothes that were sewn with a straight hem," recalls Whitaker. "That was considered trash. Even poor people didn't wear clothes with a hem like that. Now that's the norm." Today, by contrast, most mass-market clothes are finished with a quick, simple straight hem and seams are closed with a serger, a type of machine that joins fabric with an over-lock stitch and then cuts away any extra material. Without loose material left on the side seams or hems, as used to be the standard, clothes can no longer be let out, and few people make an attempt to get them altered. "My dolls wore clothes that were better made than today's clothing," says Whitaker, and she means that literally. Her dolls' clothes were finished with blind hems.

Back in the post–World War I period, the average price of dresses dropped to around $16.95 ($182 in today's dollars), and a lot of women started buying poorer-quality cheap dresses, that might last only a season, to keep up with trends.[28] Poor-quality garments bought in an attempt to chase fads? Was it possible that cheap fashion of today was just repeating history? Whitaker quickly corrected me. "The average run of cheap clothes today is made way worse than clothes used to be made," she says. In the 1920s, for example, when Europe was recovering from World War I, America imported a lot of so-called cheap hand-beaded dresses from Paris. "Today, we would be amazed at how well those were made," Whitaker says.

Consumers once bought the best clothing they could for their money, which started with an intimate knowledge of fiber content. When clothes were more expensive and kept for years and worn year-round, we were naturally more invested in what they were made of. The fabrication label with its list of fibers and care instructions is a legacy of this largely bygone era.

Around the middle of the twentieth century, newfangled man-made fibers such as acetate and rayon were heavily advertised by domestic clothing and chemical companies as easy-to-care-for miracle products. This was partially a cultural change as American lifestyles became more leisurely and lent themselves to more practical and low-maintenance garments.[29] Despite huge advancements in textile technology, man-made fibers never quite had the cachet of cotton, wool, or silk, and cellulose-based fabrics such as rayon never had anything more than a niche role. As the cotton industry improved the performance of its product, and synthetic fiber production moved to Asia in recent decades, synthetics took on a lower profile. But they didn't disappear. Synthetics have been quietly slipped back into the clothing supply in recent years, mostly in the form of polyester.

In my own closet I discovered a few of my tank tops are made from viscose, rayon, Modal, and Tencel. These fabrics are all cellulosic (there are two families of man-made fibers: plastics and cellulosic), which are produced from chemically processed wood pulp or other naturally sourced by-products like cotton scraps and sawdust. Modal and Tencel are environmentally friendly trademarked rayons made by the Austria-based Lenzing Corporation. They're generally not cheaper than cotton. Though cellulosic fibers were popular midcentury, their usage is minimal now, comprising only around 5 percent of worldwide fiber consumption.[30]

I mostly found polyester and its relatives in the plastic family lurking in my closet. It turns out that my sweaters are blended with a high percentage of acrylic, a plastic-based fiber that mimics the feel of wool or cashmere. My blouses and dresses are almost all 100 percent polyester. I imagined my low-cost winter jackets were pure wool. They are not. A gray hooded one from H&M is 65 percent wool, 20 percent polyester, and 15 percent nylon. A black balloon-cut number from Zara is 70 percent polyester, 24 percent wool, and 6 percent viscose—and is also covered in those unsightly bumps of fabric known as pills. Another bathrobe-style coat turns out to be 70 percent wool and 30 percent nylon. Nylon, also in the plastics family, is a very strong fiber used often in products like carpet but is rarely used in large quantities in everyday clothing. I intentionally avoid buying plastic products such as bottled water because they are oil-dependent and not biodegradable, yet here I was with a closet full of the stuff.

The production of man-made fibers has almost doubled over the past 15 years, with polyester production taking the lion's share of the growth. Polyester now accounts for more than 40 percent of all fiber produced in the world.[31] What does it mean that so many of us are wearing polyester? It is commonly blended into fabrics to improve strength and drape or to make clothes easier to care for, but it also brings down the price when blended with wool, silk, or cotton.

Perhaps the main reason we are wearing polyester is because Asia, where a majority of our textiles are now produced, has poured enormous investments into polyester in recent years. In 2004 *Textile World* covered the "explosive growth" in Asian man-made fiber production, noting that polyester "virtually has become the fiber of choice, albeit often combined with cotton." Polyester production now exceeds 50 billion pounds a year, the article noted, with China producing well over half of that volume.[32]

Sal Giardina, an adjunct professor at the Fashion Institute of Technology and the design director of a high-end custom men's suit company called Nantsun America, says the prevalence of synthetics like polyester is absolutely due to the cost-cutting pressures retailers endure. "It's not because people are waking up and saying, 'I want to wear polyester,'" he told me, chuckling. And with consumers increasingly uneducated about or uninterested in fabrics, the goal for designers is to choose materials that are inexpensive enough to hit the desired price point, without tipping consumers off that they're getting a less-desired fabric. "What the industry has created to address the real low-price garment is a fabric called polyester and viscose," Giardina told me of mass-market men's suits. Viscose is cellulosic and gives the fabric a wool-like feel; polyester makes it easy to care for and cheap. "There have been so many advances in the fabric that it looks almost like wool. Except it's more like three dollars a yard, compared to ten dollars a yard for wool. And wear it on a hot day and you'll really feel a difference."

Though dresses midway through the twentieth century weren't always made of the best fabrics, they were very structured and tailored, often featured extraordinary detail, and were made from veritable reams of fabric compared to today's skimpy duds. These more elaborate garments were not cheap to make, yet they were not outlandishly priced. In the January 1955 issue of *Seventeen* magazine, a plethora of gorgeous, voluminous dresses for juniors were advertised from a variety of manufacturers, and they were almost all priced between $8 and $11, which works out to about $65 to $90 today, the very definition of middle-market prices.

Upmarket clothes were also far more popularly priced. In 1961 a refined gray tweed dress by Abe Schrader sold for about $55, or $396 today. That would certainly put a dent in the middle-class pocketbook, but it was a good value, compared to the $994 cotton knit dress that characterizes the high-end market today. If a girl was too broke to buy an Abe Schrader, she could once again turn to her sewing machine. The cover story from the January 1955 *Seventeen* was "Sew it—Suds it," an eight-page spread of home sewing patterns of the season's hottest full-skirted dresses. The article trails a cash-poor teenager named Polly who, "By sewing her own clothes (and supplementing her wardrobe), got her allowance to s-t-r-e-t-c-h!"

The wardrobes on the '60s-set television show *Mad Men*, created by lauded costume designer Janie Bryant, capture the decades before we became an übercasual nation of T-shirts and jeans lovers. *Mad Men* is about the rise of the Madison Avenue advertising industry, and one of the accounts on the show is Jantzen swimwear. The ascent of large clothing companies, with their fat advertising budgets, did much to nudge Americans away from the sharp styles portrayed on the show.

The show also documents the enormous cultural change that happened during this period as well. The social upheavals of the '60s and especially the '70s counterculture and feminist movements brought in street wear and youth fashions, and Valerie Steele says that following high fashion became passé during this time. "Because of the whole hippie, antifashion revolution, people no longer were willing to be so dictated to," she says. "They were much more choosy of which of the trends they wanted to follow."

Ready-to-wear designers such as miniskirt inventor Mary Quant were early to popularize youth-oriented fashions. The sportswear industry sprang up in Los Angeles, and this style's simplicity offered lower prices compared with the formal looks of earlier decades. Separates were introduced, making it cheaper to buy pants or a top instead of a one-piece dress. Darlene Knitwear was a big early player in separates, and in the October 1965 issue of *Seventeen* advertised "Holiday-happy separates" that are "extravagant-looking (but not priced!)" A blush-colored cardigan with crochet trimming went for $13, as did a fully lined flannel suit skirt, about $88.87 today. Ship'n Shore was another manufacturer that specialized in more casual styles, such as a button-down shirt with floral print and a plaid flannel henley, both $4 ($27.35).

As people moved away from making their own clothes, general public knowledge of garment construction faded. Though the connection is not entirely direct, the loss of sewing skills happened in tandem with the public accepting simpler and simpler fashions, until today—where we have collectively accepted the two-panel knit creation that is a T-shirt as fashion. Anthony Lilore, a 30-year veteran of the fashion industry and an advocate for Save the Garment Center, agrees that the increasing informalization of fashion has made consumers cheaper. "Fashion used to be tailored clothing, not bespoke, but a much more structured garment bought at department stores," he says. "That men walk around in T-shirts and elastic waistband pants has very definitely impacted the notion of what fashion is and contributed to the race to the bottom." The less skill involved in making our clothes, the cheaper they become, and the less we are willing to pay for them. The more basic clothes are, the less it matters where they're made. A tank top can be made anywhere in the world. The same cannot be said of a well-made dress, which requires a highly skilled seamstress. Does this mean we should return to wearing dresses so elaborate we have to be helped into them? Probably not, but I know that these changes are all tied up in the bulldozing powers of cheap.

As fashion became a huge and inflexible industry, it became financially dangerous to sell fashion, especially fashion that was costly to make. When running a clothing conglomerate, it is better not to take risks on a tailored dress or jacket and just stick to tried-and-true basics and cheap-to-produce styles. Every store from Target to a midmarket chain such as Ann Taylor largely sells simply constructed tops and slacks as their bread and butter. Gap of course made a virtue of selling incredibly ordinary clothes like pocket T-shirts. Forever 21 carries trendier and more varied merchandise but even it sells a lot of denim; skimpy dresses; and light, casual tops. A tank top can go from racerback, flyaway, long and drapey, short and spaghetti-strapped, to ruffled, ruched, and accented with florettes—but it's still a basic garment compared to a 1950s dress or a turn-of-the-century ready-to-wear suit, to say nothing of the bustles, crinolines, and dresses saddled with panniers that women wore the century before.

Clothing is reverse engineered from the price consumers are willing to pay, which for mass-market clothing gets lower every year. The joke in the industry is that consumers want to pay $9 for whatever they paid $10 for last year. Sean Cormier, a textile development and marketing professor at FIT, says the pressure to produce a lower-grade product comes both from cheapskate consumers and from companies wanting to increase their profits. "It's a two-way street," says Cormier. "Obviously the manufacturers are trying to make money, but the consumers are just waiting until stuff goes on sale." Clothing companies can't afford to have consumers buy their well-made stuff on sale and continue to offer the same quality product year after year. Something has to give.

Clothiers have always had to balance quality with their own bottom lines, not to mention with changing consumer tastes and the need to keep us buying. But when the severe low-price pressures of the past decades set in, simplified and lower-quality garments were no longer a symbol of changing cultural mores or women's freedom—they became design-room staples because they were cheap to make.

I was flipping through a catalog recently from Lands' End, the preppy middle-market mail-order retailer, and the ad copy for their cashmere-wool blended coats caught my eye: "At Lands' End, we insist on features and construction details that others have taken out over the years." I didn't know what to believe. *What exactly has been removed or clipped off or forgone in the ceaseless pursuit of cheap?* I wondered. I imagined a design team trying to dream up a coat or even a dress for a consumer like me. *What kind of dress can we make for $30?* they'd have to ask themselves. The answer is not much of one.

Cormier says that most of the people he knows in the industry have been in such meetings. "We'll look at the line and look at the margins that are being made and you sense that it's not enough. So, you work with the designers to take stuff off," he says. The fashion designers and the money makers of clothing companies are often at war over the quality fade and the more basic stylings. "Designers I know want the best product," Cormier says, "but then it goes to the operational people who have to cost it out and figure out where the margin is." By the time a style goes into production, a designer has often watched his creation be whittled away.

In order to shave costs, fabrics have become thinner and lighter over the years. Cormier says that he's seen companies take a six-ounce shirt and reduce it to five ounces. "Does it still meet the company's quality standards?" he asks. "Yes. But is it as aesthetically as nice? Sometimes no." Even I have noticed the great thinning of the American wardrobe. Go to a thrift store and hold in your hands a sweater or jacket made before 1990. Today's clothes by comparison feel like they're going to float away.

Bright Young Things designer Eliza Starbuck has worked for many high-end clothing brands, including Coach, and she told me the sewing is drastically compromised when a retailer is trying to reduce costs. "The sewing is what matters when it comes to whether or not the garment falls apart and becomes garbage," she says. Cheap clothing skimps on labor-intensive details such as lining, gussets, stronger seams, and apparently sometimes forgoes sewing altogether: I was shocked to find that two flowers on an Old Navy tank top of mine were affixed by tape. Because speed to market is so important today, Starbuck says factories may use a looser, faster, less-secure stitch in order to get more garments out the door. "It's a miracle the stitch lines aren't this far apart," she said, stretching out her thumb from her forefinger.

Then she told me something even more shocking: "There are very few high-quality garments being produced at all. A *very, very, very* small amount. So small that most people never even see it in their lifetimes. People are wearing rags, basically." *That is tragic,* I thought, and the more I learned about the history of fashion, the more I was convinced she was right. Quality has been whittled away little by little, to the point where the average store-bought style is an extraordinarily thin and simple, albeit bedazzled and brightly colored, facsimile of a garment. Yet I suspect few consumers born after 1980 have any idea what they're missing.

What's alarming about the quality fade in mass-market clothing is that with the cost of labor and materials going up and consumers' price expectations going down, our clothing supply can only get shoddier from here. Quality fabrics and sewing are increasingly becoming a losing game in the era of cheap, fast-moving fashion. Quality takes time. It slows things down. It adds to cost. Michael Kane, of L.A.-based women's wear brand Karen Kane, says the company has tried to introduce cheaper products without entirely eroding its quality standards, but these efforts are at odds. "It's been very difficult to deal with the change in mentality on the consumer level of what they expect for what price," he says. "At some point, there's going to be a breaking point. You can only make things for so cheap that you cannot even wear it once and it falls apart."

There's another, more unexpected source of quality fade, and it comes from the overseas garment factories where our clothes are now made—but not for the reasons we might think. Many overseas garment factories are capable of advanced construction techniques, but they also operate on impossibly thin margins and ever-tighter deadlines. They do not relish when clients demand a lot of back-and-forth on sampling, testing, and perfecting design. Long lead times to production are not ideal for factories, which are not making money unless they are making clothes.

One Chinese garment manufacturer I talked to formerly sewed apparel for Abercrombie & Fitch, a huge branded teen retailer with an extensive testing and sampling process. The factory's sales assistant Catherine told me, frustratedly, "They are very fussy," describing a dizzying combination of washes and colors on a fleece jacket that the retailer wanted to see before green-lighting an order. "Every time they make a change, the factory stops and postpones production to next month," she says. "But don't forget, next month I've got an order for the next producer. So, *crash*!" Catherine said that her factory could be left with a hole in its production and also scrambling to deal with being double-booked for the upcoming month.

Most mass-market clothing is now so poorly made and ordinary that many consumers intuit that it's not worth much money. In 1997 *Consumer Reports* did a cross-comparison of polo shirts from different brands and stores, giving a $7 polo from Target a higher rating than versions from Ralph Lauren, Tommy Hilfiger, Nautica, and Gap based on durability, fiber content, and wear.[33] Why buy a $75 Ralph Lauren polo shirt when it's not any better made than the store-brand polo on the rack at Target? Decades ago there would have been a big quality difference between these middle-market brands and the discounters. But no longer. The brands have had to reduce their quality to pad their profits. It's much easier today to make money dressing up low-end clothing. Discounters have done just that, dressing up their products to draw in consumers who now feel absolutely no shame in buying cheap.

Who can forget budget clothing's scratchy fabrics and fashion-backward design of decades past? Growing up in the 1980s and the early 1990s, a funny Tweety Bird nightgown at Walmart or a matronly blouse at a discount store was about as good as it got in my south Georgia town. My mom used to drag me to regional budget clothing chains Cato and It's Fashion, where I'd try in vain to buy something that might pass for Gap or a department store top. This is all a distant memory. On the typical cheap garment today, the threads are cut, the seams are straight, and the colors are consistent and bright. More than that, cheap clothes are now quite fashionable. There really isn't much clothing sold nowadays that is supercheap and not on trend. Today, on Cato's Web site, there's a trapeze-neck leopard-print dress that I'd wear. The price? $29.99. It's Fashion now promises to offer "the trendy looks you'll find in mall specialty stores at low prices every day." And it more or less delivers.

The Wall Street Journal picked up on the budget-apparel design revolution as early as 1995, noting that "Budget clothing, long associated with ill-fitting men's jeans and baggy, one-size-fits-all tops for women, is looking much better these days." The difference? Manufacturers had started paying attention to the details such as fancy-looking buttons, real embroidery, and lined collars and cuffs that make clothes look expensive. "The main mission is to provide the surface details that the average consumer perceives to be good quality," one apparel consultant told the paper.[34]

Today's cheap clothes are seductive and deceiving. Old Navy was one of the earliest stores to raise the beauty on ultracheap garments, disguising thin, low-grade fabrics and basic design with bright colors and prints. As a 1999 *Newsweek* article put it, the chain was doing something novel by dyeing cheap basics "some offbeat color, like acid green" and showcasing them together in "an eye-catching bundle."[35] My own closet is emblazoned with bold hues from ochre to teal to sea foam green, and unusual prints, such as one Old Navy dress in what looks to be a red-blood-cell pattern.

As *The Wall Street Journal* noted, cheap fashion also depends on embellishments that make a garment *look* more expensive. Forever 21 clothing is an assault of sequins, ruffles, grommets, and studs. These flashy add-ons remind me of something else I read in Whitaker's *Service and Style*. When Hortense Odlum took over high-end New York City department store Bonwit Teller after the Depression, she found to her horror that "buckles, clips, pins, and bows" had been added to the store's dresses to hide poor workmanship and cheap fabrics.[36] Such garish trimmings are often the selling point for today's low-end garments. It's all about the attention-grabbing surface detail that will get us to buy, and buy on the spot.

As compared to budget fashion of yesteryear, today's offerings may be advanced products. But they are not well made. We're being sold ostensibly on good design, typically at the expense of craftsmanship or quality. As Karl Lagerfeld told *The Independent* on the eve of the launch of his downmarket line for H&M, "Everybody today can be well dressed because cheaper clothes are well designed, too. OK, so maybe the material used might not be extraordinary, but it's no longer a fact that lower-priced things are lousy."[37] Quality today means something quite different than it used to. It apparently means *not lousy*.

A few weeks before Christmas in 2010, I was cautiously pulling a dress off the rack at Bottega Veneta. The 45-year-old luxury-goods company was bought by the Gucci Group in 2001 and revamped by the logo-eschewing German fashion designer Tomas Maier. In the years since, celebrities from Kim Kardashian to Sarah Jessica Parker to *Harry Potter* starlet Emma Watson have graced red carpets in gorgeous, understated Bottega Veneta gowns. Even I, a woman who won't pay more than $30 for a dress, have heard of Bottega Veneta. It has a retail location on Manhattan's Fifth Avenue, but I had never been inside.

The dress I had in my hands was eggplant purple, with a pleated skirt and frayed football-pad shoulders, and priced at $7,000. I loved it. When a very gracious saleswoman encouraged me to try it on, I smiled and said reflexively, "I don't want to be tempted." The line rang comically hollow. I didn't even have the credit limit to buy this garment. The saleswoman persisted, "This dress is almost one-of-a-kind. It's not mass-manufactured clothing, you know. I don't like mass-manufactured clothing." And there it was. I could either flee to the H&M just down the street and buy a poorly made knockoff, or I could take out a second mortgage and buy the "real thing." For a moment, I was convinced that nothing could exist outside of the current paradigm, which pits prestige and the allure of a designer name against clothing priced just as outrageously on the cheap end of the spectrum.

4

Fast Fashion

Opened by James Cash Penney in 1913, JCPenney started off as a dry-goods store that sold, among other things, blue jeans, fabric, and sewing needles. But it quickly set itself apart from its department store brethren. It was a chain store to its core, setting up posts in numerous rural towns and small cities. As the Penney's Web site boasts, at one time more than 2,000 of its stores blanketed the country. Sam Walton, the founder of the world's largest and most ruthlessly cheap retailer, Walmart, worked at the Des Moines, Iowa, JCPenney in the 1940s.

JCPenney survived the consolidation and markdown wars of the past several decades, but by the new millennium was in deep decline, so much so that a business journalist named Bill Hare wrote a book called *Celebration of Fools: An Inside Look at the Rise and Fall of JCPenney.* A few years ago, JCPenney's former CEO, Myron Ullman, determined that his company's woes were caused by his customers—they weren't shopping enough. Department store shoppers were still on the old seasonal habit of buying. "If you only deliver four times a year, there's only a reason to come to the store four times a year," lamented Ullman to *The Wall Street Journal.*[1] The natural pace of clothing consumption in the United States was suddenly being viewed as retail suicide. There was only one thing that could save Penney's: fast fashion. Ullman concluded, "Fast fashion for the young, modern woman is our highest-potential business opportunity."

In 2010 JCPenney rolled out a collaboration with the Spanish fast-fashion giant Mango. Although it only has a modest 14 retail locations in the United States, Mango is one of the largest and most popular retailers in Europe and operates 2,000 stores in 103 countries. Mango's line for JCPenney, called MNG by Mango, is replenished every two weeks. Ullman no longer had to lose sleep that his customers weren't shopping enough. They now have 26 reasons a year to come into his stores.

Fast fashion is a radical method of retailing that has broken away from seasonal selling and puts out new inventory constantly throughout the year. Fast-fashion merchandise is typically priced much lower than its competitors'. The fast-fashion concept was pioneered by Spain's Zara, which delivers new lines twice a week to its stores. H&M and Forever 21 both get daily shipments of new styles. The London-based Topshop, which has a U.S. location in Manhattan, introduces an astonishing 400 new styles a week on its Web site. Charlotte Russe and bebe, both U.S.-based, are also constantly updating their stock. On its face, it makes little sense that selling so much attractive fashion for so little could be profitable. But in fact, it seems to be the only surefire way to make it in today's retail scene: Fast-fashion retailers have more than twice the average profit margin of their more traditional competitors.[2]

There may not be one of these stores I mention on every city block in America *yet,* but the fast-fashion model has been adopted to varying degrees by retailers of all stripes. A 2006 *Newsweek* article on the growing pressures of fast fashion on U.S. stores noted that Walmart, which has struggled to win over fashionable consumers, had already shortened its delivery times down to weeks for fashionable items and that even chains like Chico's, which caters to the over-40 set, now deliver new inventory every day.[3] There are few fashion companies that aren't currently trying hard to figure out how they can get new clothes into stores faster and sell them for less than ever before.

Fashion is by its nature a perilous business. The threat is always there of a style bombing or not selling as well as predicted and markdowns and clearances stealing away profits. In 1987 merchants were notoriously burdened with huge leftover inventories after forecasters predicated the miniskirt was making a comeback. It did not.[4] As the industry consolidated, order sizes became huge, and shareholders demanded to see quarterly growth, the financial risk of fashion became great enough to make any CEO wince.

Once production was outsourced, supply chains became very long and unwieldy, with fabric sourcing, dyeing, embellishment, and sewing all potentially happening in different countries.[5] Lead times were a half a year; collections had to be dreamed up a full year ahead of time. Clothing companies began to invest deeply in trend research and professional forecasting, all in an attempt to accurately predict what we'd all want to be wearing far down the road. Naturally, fashion companies got it wrong all the time. Long lead times and huge orders doomed clothing companies to overbuying and to the incessant sales that consumers have come to expect in recent decades. The president of Nicole Miller told *The New York Times* back in 1991, "The cost of that kind of inefficient guesswork is what has led to this phony price structure with guaranteed markdowns that we have now."[6]

Amancio Ortega, the founder of the first fast-fashion store, Zara, started his career as a garment manufacturer and was almost driven to bankruptcy after a single wholesaler canceled a big order.[7] He would not be burned again. The first Zara store was opened to sell the orphaned order. And then Ortego got to work taking the risk out of selling clothes.

Zara can design, produce, and deliver a new garment and put it on display in any of its worldwide locations in two weeks. It produces relatively small batches of each design and always has something fresh on sale. Because its customers return more often to the store to see what's new, a majority of clothes sold at Zara are bought at full price. An in-depth 2004 *Harvard Business Review* article on Zara revealed how the retailer performs its magic: Its supply chain depends on a constant exchange of computerized information and phone calls between retail locations, factories, and Zara's headquarters in La Caruña, Spain. Zara's retail employees carry customized handheld computers to feed information about what's selling, customer reactions, and buzz around new styles. They'll make last-minute calls to their factories, where more than 50 percent of their fabric is waiting undyed so they can change the color midseason if need be.[8] Zara leverages all this information for one main purpose—to keep it from producing a style or a color, or even from using a zipper instead of a button-fly, when it's not going to sell.

Fast fashion is certainly an industry innovation and not possible in the globalized fashion industry without technological progress. But this is not the first time the industry has had quick, flexible supply chains. When production and textile resources were entirely in the United States, brands such as Jonathan Logan were very fast to market. Logan once owned an integrated factory in Spartanburg, South Carolina, that spun wool, made fabric, and sewed dresses all under one roof. "Raw wool in one door and finished dresses out the other," Logan president David Schwartz boasted to *Time* in 1963. The company also owned its own planes, so it could quickly airlift goods to stores.

Zara owns some of its factories, realizing what manufacturers knew a half century ago: Supply-chain control is crucial in a very finicky industry. H&M, which has its largest number of stores in Europe, likewise relies more on Turkey and other eastern European nations for quick-turn production. And Forever 21 keeps orders in Los Angeles factories for its most fashion-sensitive products. Though not as quick as Zara, Forever 21 can get styles from design to rack in six weeks, and H&M in close to eight.[9]

Fast fashion's true secret to success does not lie in advanced technology or close-by factories—it's in selling an unprecedented amount of clothing. As the *Harvard Business Review* cautions, Zara's success may only be applicable in industries "where product life cycles are very short." Fast fashion can only give us low prices if consumers continue to buy new clothes as soon as they're on the floor. Because fast-fashion goods move so quickly, stores are able to offer their best price first. At Zara unsold items account for less than 10 percent of stock, compared with the industry average of 17 to 20 percent.[10]

Fast-fashion consumers, not surprisingly, shop more than other consumers. *A lot more.* Just anecdotally, in my own life, I was shopping almost continually at H&M—on my lunch break, on my way to the subway, during an errands trip to the city; I was buying clothes all the time almost subconsciously, like a cow grazes on grass. Zara's customers shop the store 17 times a year on average. Just as the production cycle has broken away from the seasons, seasonal shopping patterns have given way to continual consumption. And fast fashion is driving these changes.

When people shop at Costco, the discount wholesaler, they often irrationally overconsume, such as buying a six-month's supply of breakfast cereal. This is called the Costco effect. Fast-fashion stores deploy their own strategies to get us to buy more clothes, even when we already have a closetful of them or own very similar styles. They rarely restock even their most popular items, in an attempt to lure consumers back into the store for "fresh" products. I recently con-

vinced myself that I had to have a black faux fleece–lined hoodie that
I spotted at Forever 21 because it *seemed* so rare. There was not another one in sight. In reality a black sweatshirt is not an innovative
product, and I already owned four.

Somehow, the low price paired with a treasure hunt to find the only
one in the store made me feel like I had to have this exact one. Consumer
psychology expert C. W. Park says most of us learn after a few belly-
aches eating the same cereal morning, noon, and night not to buy food
in such excess. There are no such built-in physiological or psychological
limits to how much clothing we will buy. There is no Costco effect for
fashion, especially if it's cheap. "In the case of clothing you can somehow use it or wear it," says Park. Of course, much of it we don't use or
wear, but the promise of utility is enough to justify a purchase.

According to the *Journal of Fashion Marketing and Management,*
order sizes for fast-fashion companies can sometimes be as small as
500.[11] Zara produces its styles in very limited numbers initially and
then scales up or down based on popularity. Forever 21 consistently
orders smaller. A Forever 21 designer I'll call Amanda (she asked me
to change her name) told me, "The largest order Forever 21 will place
is five thousand for accessories." This is not to suggest that fast fashion
is a more responsible retailing model that produces thoughtfully cu-
rated batches of unique garments. Amanda explained that Forever 21
might buy 500 slightly different variations of a single trend—a bucket-
style handbag, for example—and order several thousand of each. The
retailer oversaturates the market with numerous spins on the same
look.

H&M, Topshop, Mango, and other fashion chains operate slightly
differently from Forever 21, often ordering big, sometimes close to the
order sizes of a Gap, Nike, or Walmart. But they spread these numbers
more or less evenly over all their retail chains around the world, mak-

ing the quantity at each store limited. H&M's PR person would not give me exact numbers of how much it produces of each style, citing "competitive reasons," [12] but a Gap designer who has been in the same factories used by H&M says the chain can order as much as 50,000 or 200,000 of a given style. This is less than a Gap denim order but tremendous nonetheless. "The fast-fashion chains definitely win on units," the Gap designer told me, meaning their total annual output exceeds that of almost all of their competitors.

According to *The Independent*, H&M produced 500 million pieces of clothing a year in 2004.[13] A decade and many hundreds of store openings later, it's safe to assume its numbers are *much* higher. London's *Times* reports that Zara processes one million garments *a day* from its Spanish headquarters.[14] As of 2009, Forever 21 was buying more than 100 million pieces of clothing a year, with a single location in Tokyo packed with 50,000 to 60,000 pieces at any given moment.[15] Fast-fashion stores have dramatically accelerated an already bloated and overheated clothing production system.

Fast fashion is known not only for its constant offerings of the latest fads but for being shockingly cheap. Forever 21 can sell cute pumps for $15 and H&M can peddle a knit miniskirt for $5. These stores make gobs of money in spite of their low prices, in part because their consumers shop more and buy their clothes for full price. But their true secret is, once again, high volume. They earn their profits the same way that any mammoth discount chain store does: by taking a small sliver of profit on a large amount of goods. According to H&M, one of the reasons it can provide such low prices is because its 2,000 stores "provide high volumes."[16] Forever 21 sells its products at double the cost of production plus a couple of dollars, says Amanda. It's a standard retail markup, but one that creates astounding revenues when added up over at least 100 million pieces of clothing. Fast fashion's profitability resides in the same place as its appeal—in selling a relentless and unsustainable ocean of new clothes *week after week after week*. Or as Amanda puts it, "Forever 21's biggest secret is units all the time. They sell *so much freaking product*."

Shopping for new clothes used to be far more leisurely. If I spotted a cute fleece-lined sweatshirt in a store, I would have been able to go home and think on it. If I came back a few weeks later, the sweatshirt would likely still be there. Usually I'd just realize I didn't really need or even want the sweatshirt at all. Most fashion labels historically produced two main collections: spring/summer and autumn/winter. A department store had four major selling seasons. A mass-market retailer such as Gap updated its color scheme throughout the year, but focused on seasonal output. To an increasing degree, "the look" on display in clothing stores is rapidly changing. What's in stores this week is no longer what will be there the next. What's in style now is different from what will be in style next year. This is all the result of fast fashion, which demands a constant stream of product to turn a profit.

In early 2010 I was sitting with friends at a pub near Manhattan's Union Square debating the biggest fashion trends of the past three decades. For the '80s, it was easy—Hammer pants, neon, power dressing, poofy party dresses, and so on. For the '90s, it was grunge, floral prints, combat boots, and midriffs. We went back and forth for an hour trying to come up with the defining trend of the 2000s—skinny jeans, knee-high boots, oversize sunglasses were all suggested—before deciding that the biggest style trend of that decade was trends themselves—too many to count, changing ever-faster, challenging us to keep up.

The fashion industry relies on change. It always has. What is so astonishing today is the breakneck pace of change, which has shifted from seasonal and focused to constant and schizophrenic. FIT Museum Director Valerie Steele agrees that fashion is speeding up. "Trends now change more dramatically in terms of silhouettes and hemline," says Steele, "whereas in the past trends changed more in terms of details like sleeves and decorations. But fashion even today doesn't really make radical changes."

At first Steele's statements seemed like a contradiction, but then I began to make my own sense of them. We're rotating through entire paradigms of fashion now within a few seasons (boho, androgynous, hippie-chic, sailor-inspired), while we're also seeing fashion within a single season change in almost capricious ways. In Lee Councell's magnanimous blazer collection, she not only has myriad colors and prints (beige, black, light gray, dark gray, army green, pinstripe), she also has a hybrid blazer that is crossed with a corset and laced up the back and a blazer that is crossed with an army jacket and covered in cargo pockets.

Before fashion met Hollywood and the Internet, Steele says that information about new looks was tightly controlled by fashion magazines and their editors, who would dictate a few winners and a fairly singular vision of where fashion was headed. That's no longer the case. "You can no longer have someone like Dior launching a New Look," Steele explains, referring to French designer Christian Dior's revolutionary 1947 collection that singularly inspired the hyperfeminine wasp-waisted tops and ballerina-like skirts of the following decade.

The Internet age and the dissemination of information through blogs, social networking sites, and tabloids is pushing fashion forward at great speeds. It's also exposing us to many more ideas simultaneously. "The empire of fashion has broken down into a bunch of warring style tribes," says Steele. Today, any runway designer or trendsetting celebrity, stylist, or fashion blogger can influence the fashion winds through our 24/7 media world.

But without fast-fashion stores, without a tangible product affordable to so many people, trends would not be established and spread across the country and now the world so quickly. In order to have something new for us to buy, Forever 21, H&M, and Zara must always be on the hunt for some fresh concept, whether it comes from the streets, the media, or the runways, and to somehow differentiate all that product. It's a tall order and a highly contentious one.

———————

Forever 21 was founded in 1984 by South Korean–born power couple Do Won "Don" and Jin Sook Chang, who now run it with the help of their twentysomething daughters Esther and Linda. The headquarters is located in shabby downtown L.A., a stone's throw from the minimum-wage factories that still stitch some of the retailers' duds. The offices are not the most relaxed environs. Employees clock in with a fingerprint ID system, Amanda says. They're required to wear an ID badge. A bell rings to notify them of their two ten-minute breaks, one at 10 a.m. and one at 3 p.m. There are security cameras to make sure that everyone is at their desk when they're supposed to be.

Amanda described working for Forever 21 this way: "It's very much set up like a sweatshop. When we take our lunch break, which we're supposed to take four hours and forty-five minutes after we start, it's in a cafeteria where they serve us stuff worse than jail food." Amanda was hired to design original products for the company, but she says Forever 21 is so much faster at getting a "cheap, close knock-off" into stores that it made her designs "unnecessary." Likewise, her department head's sketches for new designs were tossed on top of a shelf and left there to languish for eight months. That's because Forever 21 is largely structured to pounce on trends and get them into stores before anyone else, and the fastest way to do this is to buy existing designs or to copy them from other places.

Forever 21 is notorious for ripping off fashion designers. To date, the company has been sued more than 50 times for copyright violations. Yet it has never been found liable for copyright infringement.[17] U.S. copyright law does not protect fashion design, only fabric prints and jewelry, and Susan Scafidi, a Fordham University law professor and founder of the Fashion Law Institute, says U.S. copyright law has always been firm on this point. "The copyright office has always said very consistently that clothing is just functional and therefore can't be copyrighted," Scafidi explains. To anyone who's ever worn a four-inch stiletto or craved a sweatshirt simply because the fleece lining is cute, that fashion is primarily utilitarian is laughable. In Europe, as well as in India, Singapore, and with certain limitations in Canada, fashion design *is* largely covered by copyright rules, although Scafidi says they are loosely enforced. France, perhaps not surprisingly, has had copyright protection on its fashions for a century.

The reason America lags behind other nations on fashion copyright law is, in Scafidi's view, because historically it was a manufacturing hub rather than a design center. Europe had the designers; the United States had the factories that mass-manufactured the European designs. Garment makers benefit from relaxed copyright laws because it means they can either skip hiring designers or simply hire sketch artists to copy the latest looks. "They can just go out and choose what's hot—it used to be what's hot from Paris, now it's what's hot from anywhere—and make the copy," says Scafidi. Now that you're more likely to find a fashion designer than a garment worker in the United States, Scafidi believes that this has shifted the balance of power toward designers, many of whom are demanding that we reexamine our laws.

A clothing brand such as Gap arguably has its own "look" that is updated and only slightly impacted by prevailing trends. But fast fashion doesn't have *a* look. It feeds off existing fads and new trends, no matter where they're coming from. The degree to which fast-fashion retailers directly copy depends on the company in question. Fast-fashion stores from Charlotte Russe to Zara all carry core basics such as denim, sweaters, or outerwear that can be planned in advance and updated with a handful of the season's established trends—such as leopard print, bondage, or lace, as it was in the fall of 2011.

H&M claims to work much like runway designers, scouting fashion schools, street styles, blogs, and rock shows, and looking at art and literature, with the goal of creating something fresh without moving too far from the fashion zeitgeist. It also has the advantage of a gargantuan design team, which has ballooned in recent years to 140 people.[18] A company like J.Crew might have two dozen designers on its women's team by comparison; a high-end designer might work with a handful of assistants at most.

Zara has 250 in-house designers.[19] Zara is well-known for producing close approximations of entire runway shows, as it did with French luxury label Céline's spring 2011 collection. Strikingly similar leather shorts and skirts and extra-wide-legged pants, all in a muted color palette of camel, coffee, and beige, landed in Zara stores in March 2011, at the same time the originals were released. Zara commonly sells very similar takes on designers' signature pieces, such as Prada's striped sombrero from its spring 2011 collection. Zara's version was black and white instead of neon colored. The chain has been both criticized for its lack of originality and lauded for bringing designer fashion to the masses, yet because the store rarely engages in exact copies, Zara was not sued for copyright infringement even once between 2003 and 2008.[20]

Forever 21 works very differently from the European fast-fashion giants. As late as 2007, it had no in-house design team.[21] Most of this chain's clothing is ordered from vendors, essentially manufacturers and agents who either have their own factories or design teams who peddle new styles. Mrs. Chang is Forever 21's head buyer and she approves every single style found in the company's stores, which is as many as 400 new items a day according to the UK's *Observer*. The company often blames the copycat designs on its vendors,[22] but often the vendors are copying based on Forever 21's request. "[Mrs. Chang] will go shopping all over the world, circle things in magazines, buy samples, and take pictures," Amanda says, and then hands over her research to her buying team to find a vendor who can produce a replica. And unless the copy is of a fabric print or jewelry, the company is within its legal rights. Scafidi told Jezebel.com in July 2011 that the only way a company like Forever 21 would allow itself to be sued again and again is because it has a "business strategy" of copying and settling if it gets "caught." She comments in the article that paying designers a settlement is "probably cheaper" than licensing the design in the first place.[23]

In the late '80s, H&M worked the same way as Forever 21, buying existing collections from Southeast Asian agents and then "putting them together in the store like pieces of a mismatched puzzle."[24] It has since changed its strategy, possibly because European copyright law made it more legally problematic. Scafidi told me that because they operate under a much stricter legal environment, the designers at the European fast-fashion chains (including H&M, Zara, and Mango), are instructed to produce a spin on designer styles as opposed to doing direct copies.

Of course, Forever 21 doesn't *just* sell carbon copies of high-end looks. Runway designers produce small collections of 30 to 40 pieces per season, insufficient material for the bottomless pit of new styles needed in the 24/7 fast-fashion world. The reason why fast-fashion stores seem so presciently on trend is not *always* because they're lurking in the water, waiting to copy. It's sometimes for the same peculiar reasons that runway designers will all suddenly be using loud geometric prints or leather at the same time.

Celebrity designer Tom Ford explained fashion coincidences at a 2005 conference at the University of Southern California called "Ready to Share: Fashion and the Ownership of Creativity." "The clues to where we are going to be next year are here now," he said. "And to all good sleuths and people with a certain amount of intuition, they will tend to find the same thing. In order for a design to be successful, it has to be appealing to the mass population."[25] Fast-fashion design teams and buyers can be master sleuths at spotting trends as well as the high end. And fast-fashion retailers, with their quick-turnaround production systems and virtual lack of testing or quality standards, do have the advantage of waiting to finalize a collection after they've seen the catwalk or are certain of which trends are taking off.

Copying fashion was once a more inexact science, but it's always been a widespread practice, especially in America. The wholesale garment trade in the United States copied Parisian couture for much of its early history, with Christian Dior's hobble skirt on sale at Macy's before his clients received their originals.[26] According to Scafidi, before World War II a hired gun might sneak into a French fashion show, sneak back out, quickly make some sketches, and use a telegraph to transmit the sketches to a manufacturer. "Or they might intercept a dress at the docks and snap a photograph," she says. Parisian designers also sold licensed copies of their dresses to department stores from which to make exact replicas, but illegal copying was rampant.

What's different today is partly the sophistication of the copies. The Internet, while driving the heightened profile that fashion designers now enjoy, is giving the designers' competitors the tools to better rip them off. "Today, people can look at the pictures online from a fashion show, which are posted almost instantaneously, and copy them directly in a factory in Asia," says Scafidi. "And the photographs are so good. You have photographs in three hundred and sixty degrees. You have photographs in high-definition on which you can zoom in and see what kind of buttons they used." The result is uncannily similar copies, down to distinctive trim and embellishments. The only case against Forever 21 that made it to trial was in 2008, and it was because the retailer was selling copies of California-based label Trovata's shirts so exact that both the original and Forever 21's version featured a string of buttons in descending size, each one a different color, including yellow, green, red, and cream. Forever 21 eventually settled out of court with Trovata, which the retailer has done in all of the prior cases against it.[27]

Many of us who shop at fast-fashion stores end up in copies without even knowing it. It was only months after buying a boxy cream-colored top with patch pockets from H&M that I saw an almost identical one by American designer Adam Lippes in Bergdorf Goodman. And perhaps Lippes himself had copied the design from someone else. It's been a largely accepted part of the fashion industry for more than a century now. At a tribute to Ralph Lauren at Lincoln Center in October 2011, the famed American designer admitted to Oprah during an onstage interview that he owes his career to "forty-five years of copying."

The U.S. Congress is currently considering fashion-design protection under a bill called the Design Piracy Prohibition Act. Since its introduction in 2007, the bill has been whittled down to grant designers a three-year protection from copies that are "substantially similar" to their own. Close and very near approximations, which would encompass most designs, will still be legal under the bill. American designers such as Council of Fashion Designers of America president Diane von Furstenberg as well as Nicole Miller and Zac Posen are the ones leading the charge behind the act, but the design community is split on the issue. At the USC conference, Tom Ford said that nothing makes him happier than seeing copies of his designs, as the high-end consumer and knockoff consumer are not the same. During the panel at the conference which featured Tom Ford as well as author and *New York Times* style critic Guy Trebay, the moderator asked the pair how fashion would be different if there were copyright laws like the ones that protect books and movies. "There'd be no fashion," Trebay said definitively. "It's true," Ford agreed. Strong statements indeed.

The mass copying of a style is what creates a trend, and trends sell clothes today. This is why many in the industry furiously protect their right to ripping one another off. Two law professors, Kal Raustiala and Chris Sprigman, have argued against the design piracy act on the grounds that the American apparel industry "may actually benefit" from copying, as it speeds up the creation and exhaustion of trends. As they put it in their paper to Congress, "The fashion industry's entire business cycle is driven forward by consumer demand for the new, and the entire process is fueled by copying."[28]

Its easy to view copies and near copies as justified and even fair in the face of high markups and steep designer fees. Writer Christine Muhlke recounted in *The New York Times* her adventure tracking down Zara's rip-offs of the Céline collection. The original silk tuxedo shirt would have set her back $990. At Zara she could have it for 90 percent less. But what happens when the copycats in question are huge, billion-dollar companies that are gaining market share by the day? Forever 21 and Zara aren't small Seventh Avenue manufacturers aping Parisian couturiers. And they aren't just mimicking high-end designers few can afford. They're corporations that are able to under-cut virtually *all of their competitors,* whether it's a high-end luxury label, an independent designer, or anything in between.

In July 2011, Forever 21's most recent copyright victim was a small, domestically produced label called Feral Childe, whose hand-drawn "Teepees" print showed up on a Forever 21 garment. The designers' tops typically retail for between $150 and $300. Consumers have little incentive to buy Feral Childe when they can buy the same item for a tenth of the price at Forever 21. Scafidi agrees that it's the more afford-able designers and the middle market that suffer from copying. "There's a sense from the customer who might otherwise save up for something nicer, *why bother?*" says Scafidi. "Why bother when you can get an approximation of the same look quickly and very cheaply?"

Unlike the world of technology, where rapid innovation produces improvements, innovation in fashion just produces arbitrary stylistic changes. Fashion doesn't improve, it *just changes.* For some followers of fashion as well as designers themselves, this pace of change is not a welcome one. The pace has become maddening. Because of the lack of limitations on copying, paired with increasing sophistication and speed to market of copies, we're living under a tyranny of trends.

Fashion is moving faster and faster, and the pressure to produce the next "new" look has gotten so intense that designers are not only looking into each other's sketchbooks; they are increasingly looking backward and pillaging the past. This became especially apparent to me when fashion of the 1990s came back into style in 2010, right down to the tiny floral-print dresses, loose-fitting midriffs, high-waisted shorts, and combat boots. And girls were buying it up as if we weren't just looking back and snickering a few years ago at how the cast of *Friends* dressed.

It's common for fashion designers and buyers to prowl vintage outposts looking for inspiration, and Brooklyn-based vintage dealer Sara Bereket says her stall at the popular market Brooklyn Flea is a frequent victim. "We know they copy the runway, but nobody talks about how they bluntly copy everything vintage," she says of not only fast-fashion companies but high-end designers as well. One customer bought a '70s cashmere sweater by Calvin Klein from Bereket's stall and then admitted she was shipping it to China the next day to be replicated. Bereket said exasperatedly, "That's the world we live in now."

In her Brooklyn apartment, Bereket was standing in a mountain of finds from a day of digging through used-clothing bins at textile recyclers. She showed me a green silk dress in her closet from the 1980s. A friend of hers owns a shirt from H&M with an identical print. Scafidi told me that vintage is in the public domain and can be freely copied. Bereket then picked through the pile on her floor and held up numerous '90s floral dresses and tops as well as jumpsuits from the 1980s, all hot sellers in regular retailers at the moment. "What styles did we have from the 2000s era? Low pants?" Bereket wonders. "Other than that, it was all copied from the past."

Bereket didn't use to be such a cynic about the fashion industry. Her aunt is a fashion designer, and growing up in Amsterdam, Bereket used to travel to Italy a few times a year to shop in high-end boutiques. "I've always loved coming up with creative, fun things to wear," she told me. When she first moved to the United States five years ago, she was turned off by cheap fashion. "I was disgusted," she says. "We buy a top at Forever 21, wear it three times, and throw it away." But she quickly got sucked into the same habits, shopping almost exclusively at the retailer. It wasn't until Bereket became a secondhand clothing buyer, and started to see styles copied stitch-for-stitch in the stores she shopped in, that she decided to stop buying new clothes altogether for several years. She says, "I felt like I'll buy something new if you make something different."

It's easy for a cheapskate like me to criticize fashion designers as unoriginal or profiteering, especially when you consider the fact that many luxury goods doubled in price between 1998 and 2008. To the outsider, the fashion designer's life is glamorous. But the field is over-crowded and competitive. The celebrity focus on fashion and such reality shows as *Project Runway* have spiked enrollment in fashion schools, which means the competition is getting tougher by the day. Designers who are just starting out are up against enormous odds. Starting a line takes a huge financial commitment that can push a person into debt—I know a designer who is $50,000 in debt from her first fashion line. Without producing a lot of clothes, adding very high markups, or somehow finding fame and investors quickly, it's difficult for a new designer to make any profit or even to walk away without totally losing her hat.

Stores such as Forever 21, H&M, and Target have unbeatable economies of scale that no one but other huge corporate players can compete with. When H&M actually lowered its prices in August 2010, in the midst of rising costs in China, it explained its cost-cutting capacities to Vogue.com this way: "We have over 2,000 stores in 37 countries. This provides high volume and there is no middleman. We have our own team of over 100 in-house designers and we do all our own production."[29] Not surprisingly, no independent designer (not to mention most other retailers, brands, or manufacturers) has these resources at her disposal.

Most independent designers also sell their clothes through a department store or boutique—which means after the standard retail markup, consumers are paying a much higher price for something than they'd find at a store that sells its own brand, such as H&M. Of the American designers who produce in New York, Theory sells a number of dresses for less than $350, as do Alice + Olivia, Tucker by Gaby Basora, Nanette Lepore, and many others. It's actually not easy to keep prices at this level when producing in small quantities and selling through a limited number of retail outlets. Eviana Hartman, a former *Vogue* fashion writer and the mastermind behind the Bodkin label, says that selling through brick-and-mortar stores is very difficult for up-and-coming designers. "The inevitable retail markup means your wholesale price is expected to be low, much lower than would really be ideal," says Hartman, whose contemporary designs include asymmetrical dresses and jumpsuits made from environmentally sustainable fabrics that mostly retail for less than $300. Hartman says designers like her are turning to online sales and trunk shows to help pad margins.

The ubiquity of cheap, attractive fashion means that designer clothes must also be more showstopping to gain consumer loyalty and to keep people from shopping only at places like Forever 21. This further drives up the cost of designer clothes says Hartman. "It's difficult to be more than a niche player when the majority of consumers are acclimated to dresses costing twenty dollars," she explains. "When starting out, in order to distinguish your work, you have to make pieces with a 'wow' factor, and those are never going to be cheap."

How does a designer compete, for example, with a $10.50 Black Fab Skinny Jean from Forever 21? Apparently the answer is to produce jeans in such an over-the-top manner that they can fetch prices well above $300 a pair. The Phantom jean by high-end denim company True Religion, for example, typically retails for $375. Premium jeans are often made from fabric produced at a North Carolina textile plant where a shuttle loom from the 1950s creates quirky irregularities that give the jeans extra character. The denim features special washes, stitches, and distressing methods.[30] Necessary and discernible to most consumers? No. But sometimes an absurdly extravagant product is the only way a company or designer can stand out from low-cost, corporate fashion.

The intense pressure of today's apparel industry seems to be affecting even those at the top of the fashion pyramid. *New York Times* style writer Suzy Menkes noted in a March 2011 article, "The pressure from fast fashion and from the instant Internet age to create new things constantly" is wearing down fashion's famous names. Menkes says these pressures are partially to blame for Calvin Klein's stint in rehab, Alexander McQueen's 2009 suicide, and the downfall of John Galliano, who was fired from his post as the creative director of Christian Dior the month of her article's release for engaging in a drunken anti-Semitic rant.[31]

In 1904 German sociologist Georg Simmel wrote a landmark article, "Fashion," for *The American Journal of Sociology*. In it, he laid out a clear view on how price and the pace of fashion are tied: "The more an article becomes subject to rapid changes of fashion, the greater the demand for *cheap* products of its kind." How right he was. Today, it's very difficult to convince the average consumer to buy clothing at a reasonable price, and fast fashion gets around this conundrum by selling a treadmill of fresh trends for cheap. But in their race to sell new products, they speed up the pace of fashion, which in turn makes the average consumer even cheaper. Why pay good money for clothes that aren't going to be in style next season? It's a vicious feedback loop.

This takes me back to Councell and the $59.95 blazer left hanging on the rack. Blazers, like everything else, are no longer a classic piece of clothing. They are a trend, doomed to become dated. I would be surprised if they aren't "out" by the time you read this. Today's styles have a very short shelf life, and it behooves consumers to pay as little as possible for them. Councell told me that because she prefers to shop for trendy garments, she sees no point in spending a lot of money on fashion. "I like really trendy stuff that's in this spring, and next spring will probably be out," she said. "That's why I won't invest a lot of money in one thing." With so many competing trends in existence at any given moment, some consumers prefer to shop cheap so they can cash in on them all. Councell's friend Sidia, 22, is one of them. "I don't want to pay so much to buy one shirt because the style is going to change," she told me, "So, I like to spend on cheaper clothing since I buy *a lot*."

The pace of fashion is also making quality and craftsmanship obsolete. A 2006 report on fast fashion by researchers at the UK's Manchester Metropolitan University found that fast-fashion companies are indeed eliminating product development and quality control. The researchers interviewed one fast-fashion designer anonymously, who admitted: "We sometimes have huge quality issues with garments that have maybe skipped a test or fit session to get into the shops quicker as the lead times we have been given are very tight."[32] There is evidence that some overseas factories prefer working with fast-fashion retailers precisely because they send things into production with little testing or fitting. According to *New York* magazine, H&M rarely cancels or returns orders. Factories sometimes charge such retailers only half their usual fees, in part because they are such low-maintenance customers.[33]

Yet many fast-fashion stores use their quality as a selling point. H&M's tagline, for example, is "Fashion and quality at the best price."

In the spring of 2011, H&M launched its Conscious Collection, a line of clothing made from recycled plastic and organic cotton. The collection was up on its Web site and made a big splash in the media for about a week. Two weeks later the Web site was promoting summer shorts and knits. I e-mailed H&M's PR person and said that in my humble opinion, sustainable design and the high-volume production associated with fast fashion seemed to be opposing design approaches. *How do you reconcile the two?* I wanted to know.

I received this fascinating exercise in doublespeak in response: "We do not see ourselves as a fast-fashion company, we make modern designs of good quality. We do not believe that low prices can be equated with a throwaway society, because price and the life span of a garment are not related to each other . . . H&M offers fashion and quality at the best price—good quality means longevity, and we take responsibility that our products will be manufactured in an environmentally, socially and economically sustainable way."

No one expects to take an H&M shirt to the grave. At prices that often circle around $20, we know the product is not *good quality*. Instead, the quality is *good enough*. According to C. W. Park, we accept a substandard product partly because we're so amazed by how well-made cheap fashion is for the price. "Obviously, [the consumer's] expectation of quality may not be that high. But for the price, the product has a very reasonable quality," Park says. This is how quality is defined and why it has been eroded in the cheap-fashion era. Despite what H&M's PR rep would have us believe, low price also signals to consumers that a product is disposable. Low price and fast trends have made clothing throwaway items, allowing us to set aside such serious questions as *How long will this last?* or even *Will I like it when I get it home?* Park agrees, "You may try it and if you don't like it, you can still throw it away because you bought it for such a low price."

My father remembers the terror of spilling something on his $5 Gant button-up as a kid in the 1960s, when the minimum wage was less than two dollars an hour. Stains were grounds for punishment. But the quality was impeccable, he recalls, and he wore the shirt totally out. He bought a three-piece suit for his high school prom in 1965 and wore the vest until the mid-1980s, and it never looked dated. Quality is ultimately relative, and we have less use for it than ever before. Sean Cormier, the FIT marketing professor and quality-control expert, says in the industry quality is simply defined by customer satisfaction. If we do not return a garment to the store, it has met the quality standard.

In my experience, if I pay less than $30 for a garment, I'm not likely to bother returning it if I'm less than satisfied. I'm probably not going to take good care of it either. I'll wear it once and put it in the back of my closet. Stores like H&M are able to say they are "good quality" because in the era of fast fashion, its product will serve us well enough through a handful of wears—until the seams split open, a stubborn stain sets in, or the style changes and we grow of sick it. It is quality measured in number of washes.

5

The Afterlife of Cheap Clothes

I t was early morning at the Quincy Street Salvation Army, an easy-to-miss location tucked away on a Brooklyn side street. The only donations that had come in so far were books, an entire truckful from one single apartment. Charitable clothing donations usually roll in with fits and starts, with the changing of the seasons and at the end of the year, when people are looking for tax write-offs. It was a weekday morning in the middle of the fall, the off hours for clothing donations. But I didn't have to witness someone pulling up in her car and shoveling bags full of clothes from the trunk. I'd been that person innumerable times, lugging overloaded trash bags pierced by the heels of cheap pumps, sleeves and pant legs hanging out, to a local charity. I never knew what happens after I drive away and leave my old clothing orphaned on the Salvation Army's doorstep.

I shopped religiously at charity thrift stores like Salvation Army and Goodwill in high school and college, roving through the racks looking for baggy corduroys and weird T-shirts silk-screened with the logos of recreational sports teams and local auto-body shops. Shopping at thrift stores allowed me to dress uniquely and cheaply, but I abandoned them in lockstep with the declining price of fashion and with the improvement in the design and variety of cheap clothes.

Vintage-inspired and quirky T-shirts can be bought new these days, even ones that look like they're from the local auto-body shop.

I had a few minutes to down a coffee from the corner deli before Michael "Maui" Noneza, one of the donation center's assistant supervisors, bounced into the warehouse. "You ready?" the cheery Pacific Islander asked before ushering me over to a massive freight elevator and pressing the button for the third floor. The elevator jolted upward and the doors opened on a scene that looked a bit like a threadbare Santa's workshop. Dozens of Hispanic women were standing behind a row of wooden slides, pulling clothes out of elephantine gray bins and separating them into broad categories such as jackets, pants, and children's wear. "We keep only the best," Maui told me. "Then it's ticketed and priced." The pricers, perched on what looked like adult high chairs, quickly and methodically moved through racks of 80 garments each, making snap judgments based on condition and brand. Anyone who's shopped at a Salvation Army or almost any charity thrift store knows that these judgments are often wonderfully off. I've found a pure silk shirt with the tags still on for $5 and a genuine leather vest by a high-end designer for $15.

The Quincy Street Salvation Army may be on a quiet street, but it is in fact a major distribution center serving eight Salvation Army locations in Brooklyn and Queens. It processes an average of *five tons* of outcast clothing every single day of the year and much more during the holiday season when donations spike. From that astonishing mass, the sorters choose exactly 11,200 garments a day to be divided up equally between the eight thrift stores they serve. I asked Maui if they've ever hit a dry spell, where the donations dipped too low to fully restock each store with its share of the 11,200 items. He laughed. "We never run out of clothes. There are *always* enough clothes."

What American doesn't have something hanging in his or her closet worn only once or twice, a pair of pants waiting for a diet, or even a brand-new dress or jacket with the tags still on? Common sense and everyday experience tell us that we have so much clothing that a majority goes underused and neglected. According to a 2010 national survey in *ShopSmart* magazine, one in four American women own seven pairs of jeans, but we only wear four of them regularly.[1] I wear about ten to 15 garments of the hundreds I own, less than 4 percent of my wardrobe. Not surprisingly, charities regularly see brand-new clothes come in with tags still affixed. "We see people throwing away new stuff every day," Maui says. "I saw a dress come through here the other day—the price tag said eight hundred dollars. Never worn. We sold it for forty dollars."

There is an enormous disconnect between increasing clothing consumption and the resultant waste, partially because unworn clothes aren't immediately thrown out like other disposable products. Instead, they accumulate in our closets or wherever we can find space for them. The surplus of clothing weighing down our homes feels distinctly new, and for me worsens by the year. My clothes fit in the tiny closet of my first New York apartment when I moved there back in 2002. Today, even with extra storage containers, hanging shoe organizers, and myriad other "space savers," I don't have room for all of my clothes. They pile up on the bed, the dresser, and the floor.

Closet-organization professionals and storage-component companies have sprung into action to relieve of us of our overconsumption woes; retailers such as IKEA and the Container Store and companies including Rubbermaid have made a killing off consumers trying to reclaim precious space taken over by all their clothing. Homes built in the past 15 years have walk-in closets that are bigger than my living room. Master closets now average about six feet by eight feet, a size more typical of a guest bedroom 40 years ago.[2] Homes with small closets are an increasingly tough sell. When I rented the small second bedroom in my apartment, the closet's single rod and three feet of space were enough to send most candidates running.

A roommate of mine once told me she was applying for a job at a Web site called shoedazzle.com, an online club that ships members a new pair of shoes every single month, selected by a celebrity stylist, for $39.95. This was the same roommate who told me she found it overwhelming to own too much clothing. I looked at her dumbfounded. "What do you do with last month's shoes?" I asked. And she looked back at me, dumbfounded. No one seems to be asking, "What happens to all of these shoes and clothes after we no longer want them?"

For many consumers, part of the appeal of cheap fashion is that it allows them to get rid of their purchases when newer, more with-it items come along. In one epic, 16-minute-long YouTube haul, a wide-eyed 24-year-old brunette who goes by the name DulceCandy flashes for the camera a dozen party dresses and cardigans and countless pairs of shoes and accessories that she bought in one single day of shopping at Forever 21. "I like fast fashion. I like things that are disposable. So I can wear this shirt two times and then throw it away," she says. Consumers throw plenty of used clothing directly into the trash, from soiled and threadbare socks to tattered bras and underwear and stained shirts, alongside perfectly usable textiles and clothing. Though these numbers include all textiles like sheets and towels, they're astonishing nonetheless: Every year, Americans throw away 12.7 million tons, or 68 pounds of textiles per person, according to the Environmental Protection Agency, which also estimates that 1.6 million tons of this waste could be recycled or reused.[3]

There's an equally large disconnect between expanding wardrobes and the additional demands for fossil fuels, energy, and water. In the winter of 2010, I had a lovely high school intern who interviewed her friends about how they bought and disposed of clothing. One of the interviewees, a 17-year-old high school senior, stated, "Clothing is not bad for the environment because it can be reused." This is common public perception. A tremendous amount of clothing is in fact *not* getting recycled but getting trashed, and the environmental impact of *making* clothes is being entirely overlooked. Even though plastic can be reused, making it is not environmentally benign. Disturbingly, about half of our wardrobe is now made out of plastic, in the form of polyester.

The process of making textiles has never been green. Avtex Fibers, based in Front Royal, Virginia, once the world's largest rayon factory, was shut down in 1989 for poisoning the surrounding water and soil and is still listed as an EPA Superfund site.[4] The technology and regulations to make textile manufacturing less environmentally harmful have improved dramatically in the United States, but the textile industry has largely moved overseas in recent decades to countries that are ill-equipped or simply too poor to reduce the impact of the fiber-making process. In Bangladesh I drove out to Narsingdi, the site of the country's historic textile industry that is now becoming increasingly export oriented. Textile mills lined the highways and long pipes dumped colored dyes into the ditches and lagoons. Monstrous textile machinery filled a dozen warehouse-size rooms in one mill, sucking up electricity and water.

China, where 10 percent of the world's textiles are now produced, is an environmental disaster.[5] When I traveled to Guangdong Province in 2011, the air pollution was so thick I couldn't photograph anything a quarter mile off the highway—it was lost in the smog. As I drove along the expressway between the industrial cities of Shenzhen and Dongguan, I inhaled unfiltered exhaust not just from unseen polyester plants but also from electronics factories, which are highly concentrated in this part of China. My throat ached instantly, my eyes burned, my nose drizzled, and my head pulsed. I had a sinus infection for months after returning home. Still, in the United States we are not insulated from global environmental problems. Carbon monoxide and other pollutants from Asia have been documented on the West Coast since the late 1990s and are actually affecting weather patterns there as well. Global climate change as a result of global industrialization is now a reality, no matter where we live.

I asked Lily, a factory sales girl I met in China, about her country's air pollution, but she didn't understand the word "pollution." I gestured toward the gray sky and coughed violently. Lily lit up and said, "Ah, there are so many factories here. The air is *not so fresh*. It is our dream that one day China will have fresh air," she said, followed by a long pause. "Maybe in one hundred years." And then she giggled. *China can't possibly sustain another century of this*, I thought. Virtually no city in Guangdong treats waste water.[6] Dye effluents are often pumped straight into waterways. The runoff from dyeing plants has colored Guangdong's Pearl River red and indigo in recent years. Lily offered to take me mountain climbing nearby. My lungs quivered at the thought, and I politely declined.

Cellulosic fibers, a family of artificial fibers sourced from natural by-products, include rayon, viscose, acetate, cupro, and the more recently developed bamboo. To make these fibers, substances such as wood pulp and scrap cotton must first be treated with toxic chemicals and pushed through an extruder to form strands. The second and much more dominant family of man-made fibers is made from plastic and sourced from oil, which has its own implications for sustainability, as oil is nonrenewable and plastics take hundreds of years to biodegrade. And all those blends of wonderful low-maintenance Frankenfabrics we're now buying—the polyester-viscose blends and the wool-nylon-acetate blends in my own closet, for example—aren't recyclable, as the technology does not exist to separate the fibers back into their original state.

This massive pollution created by the textile industry can't be pegged on a single type of fiber. Each fabric has its own complex and hefty ecological footprint. Environmental reporter Stan Cox has noted that sheep farmed for wool can cause soil erosion, water pollution, and biodiversity loss; leather tanning involves toxic heavy metals; all man-made fiber production emits greenhouse gasses and pollutes water; and the U.S. cotton crop demands 22 billion pounds of weed killer per year.[7] Most fiber is bleached or dyed and treated in toxic chemical baths to make it brighter, softer, more fade-resistant and waterproof, less prone to wrinkles, and any other number of qualities that we demand of modern clothing. Then it has to be dried under heat lamps—a huge energy suck.[8]

Textiles have always had an unflattering environmental footprint, but the more pressing problem is the terrifying scale at which they are now being produced. As China and India develop consumer classes and gain a taste for fashion, the total quantities of fiber production are growing dramatically along with the burden on resources. According to Oerlikon's *The Fiber Year 2009/10 Report*, in 1950 world fiber use was close to 10 million tons. Today, that number has soared to more than 70 million tons. It's hard to choose which shocking figure best sums up the environmental toll of today's monstrous global fashion industry, but here's a particularly compelling one: UK journalist Lucy Siegle found that the natural resources that go into fiber production every year now demand approximately 145 million tons of coal and somewhere between 1.5 trillion and 2 trillion gallons of water.[9]

Maui and I took the elevator back downstairs and walked into a dimly lit warehouse hidden away on the far side of the donation drop-off area. This room, Maui informed me, is where the "rag-out" ends up, the donated clothing that languishes on thrift-store racks without getting sold or is too threadbare and stained or out of season to sell in the first place. Garments that make it into the Salvation Army thrift stores have exactly one month to sell. At Goodwill, clothes are given a similar three- to five-week window to prove themselves. Then they're pulled from their hangers, tossed in bins, and end up in a room such as this one.

In the rag-out room, two men were silently pushing T-shirts, dresses, and every other manner of apparel into a compressor that works like the back of a garbage truck, squeezing out neat cubes of rejected clothing that weigh a half ton each. The cubes were then lifted and moved via forklift to the middle of the room, where a wall of wrapped and bound half-ton bales towered. I saw tags from Old Navy, Sean Jean, and Diesel peeking out of the bales, as well as slivers of denim, knits in bright maroons and bold stripes, and the smooth surfaces of Windbreakers. Smashed together like this, stripped of its symbolic meaning, stacked up like bulk dog food, I was reminded that clothing is ultimately just fabric that comes from resources and can result in horrifying volumes of waste. Clothing stores completely separate us from this reality, but a rag-out room brings it home in an instant. The Quincy Street Salvation Army builds a completed wall made of 18 tons, or 36 bales, of unwanted clothing *every three days*. And this is just a small portion of the cast-offs of one single Salvation Army location in one city in the United States.

Since the end of the nineteenth century in both Europe and the United States, philanthropic groups have been involved in the collection and distribution of clothes to the poor. The Salvation Army started up in the United States in 1880, at a time when the U.S. population was just over 50 million and almost all clothing was still handmade. It wasn't until the late 1950s that charities opened retail outlets, and their income began to come primarily from the sale of used clothing.[10] Charitable clothing donations from that point were used indirectly, by first selling clothes and then using the proceeds to fund charitable works. This is how clothing donations function today.

Then consumer culture set in. During the postwar period, growing incomes allowed Americans to buy more clothes. Our wardrobes became diversified, with juniors' clothes, office clothes, sports clothes, and street wear becoming common.[11] This was when charities started processing enormous yields of used but still wearable clothing. But it wasn't until clothing prices started declining in recent decades that charities started seeing barely used and even unworn discarded clothing. Throughout the 1990s, donations to Goodwill increased 10 percent per year. In 2011, Goodwill sold 173 million pounds of used clothing and household goods through their retail stores.[12]

I once thought that for every garment I grew bored of and donated, there was either some poor, shivering person in need of it or a thrifty woman out there thrilled to give it a second life. I've come to call this logic the "clothing deficit myth," and I'm not the only one who falls prey to it. In a 2007 column in *The New York Times*, a reader wrote in concerned that her clothing donations were being sold for profit in Africa. In response, "The Ethicist" columnist Randy Cohen directed the reader to one international labor leader who recommended finding charities that "bypass middlemen and distribute donations directly to people in need, particularly to people in your community."[13] Most Americans are thoroughly convinced there is another person in their direct vicinity who truly needs and wants all of our unwanted clothes. This couldn't be further from the truth.

Charities long ago passed the point of being able to sell all of our wearable used clothes. According to John Paben, co-owner of used-clothing processer Mid-West Textile, "They never could." He says that charities had excess donations even before World War II, but they often threw away what they couldn't sell. "The public wasn't happy about that either," Paben told me. He says public disapproval of how charities handle donations is nothing new. Charities started to look for other solutions. A wiping-rag industry sprang up to turn unsellable clothing into rags for industrial purposes. Still, anything leftover went into a landfill.

Increasingly, textile recyclers and rag graders including Mid-West Textile cropped up to help charities process the excess. "The rag graders came along and figured out how to separate clothes and find markets around the world that'd be interested in buying it," says Paben, whose company began operations in 1982. "Gradually you had fewer and fewer goods going to the landfill." Today, it's textile graders who end up finding a home for *most* of our donated clothing. Of all the clothing that we dump on charities' doorsteps, Paben says, less than 20 percent gets sold through thrift stores. About half of it doesn't even get a shot at the stores, going straight into the postconsumer waste stream and on to such facilities as Mid-West Textile.

Though their industry is largely hidden from public view, textile recyclers have been around for as long as textiles themselves. It is the original and oldest recycling industry. A 1904 *New York Times* article entitled "Use of Shoddy Is Greatest in America" describes the already flourishing trade for secondhand wool. Then, "shoddy" meant recycled wool cloth made from rags and woolen clothing scraps imported mostly from England and France. The wool was ground up into a fibrous mass and respun into new fiber, sometimes by mixing it with cotton. The resulting fiber allegedly looked a lot like real wool but was far more inexpensive. A shoddy manufacturer told *The New York Times*, "Our people demand a cheap suit of wool or something that looks like wool, and that is the reason that we must use shoddy in constantly increasing quantities."[14]

There are thousands of secondhand textile processors in the United States today, mostly small family businesses, many of them several generations old. I visited Trans-Americas Trading Co., a third-generation textile recycler in Clifton, New Jersey, which employs 85 people and processes close to 17 million pounds of used clothing a year. Inside Trans-Americas, there is a wall of cubed-up clothing five bales tall and more than 20 bales long. "This is literally several hundred thousand pounds of textile waste, and we bring in two trailer loads of this much every day," Trans-Americas president Eric Stubin told me. The volume it processes has gone up over the years alongside our consumption of clothing.

Stubin spends a lot of time doing media outreach to keep the public from seeing his recycling business as parasitic and profiteering, responding for example to "The Ethicist" column. "We provide a tremendous service to the charitable industry," Stubin told me, as he walked me through his company's cavernous warehouse of used clothes. It looked much like the Salvation Army sorting room, with slides, bins, chutes, and walls of shrink-wrapped clothes, but on a scale maybe ten times larger. Stubin explains, "We're buying their salvaged clothing and paying them for it, so they can generate literally millions of dollars in revenue annually for their salvage, which otherwise would have ended up in the landfill."

Seeing a veritable Great Wall of China made of clothing castoffs brought me back to the plastic analogy. When we put a plastic bottle in the recycling bin, we're not concerned that recyclers will melt it down and sell it for a profit to companies who might find a useful purpose for it. Yet there's something about for-profit clothing recy-cling that bothers consumers. "There isn't a recycling industry around today of which private enterprise is not a major part," Stubin pointed out. Without textile recyclers, charities would be quickly over-whelmed and forced to throw away everything that couldn't be sold. Charities might have to turn many donations away. The only benefit to this doomsday scenario is that our clothes would pile up in our homes or in landfills, finally forcing us to face down just how much textile waste we create.

A majority of the clothing processed at Trans-Americas comes from overburdened charities within a 1,000-mile radius of New York City. Used clothes come into the warehouse in mixed bales like those I saw at the Quincy Street Salvation Army. "I like to call it the good, the bad, and the ugly," Stubin said, as we sailed past women separating pants from shirts and sending them down long slides. "We get every-thing from torn sweaters to spoiled and stained towels to good useable clothing." Stubin's sorters separate the wearable stuff into 200 broad categories such as cotton blouses, baby clothes, jackets, sweaters, khaki pants, and denim. "From there, sorters begin to look for quality and start sorting the worn from the torn and making various grades," Stubin explained. The higher-skilled employees "develop an eye," he says, for coveted brands, cashmere, and the gold-mine vintage finds. But at least half of what Trans-America processes is "the bad and the ugly." This is the situation in general in the textile recycling industry today.

According to the trade organization Secondary Materials and Re-cycled Textiles (SMART), less than half of the clothing processed by textile recyclers is of a high enough quality to continue as clothing. About 20 percent of postconsumer apparel is so busted up it is sold to fiber buyers, who break it down into component fibers for reuse in a variety of products from insulation to carpet padding and building materials. Another 30 percent is sold to the industrial wiping-rag industry for about eight cents per pound, says Stubin. Only a small sliver, 5 percent, is thrown away.[15]

Textile recycling is a tough business, and it's gotten tougher over time. The dramatic increase in the volume of secondhand clothing has driven down its value by an estimated 71 percent in the last 15 years.[16] Stubin estimates that more than half the clothing that his company receives gets sold for less than what it costs him to buy and process. He only gets two to four cents a pound for clothes sold to fiber buyers. But the decreasing quality of donations is also pushing prices through the floor.

Charity shop racks are now filled with the cheap fashion and budget basics we prefer. In my own experience the good "finds" at charity thrift stores are getting fewer and farther between. Countless times I've gravitated like a moth to a flame to what looks like a nice blouse or a wool sweater at the Salvation Army only to see the H&M or Target-brand Mossimo tag popping out. At the Goodwill on West Twenty-fifth Street near Union Square in New York, I examined the labels of the first 100 garments in its women's tops sections and found that one in five came from Old Navy, H&M, Forever 21, or Target.

This junking up of the secondhand clothing supply has not gone unnoticed by textile recyclers. Paben says, "I can tell you that the quality coming through the donation stream has been trending down." I asked Paben if he's speaking specifically of our purchases from discount and cheap-fashion chains. "Exactly," he said, but continued more carefully. "As the Walmarts, Kmarts, and Targets have grown their store bases, and taken market share of the clothing purchases, then there is a pretty good correlation there."

Alongside our unworn castoffs, charities are also seeing donations arriving in unbelievably ragtag condition. Americans as a whole no longer repair clothes, and I've personally donated items with the buttons dangling off, zippers off their tracks, and seams busted open. Charities have become our dumps. Goodwill executives told *The Washington Post* in 2002 that the organization had spent $500,000 that year alone hauling away worthless rubbish, including soiled clothing that couldn't be resold.[17] In an effort to curb the amount of trash that charities were having to process on our behalf, federal legislation was passed in 2006 so that only donations in good usable condition could be claimed for federal tax deductions.

I pay around 50 bucks for winter boots every year (a fortune in my book), and they're usually wrecked by the end of the season. One pair is made of such cheap leather that they've turned a silvery, dappled color and the heels are worn to a knee-wrecking slant. Don Rinaldi, the head of the Shoe Service Institute of America, admonishes, "You have to know that at that price your shoes are not going to last. They're not sewn properly. The soles are probably thermoplastic." Rinaldi's organization is dedicated to educating Americans about the lost art of shoe repair. Plastic soles are virtually irreparable, Rinaldi explains, making cheap shoes like mine inherently disposable.

In the 1970s it became fashionable to wear sneakers as everyday footwear. Unfortunately, the soles on athletic shoes cannot easily be replaced. As the price of footwear plummeted (all but 15 percent of our shoes are made in China), consumers have chosen to buy new ones instead of maintaining the pairs they own. "People have started to think that since they can get a new pair of shoes for sixty dollars, why get them repaired for fifty dollars?" says Rinaldi. Shoe repair peaked in the 1960s with almost 60,000 repairers in the United States. Since then, Rinaldi says the numbers have declined nearly 90 percent, and he can't even get his own children into the ethos of repair. "Style changes so quickly," he says. "My daughters will not wear last year's shoes. Every summer they go out and buy the new styles. Our society is just like that now."

Every now and then, among the tattered boots and stained blouses, a true gem will get tossed out and find its way to Trans-Americas. I'm talking of course about vintage clothing. Not surprisingly, some of the most highly valued used clothing is anything made prior to the corporate takeover of fashion. "This is what half of Brooklyn is wearing," Stubin told me, as I picked through silk dresses and print scarves and thick leather belts separated into cardboard boxes in a far corner of the Trans-Americas facility. "If you go to your local vintage retailer, they're probably buying from us," he boasted.

As the value of used clothing has gone down, textile graders have increasingly relied on the small sliver of well-cared-for vintage clothes that comes through the waste stream. "As a textile recycler, vintage is one of the few ways that you can stay in business," Stubin confessed. Our collective lust for vintage is taken for granted, but valuing old clothing as we do now really only dates back to the 1990s.[18] Today, in Brooklyn's vibrant vintage retail scene, I've lusted over a $400 1940s two-piece bathing suit and even pricier silver glitter '70s platform boots.

We can't go back in time and make more pre-1990s clothing. And as the demand goes up, vintage is getting harder and pricier to find. The textile graders are raising vintage prices in order to offset the decline in value of the other clothing they process. Paben justifies it as "a classic supply and demand issue." Vintage clothing, like designer clothing, is in danger of becoming a rich person's sport, forcing well-made used clothing even further out of the reach of the average consumer.

Sara Bereket, the vintage dealer who sells at the Brooklyn Flea, is struggling to offer her customers reasonably priced secondhand clothes. "If you want to charge me fifty dollars for a dress, I'm just not going to buy it," Bereket told me of the increased prices she's seeing at some textile recyclers, where she buys most of her vintage pieces. "That means I have to charge my customers one hundred and fifty at the flea market." As the vintage supply in the New York City area gets more overpicked, Bereket's turned to sourcing from vintage dealers in the Midwest.

Bereket has also adapted to the overheated vintage market by buying passed-over items and less valued pieces from the '80s and '90s and freshening up and altering them. She's turned an '80s sequin dress into a tube top, replaced broken buttons on a plaid Yves Saint Laurent jacket, and taken the sides in and the hem up on countless dresses. She calls her products "reconstructed vintage" and about 70 percent of Bereket's business is refashioned in some way. "The clothes I buy have potential, but they need tweaking to make them perfect," says Bereket. "Maybe the fabric is really nice or the print is really nice. Then you just work it."

Vintage's appeal is about nostalgia and exclusivity, but there's also a certain "they don't make 'em like they used to" allure to owning something from our garment industry's heyday. Clothing made in the era before chain-store mass fashion seems, and in many cases is, better made and unique. "There are no details anymore," Bereket told me wistfully as she flipped through her walk-in closet of reconstructed vintage furs, '70s designer dresses, and home-sewn '50s housedresses. "There used to be pleating, side zippers, interesting clasps and buttons," she says. "We forget that people use to buy stuff and have the tailor take it in so it would exactly fit their shape."

Much of our donated clothing does not end up in vintage shops, as car-seat stuffing, or even as an industrial wiping rag. It is sold overseas. After the prized vintage clothing is plucked out and the outcasts are sent to the fiber and wiping-rag companies, the remaining clothing is sorted, shrink-wrapped, tied up, baled, and sold to used-clothing vendors around the world. The secondhand clothing industry has been export oriented almost since the introduction of mass-produced garments.[19] And by one estimate, used clothing is now the United States' number one export by volume,[20] with the overwhelming majority sent to ports in sub-Saharan Africa. Tanzanians and Kenyans call used clothing *mitumba,* which means "bales," as it comes off the cargo ships in the shrink-wrapped cubes like the ones I saw at Trans-Americas and Salvation Army. In Zambia, the word for secondhand is *salaula,* which literally translates as "to select from a pile in the manner of rummaging." Both words reference the fact that African vendors select the bales by only eyeing what's on the outside. The bales are cut open in front of an eager clientele and buyers, who pick through it for higher-value finds.

Once again, while many Americans might like to imagine that there is some poor, underdressed African who wants our worn and tattered duds, the African used clothing market is very particular and is demanding higher quality and more fashion-forward styles. Paben told me that access to the Internet and cell phones has made the continent fiercely fashion-forward in recent years. "There's been a change in what you can sell there," he says, and the bales have to be much more carefully sorted based on style, brand, and condition. In Mali, journalist Lucy Siegle found that the men wore belted trench coats with three-quarter-length sleeves, while the teen girls preferred hot pink shirts and flared jeans.[21]

The quality of the clothing sent to Africa depends first of all on the quality of the sorting done at textile graders in the United States. "When a customer buys a container of used clothing, they're taking a gamble because they're paying for it before it leaves the factory," says Paben. "They could open up the container, and it could be lots of really bad stuff." Mid-West Textile, says Paben, specializes in taking the "risk out for our customer" by doing a more rigorous sort for the African market.

Other textile recyclers are not as ethical, with some hiding used clothes beyond wearable condition inside bales, essentially using African countries as their own dumping ground.[22] As the quality of clothing Americans buy and donate goes down, the stuff that ends up on Africa's shores can be quite shoddy. According to Siegle, rag buyers in Africa are more frequently seeing broken zippers, discolored fabrics, and flimsy clothes that stain and rip more easily.[23] As incomes rise in Africa, tastes become more savvy, cheap Chinese imports of new clothes flood those countries, and our own high-quality clothing supply is depleted, it's foreseeable that the African solution to our overconsumption may come to an end. What then?

On a recent Saturday morning, I was back at the Quincy Street Salvation Army shopping for a vintage coat, hoping to find quality and craftsmanship inherent in older clothes. This particular Salvation Army is roughly the size of an airplane hangar, and deathly quiet in the mornings. I hoped to make a score while the rest of Brooklyn slept off their Friday night. I found a handful of Italian- and American-made, sharply lined, wool-blend coats with beautiful cloth-covered buttons. But none of them were quite my style. As I flipped through the women's tops nearby, I noticed a Salvation Army employee in a smock, methodically walking past me. At first I thought she was straightening the racks and hanging up clothes that had been pulled to the floor, but then I realized she was carrying clothes away. She looked at the color of the price tags stapled onto each garment, which Maui explained is how their stores keep track of which week of the month an item was put on the floor. Then she plucked out the garments that had been sitting there too long unsold, like eggs gone bad, and chucked them into one of those huge gray Dumpsters I had seen in the sorting room upstairs. Soon enough, I thought, they would be shredded or on their way overseas.

6

Sewing Is a Good Job, a Great Job

The workday begins early at Alta Gracia, a garment factory located in a tiny villa in the rolling hills north of Santo Domingo, Dominican Republic. I arrived at 7:30 a.m. to *bachata* music blaring and the sun streaming into the wide ground-floor factory. The staff of 107 sewing-machine operators was already running batches of T-shirts under the needles of their machines. They sat, young and not so young, men and women, in a half-dozen lines, each one sewing a single part of a shirt and passing it on. Off to the right, the cutters were slicing their electric blades through thick, 20-foot-long stacks of fabric. Off to the left, rolls of colorful jersey knit and boxes of finished goods were piled on shelves.

The factory trainer, a cute, curly-haired guy named Julio Cesar Sanchez, asked me, "Have you ever sewn before?" I have. Sort of. *Un poquito*, I told him in my high school remnants of Spanish. "It's like a puzzle," Julio continued, and I realized he wanted to know if I've ever sewn an entire garment together. The answer, as for most Americans of my generation, was no. I've sewn on a button using a needle and thread, and I have some recollection of trying to sew patches on my jeans using my mother's sewing machine in high school.

I followed Julio to the back of the factory, where a quadrant of machines lay vacant. He sat down at one that looked like a compact loaf of bread recessed into a white plastic table. It had four protruding knobs and four large red spools feeding it yarn. Julio gave the loaf two wide pieces of chocolate-brown scrap fabric, pressed the pedal under the table, and sewed an arrow-straight seam. Then it was my turn. "Pick up the foot," he directed in Spanish, and I lifted the little metal tab that holds the cloth under the needle. "*Coser!*" he said, meaning "Sew!" I pressed the pedal under the table, and the needle took off like a shot, rising and falling rapidly, the cloth speeding out from under my hands. The resulting seam looked like a cartoon frowny-face.

I peered sheepishly at Julio. He'd clearly seen this kind of incompetence before. With his hand, he made a subtle downward gesture to indicate I needed to press more *gently,* and then he took my hands and guided the same stretch of cloth back through the machine.

I asked Julio if I was the worst trainee he'd seen. "No," he told me. "Some people, you tell them to lift up the foot and they lift up their *actual* foot," he said, bringing his knee high up into the air. We laughed for no more than two seconds before my no-nonsense trainer rushed me over to the side-seam station, where I sewed in the fabrication tag (100% cotton) on the trunk of a shirt. I sewed four more seams on four different machines before realizing that I wasn't sewing scrap cloth. I was creating actual T-shirts, four of them—two red and two brown with red trim.

At Alta Gracia, a simple men's T-shirt is created using a 14-person process and a number of different types of machines, including a heat press that transfers the brand logo from a translucent plastic film onto the inside back collar of the shirt. When producing large volumes of clothes, this kind of assembly line production is very efficient. Each person becomes master of his or her operation and machine, which also makes it easy to trace any quality problems to their origins. The right sleeve seam doesn't match up with the shoulder seam? The person behind machine 11 has got some explaining to do. Of course, modular production can create a lot of pressure and competition too. If one person is slower or less skilled than the others, they hold up the line.

I didn't have the help of an assembly line. And Julio was training me with the intensity he would use on a new hire. I was going to sew these shirts myself from start to finish. But after I got a handle on the pedal and wasn't sending fabric flying, I was having fun. "Look, you're getting better," Julio said, proudly. "I wish everyone learned as fast as you do." But I was still the least talented person at Alta Gracia. By the time people were popping out of their chairs for lunch, more than four hours later, the rest of the sewing machine operators were halfway through producing their flabbergasting 1,300-shirt quota for the day. My four shirts still didn't have any sleeves.

Alta Gracia is not a typical garment factory. Aside from being an open book to media and labor rights groups, it is the only unionized factory I visited outside the United States. The factory has a formal process for dealing with complaints and making workplace improvements, and the managers and sewing-machine operators work collaboratively to make the factory succeed. Everyone has a say in how the factory is run, down to deciding what tunes are played over the loudspeaker every day. The Christians choose the morning tunes and the nonreligious folks control the airways in the afternoons.

Alta Gracia is owned and operated by an American company—South Carolina–based Knights Apparel, the leading producer of college-logo clothing sold at American universities. Knights hand-selected the factory's location and oversaw every step of its setup, from the type of chairs purchased to the dexterity tests given to potential hires. Knights supports the factory's labor union and the Worker Rights Consortium, an independent labor group, has someone onsite at the factory on an almost daily basis to verify that the company's standards are met. Of course, when you're there, all this seems normal. Alta Gracia just seems like a nice place to work.

Gemma Castro, one of Alta Gracia's production managers, has worked in the Dominican garment industry since 1994—at a lingerie factory, a children's and baby clothes factory, a T-shirt factory that produced for Gap and Old Navy, and Grupo M, once one of the largest private employers in the Dominican Republic and the manufacturer of clothes for virtually every large American brand, including Donna Karan, American Eagle, Calvin Klein, and Tommy Hilfiger.

During her lunch break, I asked Castro if any of these huge brands she's made clothes for in the past would ever place an order in a factory like Alta Gracia. There was a long pause, then a nervous laugh. She said, "I don't think so. This is a very *different* factory." In her experience, big clothing brands *are* strict about following health and safety codes and the local labor and wage laws in the countries where they source their goods. But when it comes to wages, the legal minimum is as far as they take their responsibility. "These factories that I used to work with use the legal requirements of the country they work in," says Castro. "And in most countries, the minimum wage is not enough for people to live decently."

To calculate the wages of the people who make your clothing, just look at the "made in" label and then do an Internet search for that country's minimum wage. Virtually no clothing company volunteers to pay much more than the minimum plus any mandated overtime. This is what truly sets Alta Gracia apart: It is one of the *only* factories in the developing world where its employees aren't just paid the legal minimum or just above or below it. Its workers earn three and a half times the Dominican minimum wage, roughly $2.83 an hour or $500 a month.

This type of pay structure is known as a "living wage," and in Alta Gracia's case it is independently determined by the Worker Rights Consortium. Though the definition varies slightly between groups that study non-poverty income levels, a living wage is broadly understood as pay high enough to cover the cost of a family's basic needs such as food and water, housing and energy, clothing, health care, transportation, education, and child care, as well as modest funds for savings and discretionary spending.[1] It varies from country to country based on cost of living. Instead of trapping garment workers in a hand-to-mouth existence, which has been the case in most overseas garment factories that produce for export, a living wage allows factory workers to achieve longer-term goals and invest in their children's futures.

———

When I met Andy Ward, he told me something that stuck with me about garment work. "Sewing should be a good job; it should be a great job," he said. As anyone who's ever sewed can attest, using a sewing machine isn't an unskilled job. Sewing clothes isn't an inherently grueling task either. The experience ranges anywhere from tedium to pure joy depending on how long you have to keep at it and what it is that you're creating, as well as how much you're getting paid. Most Americans today link sewing inextricably with sweatshops and human misery—yet it hasn't always been this way.

In 1909, 20,000 New York City garment workers, many of them teenage girls, went on strike and demanded better pay and working conditions at their jobs. Garment workers at the time worked 13-hour days, had no days off, and made about $6 a week, according to historical information collected by the AFL-CIO. Some of the strikers were beaten up and taken to jail; some were even shot. Among the strikers were workers from the doomed Triangle Shirtwaist Factory, which made those ubiquitous turn-of-the-century blouses with the high collar, puffed sleeves, and cinched waists.

Two years after the "Uprising of the 20,000," the infamous fire at the Triangle factory occurred. The fire caused national outrage, with 400,000 people attending the funeral procession in New York. It was the catalyst for quick and wide-reaching social change. A Factory Investigating Commission was set up and more than 30 state workplace safety and employment laws were passed within two years. Robert Wagner, who chaired the commission, went on to sponsor Social Security, the National Labor Relations Act, and many other New Deal legislations. Francis Perkins, also on the commission, went on to become the Secretary of Labor under Franklin D. Roosevelt and established the 40-hour workweek, as well as the first minimum wage and overtime laws.

In 1938 the Department of Labor's Women's Bureau produced a short film called *What's in a Dress?* to show the public, after more than two decades of labor activism and strengthened industry regulations, just how much the garment industry had improved. The camera pans over a large dressmaking factory, presumably in New York City, as the narrator boasts, "For making these dresses, women are well paid." A few garment workers are then shown sitting around a table with their managers disagreeing on the rate to sew a belted dress with pearl buttons. An arbitrator is called in to examine the dress and set the final rate. Then the camera cuts to a classic Hollywood-style beauty wearing a silky cape and tiara. Text runs across the screen that reads: "Dame Fashion rejoices that sweatshop wages are being rapidly abolished in the dress industry."

By the 1960s the garment industry achieved in many American cities what Katie Quan, the associate chair of the University of California at Berkeley's Labor Center, calls a "closed market," meaning non-union brands, factories, and middlemen were entirely shut out of the business of making clothes. "The unions required the brands to use only union contractors, and the contractors were required to use only union brands," explains Quan. "You couldn't do any business in New York City or Boston or Chicago without being union." Garment workers were able to negotiate guaranteed annual pay increases, as well as medical, retirement, and vacation benefits.

Today, apparel manufacturers have comparatively little power. Economic globalization, which has happened without globalizing first-world labor protections, has left workers around the world to compete against one another. As garment worker unions declined in power during the second half of the twentieth century, factories lost their ability to bargain with clothing companies and garment worker wages were driven down.

Robert Ross, Director of International Studies at Clark University, says consolidation of the clothing industry, which has resulted in large and powerful entities, puts factory workers at an enormous disadvantage. "Today, we've got eight or ten of these big chains, and the discounters in particular, that buy up roughly as much as seventy percent of clothing bought at wholesale," Ross explains. "If Walmart wants to buy T-shirts from you, they can basically buy a whole factory's output for a year, so they have tremendous leverage." By comparison, even the most powerful clothing buyer in the 1970s or '80s controlled just a fraction of the total apparel market, ordering at most several hundred thousand dresses for all of their stores, says Ross. Today, huge clothing brands can and will simply move production if factories form unions or ask for more money, and have been known to demand price cuts from their factories on a yearly and sometimes even quarterly basis. [2]

As clothing companies became design and marketing houses that don't own any factories or directly make any clothing, they distanced themselves legally from their suppliers. In 2009 a federal judge ruled that Walmart was not legally responsible for bad conditions in factories that made Walmart products because the workers were not Walmart employees.[3] H&M's Web site has a video about its social responsibility program that also says as much. "Legally we don't really have a responsibility for our suppliers, but of course morally and according to our values we feel that we should take responsibility for how the garments are produced," boasts H&M's Ingrid Schullström, the company's head of ethical sourcing. Clothing companies like to highlight they don't *have to* monitor factory conditions, they volunteer to.

Most companies don't own factories, yet they certainly own the clothes that are made in them and create the time constraints and cost pressures that make factories miserable places to work. The legal loophole that doesn't hold companies accountable to factories makes it all too easy for conditions to exist that clothing consumers would never condone. In Bangladesh, many buildings are old, structurally unsound, or fire safety protocol is simply ignored by management, yet many of the stores we patronize produce in these buildings. In 2002 a Dhaka factory making children's clothing for Inditex, the company that owns Zara, collapsed, killing 64 people and injuring more than 70.[4] In 2010, 27 people were killed at a factory fire at Ha-Meem Group factory north of Dhaka, which was making clothes for Gap. Another factory, the Garib & Garib Newaj Garment Factory, which made sweaters and cardigans for H&M, went up in flames in Gazipur the same year, killing 21 people. The fire started at 9 p.m., when workers should have been home. H&M had audited this factory within the previous year and told reporters: "The findings we had at Garib & Garib on the last audit were two covered fire extinguishers but that was corrected immediately." The company says that its October 2009 audit found clearly marked escape routes and emergency exits, as well as fire extinguishers. It was later revealed that the security guards did not even know how to operate a fire extinguisher.

––––––––––

The physical and cultural distance between suppliers, clothing companies, and their consumers have led to headline-grabbing sweatshop stories that have characterized the past two decades. In 1996 Kathie Lee Gifford became an early subject of international scorn when underage workers were discovered making her clothing line for Walmart in a Honduran sweatshop. In the late nineties, 18 American clothing companies were sued for using abusive poverty-wage factories in the U.S. Commonwealth of Saipan, a tiny island between the Philippines and Hawaii, and putting "Made in the U.S.A." labels on the clothes. The list of Saipan producers included virtually every megabrand and retailer Americans shopped at in the 1990s, including Abercrombie & Fitch, Brooks Brothers, Calvin Klein, Donna Karan, Dress Barn, Gap, Banana Republic, Old Navy, JCPenney, J.Crew, Jones Apparel Group, Lane Bryant, The Limited, Liz Claiborne, May Department Stores Company, Nordstrom, Phillips-Van Heusen, Polo Ralph Lauren, Talbots, Target, and Tommy Hilfiger.[5]

As the millennium drew to a close, a powerful antisweatshop movement, the biggest protest movement since the 1960s, was raging on college campuses. Huge antiglobalization protests, critical of the free-trade deals that seemed to make it too easy for international corporations to exploit overseas workers, were front-page news around the country with such clothiers as Gap and Nike held in the cross-hairs. Many schools, including Syracuse University, where I was a student, demanded higher standards for the factories where collegiate apparel is made.

Sweatshop allegations are certainly bad PR for clothing companies and ultimately bad for business. To counter the mounting negative press, boycotts, and picketers at the insistence of consumers, activists, and religious groups, it became common policy for large clothing companies to draft what are known as "codes of conduct." These are essentially guidelines regarding human rights, health and safety, and wages and overtime that factories must follow in order to do business with big Western brands. Today, just about every major clothier has a Web page dedicated to "social responsibility" where the company's code of conduct is posted. Most of them hire huge teams of compliance auditors who visit their factories to verify that the law and any additional standards are being followed. Nike, according to its 2009 *Corporate Responsibility Report,* monitors each of its 600-plus suppliers an average of 1.77 times a year; Walmart, according to its 2010 *Social Responsibility Report,* conducts more than 8,000 audits of its factories annually; and H&M's annual report notes that the company has 76 people on its auditing team and reviewed more than 1,900 factories in 2010.

However, according to a 2006 article in the *Journal of Fashion Marketing and Management* on how fast fashion is affecting supply chains, the pressure to produce goods at an increasingly furious pace is placing ethical practices "at greater risk of being ignored."[6] An industry insider and designer for a major national brand says that competition in the industry is so fierce that extreme overtime has become an industry necessity. "Most companies tell their factories to just *work 'em over the weekend,*" she told me. "That's what these factories hear from American companies all the time. I hear it in the office all the time. *Whatever you have to do. Get it done. Ship it on time.*"

Journalist T. A. Frank wrote a piece for the *Washington Monthly* in April 2008 describing his experience working for a private company that audits factories. Its clients include Walmart and major brands like Nike. Frank found that social responsibility was an easy-to-play game for companies that don't take it seriously—noting that the most unethical ones announce the audits before they happen and will use a bad factory long enough to get an order done and then cut ties, claiming a string of failed audits as the reason. Walmart, for example, announces almost three-fourths of its audits. Frank writes that "monitoring by itself is meaningless," and is only effective if the company that commissioned it is dedicated to ethical sourcing.[7]

I visited a large, socially compliant garment factory smack in the middle of the downtown business district of Gulshan Circle in Dhaka, Bangladesh. Direct Sportswear Limited, the factory owned by Ashraful "Jewel" Kabir, employs several hundred people in a large, two-floor space and produces for big American brands, including Echo, Varsity, and Warner Brothers. Its main client is Umbro, an athletic brand owned by Nike.

Frank notes that Nike has done an about-face since the 1990s and has become an industry leader in responsible sourcing. It prescreens its factories for compliance, conducts unannounced audits, and builds long-term relationships with its suppliers so that they have incentive to improve. It makes public the names and addresses of all of its suppliers. The day I visited DSL, the staff of mostly female workers wrapped in burnt-orange saris were sewing, trimming, and packing pairs of blue track pants. Men had the better-paying cutting and ironing jobs. Tacked up near the entrance of the workroom were Nike and Umbro's Codes of Conduct, printed in Bengali. Exaggeratedly large signs around the room indicated the "fire extinguisher" and "fire alarm switch"—oddly, both in English. On the roof of DSL is an open-air canteen, where rows of picnic tables face a nice view of the snarling traffic in Gulshan Circle. Up there, Jewel proudly showed me the "children's room," an empty glassed-in cube, and the "doctor's room," also a small cube that holds a table and a white curtain with a red cross. It was unclear whether either room is ever used or if they're even helpful, but it was obvious they were there to reassure Western-ers like me that progress is being made.

Jewel made all of these changes to his factory to be labeled socially compliant, the requirement for doing business with big Western brands. I asked him what he thought of all of the required upgrades. "It's good," he said. "It should be. Now we are feeling we are doing some betterment for the workers. We also feel good." But there's a natural limit to a factory owner's feelings of goodwill about social compliance, as the factories are the ones that incur the costs of getting their facilities up to the retailers' standards. Many companies now require factories to pay to be audited, especially if they've violated their client's code of conduct in the past.[8] According to a 2009 report by the UK-based organization Labour Behind the Label, clothing companies are demanding that suppliers pay their workers more with-out increasing the amount they pay for their products.[9] The boost in pay comes out of the already stretched-thin factory's pocket. Jewel later admitted, "It is difficult to negotiate with brands when they're asking for low prices and also for the factory to increase their costs, asking for better wages and compliance and all this."

Production specialist Sally Reid, who worked for a manufacturer that produced for Ann Taylor, traveled to factories around the world throughout the '90s, when brands were moving the bulk of their busi-ness overseas. Reid says she never saw "people chained to their ma-chines" or any other abusive conditions, but she does remember factories in earlier years being very dirty and inhumanely hot, and payroll records either were kept ineffectively or weren't kept at all. Fire safety was practically nonexistent. "The factories were nasty," Reid recalls, especially shoe factories, where workers handle toxic chemicals and inhale tanning agents.

Since the early days of outsourcing Reid has seen the health and safety of factories improve, with many of those in Bangladesh and China today being very clean and "sanitized-looking." Reid says, "In the beginning, [compliance] was a joke to everybody. But over time, it started to take hold." The factories I went to in Bangladesh and China were indeed cleaner, more modern, and more closely followed fire and safety codes than the ones I saw in Los Angeles. They were all new or recently renovated, highly organized, and brightly lit, and the floors were clearly marked with fire exit routes and safety equipment. I was always at the Chinese factories at lunchtime and like clockwork, the workers would reach up, turn off the lights above their machines and file out for their meals. Because it happened at all the facilities I visited, I have a hunch the lunch-break procession is for show.

It's not unlikely that what I saw in China were "demonstration" factories—more regulated showpiece factories shown to Western clients. My actual order, if I'd had one, might very well have been completed in a network of illegally run factories in the surrounding area. By one account, an estimated 99 percent of Chinese factories subcontract, meaning they use other suppliers that the client never sees.[10] Often a subcontractor is paying workers less or, more commonly, using excessive overtime to complete orders faster and cheaper. Factories subcontract this for the same reasons clothing brands outsource to other countries: to save money[11] and to stay competitive.

No amount of social compliance, sparkling showpiece factories, or glassed-in doctor's cubes changes the fact that it is entirely legal to pay poverty wages in most of the world's factories. The minimum wage in the Dominican Republic free-trade zones is less than $150 per month. One Alta Gracia employee named Kuki told me that when she earned a minimum wage at the factory she worked at previously, she wasn't making enough money to buy food for her and her four kids every week. "And that's just food," she said. It's unclear whether workers in socially compliant factories make more than their counterparts as a whole. In some cases, they actually make *less* than their peers at shadier suppliers, as they are required to work fewer hours or are salaried and forbidden from excessive overtime. Mattel's Chinese factories are known for being safe and clean, for example, but their workers' take-home pay is less than those who toil in noncompliant factories.[12]

In 2010 the Bangladeshi minimum wage was up for review. Inflation was spiraling out of control, stretching garment workers' already paltry paychecks to the breaking point. Labor protests erupted in Dhaka with garment workers demanding a 200 percent increase in the minimum wage. It sounds like a big leap, but it would have worked out to a new minimum wage of $71 a month. According to the International Labor Rights Forum, this would have been a living wage.[13] Interestingly, H&M, Walmart, Gap, Levi's, and other Western clothing giants who source from Bangladesh wrote a joint letter to the Bangladeshi government, urging it to raise the minimum wage and reset it every year. The letter read: "It is a discomforting fact that the current minimum wage level in Bangladesh is below the poverty line calculated by the World Bank and thus does not meet the basic needs of the workers and their families." These companies did not specify what the new wage should be, but a spokeswoman for H&M said the company was willing to pay more for clothing to help support higher wages. Yet just the year before, when the economy was struggling more, Bangladeshi suppliers reported that buyers were demanding drastic *decreases* in prices, and H&M was among the 50 brands and retailers calling on

Bangladeshi exporters to reduce their prices if they wished to stay competitive.[14]

The government eventually agreed to raise the minimum wage, but to only 3,000 taka a month, or about $43. The highest-skilled and most experienced workers were to receive more, about the demanded $73 per month. The changes were to go into effect in November 2010. The deadline came and went and many workers weren't receiving the increase. According to Mehedi Hasan, a Worker Rights Consortium staffer stationed in Dhaka, "Management started to readjust the new wage scale. This readjusting process caused a massive, unaccountable demotion of skilled workers." Factory managers were either refusing to implement the changes, claiming the bad global economy made them infeasible, says Hasan, or they simply demoted their workers to the base level so as to not pay them the new minimum for skilled work.

I was supposed to meet Hasan in person to discuss Bangladesh's labor strife. It was dangerous, as labor activists have been imprisoned there recently and I was explicitly warned by labor leaders not to meet with anyone involved in the unrest face-to-face. Perhaps by luck, the Dhaka traffic made it impossible for the two of us to meet as planned, so we ended up in several late-night chat sessions online. We discussed the new wages, which include an allowance of 200 taka ($3) for medical expenses and 800 taka ($11) for housing. "Only 40 percent of housing is covered," Hasan explained. I had been told that even in slums one room could cost as much as 2,000 to 3,000 taka a month ($26 to $39). "So, most garment workers live in slums?" I asked, meaning illegal and slipshod housing common in and around Dhaka where there is no running water, electricity, or any other modern amenity. "Yes, it's slums or lower housing conditions," Hasan wrote.

According to the Bangladesh NGO Nari Uddug Kendra (the Center for Women's Initiatives), it would require 1,400 taka ($19) a month to cover food for a single person in Bangladesh.[15] Many Bangladeshi garment workers are the sole breadwinners in large families, so the new minimum wage would conceivably be entirely taken up by food expenses. I also asked Hasan what he thought of Nike's code of conduct, the one I saw posted on the wall at DSL. "It's a good-looking poster used as a decoration," he typed. "If I say they are not doing anything that would be wrong. But the changes are few."

Protests broke out again in Bangladesh, and this time they were more violent. "Workers came out into the road, engaged themselves at vandalizing vehicles, damaging property, torching cars and buses," Hasan wrote in jumbled English. "The situation went in explosively matter and so many chaoses, vandalizing had occurred at all the industrial hubs and zones in the country." The garment worker protests in Bangladesh continued well into 2011.

<hr>

At five on the nose, everyone at Alta Gracia popped out of their seats, grabbed their purses and bags, and filed out of the factory in a flurry of chatter. Each module had finished its quota. Even I had completed my four T-shirts and was beaming. A lanky young woman named Patricia invited me over to her house after work, and I happily accepted. She lived just a few miles away in a subdivision built into a patch of hills. When we pulled up in front of her house, the sun was dipping below the mountains and the street was lined with pickup trucks and loitering men filled with after-work glee. The neighborhood's houses were tiny, ramshackle, and just a few feet apart. Patricia's house was a hair's length from the crumbling sidewalk and down an even crumblier set of stairs.

She showed me inside and we followed a point of light straight through two small rooms and out the back door, which opened onto what looked at first like a junkyard with scraps of paper, cinder blocks, broken cement, and plants growing wildly. A rural Dominican back-yard makes an American backyard look like a hospital room, sani-tized and unnatural. Avocado trees and fruit trees tangled into the sky; one neighbor's yard blended into the next. Patricia sent me home with some kind of plump tropical fruit the size of a softball, which I found too interesting looking to eat.

In the midst of all of this overgrowth was a teal building the size of a toolshed. This was Patricia's new house, built with her factory wages from Alta Gracia. It's a modest but enormous improvement. Patricia and her two boys, six and five, one of whom is her late sister's, had been living in the main two-room house along with her mother. The main house, only slightly larger than Patricia's teal cottage, was too tiny for Patricia's husband to live with his family. There was no kitchen. And a hut with a hole in the ground in the backyard served as a bathroom.

Patricia used to work at BJ&B, the factory that formerly occupied the building where Alta Gracia now operates. BJ&B employed sev-eral thousand people making baseball caps for Nike and Reebok. The story gets disappointingly familiar from there. In the late 1990s, low wages, high production quotas, and verbal abuse from the fac-tory owners were rampant. The workers unionized, and in 2002 the union leaders were fired. The international labor community, with the support of college activists, intervened and reinstated the work-ers. Two years later the workers won established pay raises and med-ical and retirement benefits, a rarity in today's globalized garment industry. For a time, the factory was a model case for how student activists, factory workers, and brands in the United States could work together to improve factory conditions in other parts of the world. And then the brands pulled out of the factory, which then shut down.[16]

When the factory closed, the village of Altagracia became a ghost town. There was 95 percent unemployment, according to Knights Apparel president Donnie Hodge. Some of Patricia's neighbors ran food stands or lived off their land to get by. But other families were split apart, with parents trying to find work in Santo Domingo and leaving the kids behind with relatives, or vice versa. Others looked for work in the United States. Patricia scraped by on her mother's earnings from selling fried food at local cockfights. But a lot of times the family went hungry. She hit rock bottom when one of her little boys got sick and she had to sell all of her furniture to pay for his medical care.

"I saved the envelope from the first time I got paid," Patricia told me, as she tore apart her new house looking for the blue slip of paper that was her first Alta Gracia pay stub. "It was a big deal for me to be able to get enough food," she says, so she went to the grocery store first. Next she paid off a washer and dryer and installed a refrigerator, stove, and plumbing in her mom's house, where the family now takes its meals and bathes. Patricia also has plans to add on one more bedroom for the kids and has purchased several hundred dollars worth of concrete blocks to rebuild a sturdier home at some point down the road. She has her eye on the empty lot across the street.

I was invited to Kuki's house next. She's a talkative and motherly woman and her house is clearly the place to be in the neighborhood. There were her three children, plus three of the neighbor's kids, and a kitten bopping around while Kuki poured me orange soda and made me a plate of fried plantains. Kuki's house is larger than Patricia's and already has a kitchen and plumbing, yet there are still four people (including a teenage boy) sharing a single bedroom and a common space. She's adding extra bedrooms onto the back of the house and has used her wages toward more material comforts like two couches and some nice drapes. Kuki was also a BJ&B worker and when it went under, there was a moment when she thought she was going to lose everything. "I was going to have to give up my house and move back in with my mom because there was just no way I was going to be able to make ends meet," Kuki recalls. "I owed too much money to the grocery store, so they weren't going to give me food anymore." Many of the workers at Alta Gracia had amassed debts like these before the factory reopened.

Early in my visit with Kuki, a rolling blackout snuffed out the electricity in the neighborhood; we were talking by candlelight. Kuki's two-year-old promptly crawled onto the table and stuck his finger into the candle. When everyone calmed back down, I asked Kuki, carefully, about the elephant in the room. Her livelihood depended on American consumers buying the clothes that Alta Gracia makes. *Does this cross her mind?* "Yeah, it worries me," she said. The factory was still getting up and running, and the orders weren't yet as big as they needed to be. The workers had been filling in the production lag with other Knights products that were not under the Alta Gracia brand. She folded her hands and told me soberly, "But I have faith that it will work."

As the fashion industry exists now, the most effective way for garment factories to provide good jobs is for the companies that make the clothes or the consumers who buy them to demand better conditions. Alta Gracia is a confluence of both approaches. It is owned by Knights Apparel, which has gone several steps further than most companies by allowing its workforce to unionize, inviting labor monitors to scrutinize conditions in the factory, and by paying its workers a living wage.

From a business standpoint, it's an enormous risk. Because of the

Dominican Republic's already higher energy and labor costs, Hodge says that making a T-shirt there costs the company an estimated 10 percent more than it might in Asia. "And then I'm paying three and half times the wages on top of that," he told me. "I can tell you this, if a thousand companies looked at the numbers, the pros and cons, I don't think anybody would have done it. If we had looked at it in that light, we would not have done it." Hodge says that consistent pressure from the American college community is what motivated the company to open the factory, in addition to a personal commitment from himself and Knights CEO Joseph Bozich. "It sounds corny, but we have a different viewpoint from some people when it comes to corporate responsibility and what you should and shouldn't do," says Hodge. "Joe had some sickness in his past and I lost my second daughter in an accident when she was a teenager, and those things change your view of the world and make you more open to doing some things and taking some chances."

Knights Apparel is trying to acclimate consumers to a living-wage product by offering it at a similar price as its competitors. Alta Gracia T-shirts are high quality and on trend for the college market, so there is no sacrifice for the consumer, which is essential for ethical fashion to succeed. Knights absorbs Alta Gracia's higher costs through its other, more profitable lines. "We could have said, 'Let's retail our shirts at twenty-eight dollars' and recovered all of our costs and made the same margin that we make on other stuff, but we do not do that," Hodge told me. Instead, its T-shirts retail for $18, a price similar to Nike and Reebok's collegiate lines.

Fair-trade certification is also being extended to fashion products for the first time, offering consumers another way to support factories that supply more than the baseline minimum. The Oakland-based nonprofit Fair Trade USA has spent the past ten years working mostly to certify Fair Trade coffee growers around the world, including the popular Green Mountain Coffee brand. In 2010 the group expanded its work into apparel factories and small-scale cotton farms. Both Alta Gracia and Fair Trade certification use sewn-in labels to give consumers a shorthand way to know workers' lives actually are directly elevated with their purchase. Alta Gracia products have the WRC's certification sewn in, as well as a hangtag explaining the Alta Gracia story.

In addition to following international labor standards and submitting to regular audits, Fair Trade–certified clothing factories must also create an environment in which workers are comfortable reporting any problems in the workplace. Fair Trade USA spokesperson Stacy Wagner says, "We want to make sure there's a grievance process that gives workers the ability to give feedback and complain. We're an audit system, so it works both from employees speaking up as well as auditors going in and making sure everything is on track." Fair Trade buyers must also pay a "premium" of up to 10 percent of the cost of each garment produced. The factory workers and managers cooperatively run a community fund created by their Fair Trade premiums, which they can choose to invest either in bonus checks or in community development projects such as education or clean water.

The first Fair Trade USA–certified label was sewn into a shirt in late 2010. So far, a limited number of socially conscious brands have stepped up for certification, such as Maggie's Organics and HAE Now, which are both basics companies. *Project Runway*'s Korto Momolu has produced a line of certified graphic-print T-shirts as well. Fair Trade USA has recently been criticized for breaking off from its umbrella group, Fair Trade International, which coordinates fair-trade groups around the world and sets the standards for certification. The U.S. organization claims the move is necessary to grow demand for fair-trade products and extend certification to bigger companies. Fair Trade USA CEO Paul Rice said in an October 12, 2011, conference call with fair-trade advocates, "Competition is not a bad thing . . . Companies like Walmart, Costco, Green Mountain, Starbucks and Ben & Jerry's are expanding their offerings in terms of fair-trade products."[17] It's unclear whether certification for clothing will work for larger retailers, but Rice's comments hint that this might be the plan.

The ill effects of the fashion industry on foreign workers are well documented to the point of being tired. It's a natural assumption that a book about cheap fashion will cover the grim issues of sweatshops and child labor. A common refrain is that garment workers should be glad to have jobs. Our expectations and standards for ethics in the fashion industry are embarrassingly low, but the potential for change is also grossly underestimated. Companies are now offering alternatives that are affordable and stylish, and they'll succeed if consumers support them. "Our success will be completely determined by whether people are willing to buy the product," admits Hodge, who says he often loses sleep picturing the day when he might have to stand in front of the Alta Gracia staff and tell them their project has failed.

Consumers can afford to take on higher costs for living-wage products, yet raising the wages for garment workers does not have to have a huge impact on retail prices. Garment workers overseas are still only earning about 1 percent of the retail price of the clothing they produce.[18] The reality is that their wages are so low and many U.S. clothing companies' profits are so high that brands could afford to raise wages significantly without passing the cost on to consumers. The Worker Rights Consortium has found that garment worker wages could be doubled or even tripled with *little or no increase* for American consumers and Jeff Ballinger, a former labor studies professor at Webster University, calculates that Nike could afford to double the pay to its estimated 160,000 shoe factory employees without raising the consumer price at all.[19]

Clothing companies have enjoyed decades of cheap foreign labor and the resulting profits, but what exactly are the tangible benefits *to us*, the American consumer? We own more clothes than we can wear, the quality and craftsmanship of our wardrobes are at an all-time low, and the U.S. manufacturing base can't compete on wages with the developing world, costing countless domestic jobs. One of the tools we have to change these dynamics is not just to demand that clothing companies stop using sweatshops, but to set the bar much higher and demand they pay those who make our clothes a living wage. Raising wages abroad would be good for the U.S. economy, as it would give our own industries a much-needed chance to compete. It wouldn't be easy or simple, but it's achievable and the benefits would be far-reaching.

7

China and the End of Cheap Fashion

Lily was thrusting a dress toward me—a short, body-hugging number with a giant florette planted right in the middle of the chest. Lily's factory, due north a few hours from Hong Kong on the Chinese mainland, was producing 22,000 of these faddish garments a month. "This dress is very popular," she said, putting it in my hands. "Any color. We can do it for you." I was at the kind of factory I'd come to China to see—massive, state-of-the-art, and eager to produce gobs of cheap, trendy fashion in a flash.

Lily, a factory salesgirl, and I were standing in the sample room, where past production runs were hanging off a rack haphazardly, faded and droopy, looking spent before ever seeing a store. Some designers use factory sample rooms for ideas and to see exactly what styles and level of quality a factory is capable of, or to just copy a garment entirely. Lily pulled out a number of other trendy fashions for me to consider, including a black ruched minidress with a bodice covered in brass-colored studs, an electric-purple V-neck top covered in vertical strips of ruffles, a drapey top also bedazzled in studs, a ruched army-green dress with a zipper racing diagonally across the skirt, and a black sleeveless blouse crisscrossed in *more* studs.

Any of these styles could be sold on the racks of cheap-fashion chains in the United States. Lily's factory produces eight million garments a month for export, most of it flavor-of-the-month fashion for cheap retailers in America. In fact, I came across several Forever 21 garments while rifling through the sample racks, including a bright blue top with embroidered flowers around the neck. Forever 21 got its start producing most of its clothes in Los Angeles but now source everything but its fastest-moving trends overseas. I asked Lily what it was like working for the cheap-fashion chain. "They have an agent in China," she clarified, "so we talk to their agent." This is not uncommon. Huge corporate fashion giants, especially those who produce cheap products, routinely work through a middleman to place orders in foreign factories. Lily then offered to sell me the Forever 21 embroidered dress for $9 a pop. *That's rich,* I thought. I could make a knockoff of what might just be a knockoff. Lily also gave me a price quote for the florette dress, $11. She said, "The cost is rising, but I will try my best to give you my best price because we are friends."

Over the past two decades, American consumers have accepted, and benefited from, the race to the bottom in fashion. The competition in garment manufacturing has been beyond fierce, with only those with the lowest prices surviving. According to some Chinese suppliers, net margins are still somewhere between 3 percent and 5 percent.[1] Returned orders, cancellations, or lapses in the production lineup are common occurrences and they can all easily put a factory under. The profits that are created are kept by those in charge. Many factory owners and managers in China and the developing world have become middle class—the ones I met in China have nice cars, live in luxury high-rises, and eat at nice restaurants. The office girls like Lily are in a class above the factory workers and below the managers, and often live in the factory dorms themselves. It's common for Chinese factories (whose owners are often male and Mandarin-speaking) to hire these English-speaking young college grads with Western names to

act as liaisons to their foreign clients. It's the sewing-machine operators beneath them who are barely scraping by. Without independent
labor unions, which are outlawed in China, it was hard to imagine
wages ever improving there. It seemed our supply of low-cost clothes
was in no danger of drying up anytime soon. Yet there are signs everywhere that cheap fashion is coming to an end.

Lily had picked me up at 9 a.m. that morning at my hotel in Shenzhen, China, about a two-hour drive south from her factory. In the car
with her was her boss, wearing a black leather motorcycle jacket, fitted
jeans, and a buzz cut. Lily, beautiful and tall with a gummy smile, was
in a fashionable navy pea coat and Chinese-brand Ugg boots. I found
Lily's factory on Alibaba.com, the world's largest business-to-business
Web site, created by a Chinese entrepreneur named Jack Ma. In 2007
Alibaba became the world's second-largest Internet IPO in history
(after Google).[2] You can find any kind of supplier on the site, from
boat-paint factories and bulldozer factories to ones that make web-
cams and wigs. And you also get more than one million results when
you search for women's wear on mainland China.

I contacted factories and told them I owned a company called
Fashion Forward Inc., which of course I don't, and printed up light
pink business cards from my home computer with my apartment address and phone number. I put together a "line" of cheap fashion out
of my own closet in order to ask the factories how much it would cost
to produce my garments with each of them. I crossed my fingers that
the language barrier would help me fudge the rest.

"What are your prices?" I wrote to numerous manufacturers on
Alibaba, and with that simple inquiry I got an inbox full of eager re-
plies. One wrote to me, "Your time and inquiry means a lot to us.
Please send us the below things so we can give our best price for you:
Measurement Chart, Art Work/Design/Workmanship, Photo (if avail-

able), Printing Details, Quality of Fabrics, Quantities (minimum per color/design), and Delivery Schedule." I didn't know any of the above, but this factory didn't mind. Most of those that I contacted offered to take care of virtually the entire process of making clothes for me, even offering me a catalog of existing designs to order from.

I decided to travel to China because, despite what the labels on my clothing tell me, apparel manufacturing is not at all evenly distributed across the planet. Among my own cheap threads are "made in" labels from Bulgaria, Cambodia, Hong Kong, India, Indonesia, Israel, the Philippines, Romania, Sri Lanka, Thailand, Turkey, Vietnam, Lesotho, and Macau—countries from every continent on earth, except my own. But since the Multi Fibre Arrangement expired in 2005, China has become the colossus in the field. Chinese apparel imports to the United States have more than doubled since 2005 and now account for an astounding 41 percent of imported clothing.[3] In certain categories, China totally dominates, making 90 percent of our house slippers, 78 percent of our footwear, 71 percent of our ties, 55 percent of our gloves, and roughly 50 percent of our dresses.[4]

In many product categories, China is not associated with quality. We see "Made in China" and we think, *Proceed with caution.* I've heard stories from those in the fashion industry of Chinese factories switching to cheaper thread or fabric on the sly, churning out orders so fast that the garment barely hangs together, or producing batches of jeans or socks where the color varies dramatically from lot to lot. All of this surely happens.

Michael Kane, of L.A.-based women's wear brand Karen Kane, told me that the quality of its products produced in China has in fact declined in recent years. After a 20-year relationship with factories there, Kane says his company is now forced to inspect every single piece of clothing coming in from its Chinese suppliers, down from an inspection rate of just 10 percent when the company first moved production overseas. "All of a sudden, really in the last three or four years, the dynamic has completely changed," says Kane. "There's more competition there. They have rising labor costs, yet they need to produce things at the same price that they've always had to." The factories are reducing their costs at the expense of the Karen Kane product.

But outside Western Europe and the United States, China is a leader in garment quality and one of the only cheap-labor nations that has the technology *and* the skilled work force able to handle more complex styles. "The quality gets even harder to control in other countries," explains Kane, naming lower-cost suppliers such as India and Bangladesh. "We've tried in the past. For the price and the quality, China really is the best option." If you take a closer look at your closet, you'll notice that basics like T-shirts and sweatshirts are mostly made in Bangladesh, Cambodia, Vietnam, and other very poor developing countries. Meanwhile, things like party dresses, trendy coats and shoes, or tops with funky prints and embellishments—the more fashionable clothes—are very often made in China.

In the 1980s China produced low-value basics as well. "China was what they call a CMT country," says Sally Reid, the production specialist who was working for Ann Taylor when it opened its first offices in Hong Kong and then in Shanghai. When the country was first opened up to foreign investment in the 1980s, Chinese garment factories only "cut" the fabric, "made" the garment, and "trimmed" them. "Years ago, China didn't make fabric," says Reid. "You used to have to cut the fabric here and send it to China. All those things have changed now. China is holding all those cards." According to Oerlikon's *The Fiber Year 2009/10 Report*, China has been "the driving force of the world textile industry" for the past decade, now producing 69 percent of polyester, the world's dominant fiber.

Today, there's little that a Chinese garment factory can't and won't take on. Many of them are full package, meaning they source and cut fabric, make patterns, and do all the required testing, sewing, trimming, and packing. Full-package factories are particularly convenient for fast-fashion retailers. While a brand like Gap tries to maintain a certain consistency and quality level across all products, a retailer that operates on speed and trendiness might opt to leave the fabric sourcing, and really anything else, up to the factory.

China's factories—certainly the ones I saw—are often equipped with the latest machinery and computer software. This extends to their textile industry as well. In 2010 China placed 72 percent of the world's orders for modern spinning equipment, 84 percent of the orders for the most modern weaving looms, and three-quarters of the orders for new knitting machines.[5] At Lily's factory a sharply dressed man quietly entered the room and took a racer-back tank top out of my hands. Twenty minutes later it had magically been drawn up using design software on an Apple computer, where I could see it in different colors.

Of the five factories I visited, a number had their own design teams and sample rooms, and to this day, Skype and e-mail me regularly with spreadsheets and high-resolution photos of their latest styles. And the Chinese factories I talk to are *always* available. Katy, one of the factory sales girls, e-mails me at 10 p.m. her time, when she's watching TV in her factory-provided apartment, to see how I'm doing, to find out if I have any orders for her, and to meddle in my love life. The Chinese factories make the whole process of garment production very easy. But they can also make the process very hard, as Karen Kane has experienced. Michael Kane says, "They have such a monopoly on manufacturing now, especially in apparel, that they really can dictate whatever quality they want to put out. And you really can't challenge them. You're kind of locked in."

About five years ago, rumblings of a serious labor crunch began to be felt around China. Because of the country's one-child policy, the labor pool of young workers is finally shrinking, and young people, many of them children of first-generation migrant factory workers, are choosing to better their lives by going to college and looking for office jobs instead of factory-line work.[6] Virtually everyone who works in Chinese manufacturing, from the bosses to the salesgirls to the sewing-machine workers are migrants from the country's poor internal provinces. In Guangdong Province, there are as many as 40 million migrant workers.[7] Katy, as well as the owners and most of the employees in her factory, are from the interior province of Hubei. And now that domestic spending is increasing across the country and jobs are being created in those more remote provinces, people are choosing to stay closer to home to find work.

As a result of this confluence of massive changes in China, labor costs are surging, by as much as 10 percent to 30 percent per year.[8] Sal Giardina's custom men's wear company, Natsun, has been experiencing high turnover at its factory in Shandong Province, with many of the employees going home for the Chinese New Year and taking jobs in factories that are opening closer to home. Giardina says, "Our factories now pay our workers double because we want the workers to stay."

After decades of the price of Chinese imports being flat or falling, prices are climbing. Trading supply company Li & Fung's average costs for goods rose 15 percent in the first five months of 2011 compared with the same period the year before.[9] Kane says, "In China, prices have really started to go up incredibly. The rate it's occurred at is phenomenal. It's not even competitive to produce there anymore." Gap designer Petra Langerova told me the same thing. China is too expensive now.

China's economic miracle was concentrated on its southern coast, right across the water from Hong Kong. I traveled to this manufacturing hub in Guangdong Province, where three large manufacturing cities—Guangzhou, Dongguan, and Shenzhen—are packed tightly within a 150-mile strip. This province is where most of my Alibaba contacts were located, and according to Alexandra Harney's *The China Price*, published in 2008, home to a staggering estimated 400,000 factories.[10] Shenzhen alone has 3,000 garment manufacturers employing nearly a half a million people.[11]

"You've got someone to help you get around in China, right?" my friend Lesley Wolf asked me over beers one night, a few weeks before I was to leave for Guangdong. Lesley works for a legwear and sock design company in Manhattan's Garment Center. One of her previous employers had sent her to China, to a place called Panyu. I told her I was going to call a cab, take the subway or bus, and ask directions in English, because *Americans are such important customers to China.* "Oh," Lesley said smirking, when I told her I was essentially winging it. "You're screwed. How are you going to get where you need to go? Are you going to write down the factory name in English and show it to the cab driver?"

A few nights later I was watching TV on my laptop, and I thought of Panyu. Where was Panyu anyway? I looked it up on the Internet and a wave of panic rippled through me. Panyu is a city in Guangdong Province. In fact, Panyu is a city of more than one million people located within the boundaries of Guangzhou, the capital of Guangdong Province, and the location of several of the factory meetings I had set up. I was finally connecting China's *very* large dots.

The three cities I was planning to zip back and forth between by cab form a single megacity bigger than any metropolis in the United States. Shenzhen has a population of around 14 million people. Dongguan, located between Shenzhen and Guangzhou, has more than eight million, and Guangzhou has roughly 13 million. All told, Guangdong Province has at least 100 million inhabitants, almost a third of the United States' population crammed into a space the size of Missouri. I went into recon mode and made sure I wasn't spending a single unguided moment in southern China. Luckily, most of the factories happily agreed to pick me up from my hotel. Any that told me to take the train or a cab were cut from the list.

About a half hour into our drive from my hotel to Lily's factory in Dongguan, Shenzhen's sparkling office buildings and high-rise apartment towers dropped off and we entered a land of factories. I easily saw thousands upon thousands of them, riding back and forth a few times along this one stretch of highway. The landscape reminded me of how big-budget fantasy movies deploy CGI for battle scenes, copying and pasting goblins and armored creatures into the distance until the army spans the entire horizon. Dongguan's factories stretch as far as the eye can see, a veritable CGI army of boxy gray edifices visible a half-mile deep on either side of the arterial expressway running north from Shenzhen.

China's garment industry operates on an intimidating scale. It's several times bigger than any garment industry that's happened anywhere in the world at any point in history. They have more than 40,000 clothing manufacturers and 15 million garment industry jobs.[12] Compare that to the 1.45 million garment and textile industry jobs the United States had at peak employment some 40 years ago.[13]

China's supersize garment industry has achieved a degree of specialization that is beyond belief. There is a coastal city near Shanghai in northern China that produces most of the world's socks: nine billion pairs a year. Not too far away in Zhejiang Province is a city dedicated to children's clothing, with around 5,000 factories doing just that.[14] There's also a Sweater City and an Underwear City, where huge volumes of each are churned out in highly concentrated areas.[15] If you ever wonder how we went from living in a world of relative clothing scarcity to feeling like we're swimming in the stuff, ponder no further than China.

In 1935 the founder of Filene's department store claimed that the main economic conundrum facing the industrialized world was finding ways to distribute all the consumer goods we were able to produce.[16] This was almost 50 years before China's own industrial revolution blanketed the world with virtually every imaginable consumer product. On the ride to Dongguan, I started a game of name-that-factory with Lily. We'd pass an austere compound and I'd ask, "What does that one make?" She'd rattle off "laptop," "TV," "cell phone," and an occasional "garment!" One factory she didn't know the word for and so she made a gesture toward an electronic spire on the top of a building. An antenna factory?

For decades, China solved the conundrum of how to distribute its inexhaustible supply of factory-made goods—by making things inexpensively. At most of the factories I visited, I could in theory buy a couple of thousand skirts for $5 apiece, sell them in the United States for $20 apiece (assuming I could sell them directly and pay minimal shipping costs) and make quite a nice profit. Importing goods is not that simple, but there's an undeniable appeal to making money from China's miraculous capacity to make cheap, attractive products.

For a half century, Americans have been the world's leading consumers. We have been busy shopping while the developing world, and more recently China, has been busy making things for us to buy. We have been sucking up more than our fair share of the planet's resources, but our consumption was somewhat offset by the fact that the developing world used very little. Our consumer habits are now spreading to China, which has more than four times our population and may soon have more than four times the buying power. Ponder this for a second: a population of 1.3 billion people consuming clothes with the furious intensity that Americans do.

This is embarrassing to admit now, but when I packed for my meetings with Chinese factories, I intentionally chose the blandest things I owned. Still imagining Communist-era austerity ruling the Chinese fashion winds, I didn't want anyone to be overwhelmed by my New York fashion sensibility. But as I walked down the palm-tree-lined pedestrian plazas of Shenzhen in a pair of khakis, canvas slip-ons, and a plain black blouse, I was decidedly outdressed by sharply dressed twentysomethings in knee-high boots and chic leather messenger bags. Lily and Katy were both better dressed than I, in the latest styles for China's college-educated up-and-comers.

A decade ago China's fashion industry was almost nonexistent. Today, it's on the verge of exploding and the country has the world's fastest-growing fashion and luxury markets.[17] China has had its own edition of *Vogue* since 2005, and the Shenzhen Garment Industry Association has organized a collective runway show for the city's designers at London Fashion Week since 2010. High-end American designer Diane von Furstenberg has had a store in Shanghai since 2007.

Sal Giardina recalls that when he first traveled to China for work in 2005 very few people were driving nice cars or wearing fashionable clothes. Just a few years later, fashion had taken hold. In the factories I visited in the spring of 2011, most of the sewing-machine girls were wearing puffer jackets and bedazzled stretch denim, and the boys were in trendy tracksuits, their hair gelled into spiky points. Sewing-machine operators still make a pittance, but it's obvious that many of them are spending their spare cash on trendy clothes. Giardina agrees. "They're developing a taste level for better items."

Initially, as the trappings of Communism fell away, the Chinese followed Western styles and sought out our brands, but this too is changing. Chinese fashion brands are beginning to challenge their foreign competitors for loyalty at home.[18] And Chinese brands are also moving into the American market, such as contemporary women's wear label JNBY, which has had a flagship store in SoHo since 2010.

China's growing consumer class and incredible industrial output pose enormous sustainability issues for the global economy and the world's resources. Giardina states, "If every man, woman, and child in China bought two pair of wool socks, there would be no more wool left in the world. Think about that. So, yes, there will be problems with scarcity of resources. And what's going to happen is prices will go up." The country's growing clothing consumption is already putting upward pressure on the price of fibers, particularly cotton, as demand is outstripping supply.[19] According to the Oerlikon fiber study, cotton production is already reaching its limitations as competition for arable land intensifies.[20]

Many Americans have forgotten what industrial cities—polluted, inhuman, and deeply ugly—look like. When I was in Dongguan, I was constantly thinking that the planet has no other option but to buckle under all of this manufacturing and that it clearly already was. To see industry on a scale that looks like science fiction seems as if it would take an equally fictional solution to stop. Also deeply unsettling is the fact that fast fashion is gaining hold among Chinese consumers too. Inditex, Zara's parent company, saw a 32 percent rise in profit in 2010, largely attributed to sales in China, and opened 75 stores there in 2010 alone.[21] If China begins consuming clothing at disposable levels, which fast-fashion companies are angling for, the environmental and social problems of fashion are just going to increase exponentially from here.

———

L ily's factory is a large, four-story, pink concrete complex in Humen Town, a city within the gargantuan factory city of Dongguan. In the Chinese way, Dongguan is made up of dozens of mini-cities, each one specializing in a different type of manufacturing.[22] Humen Town's specialty is women's fashion. I liked it there instantly because, contrary to its name, it is not crawling with people. Unlike the rest of southern China, Humen Town is built on a scale I recognized, with buildings that are six stories high instead of 60, and it has a landscaped downtown with Western eateries and a wholesale clothing mall. There I saw dealers disappear into storefronts advertising stretch jeans, graphic print sweatshirts, and trendy blouses and emerge with duffle bags full, intending to sell them in stores around the country.

Humen Town's manufacturing sector, on the other hand, is Chinese-scaled. On the side streets, there is block after block after block of narrow, open-air stalls selling thick rolls of fabric and trim, as well as every other accessory of the trade, from lace and sequins to studs and zippers. According to the *South China Morning Post*, as of 2005, $1 billion worth of apparel is produced in Humen Town every year.[23] Lily's factory in Humen is about ten times bigger than any sewing floor I've seen in Los Angeles or New York. In one warehouse-size room, I saw a team of sewers individually working on white polka-dot sundresses and a gray-and-white order of the florette minidress. In another room, a handful of women were guiding 40-foot-long computerized embroidery machines to create a Venn diagram shape on fabric. On another floor, hundreds of pairs of track pants with a white stripe down the sides were being stitched up and tossed into bright blue plastic bins. We also waltzed through a sample room, where a team of 20 was looking over one another's shoulders, analyzing a tan-and-brown color-block sweater and royal blue coat. Just when I thought there couldn't be any more to see, I was shown another room with roughly a dozen workers making a gauzy dress in a blush- and cream-colored fabric that looked like chiffon, probably made from polyester. Then Lily put me back in the car and drove me to the brand-new and equally massive denim factory on the other side of town. We ended the afternoon ordering several courses at a swanky Korean bar-beque restaurant owned by the factory boss's brother, who is also a garment factory owner.

That evening, on the way back to my hotel in Shenzhen, the driver lost his way, and we ended up downtown at night. It was Lily's first time in Shenzhen too. She had just recently moved from China's interior to Dongguan, straight out of college. Shenzhen has more than 20 buildings over 650 feet tall, and almost everyone lives in skyscraper-tall apartment blocks that look like Transformers run amok. Lily and I were glued to the windows, watching the city's cloud-kissing sky-scrapers put on a spectacular Vegas-style light show. One building was laced with neon blue zigzags that danced in the rainy reflection on the car windows. Shenzhen dazzled us completely.

The city is the stuff of legend. Thirty years ago it was a little dot of a place, a fishing village of 30,000 people.[24] It was China's first special economic zone, set up in 1980 to gift foreign investors with low tax rates and exemptions on import duties for parts and materials used in export processing. From there it grew faster than anything the world had ever seen. The economy expanded on average 28 percent per year between 1980 and 2008.[25] Factories went up overnight. Cheap Chinese clothes, electronics, toys, and everything else imaginable started to flow into the United States out of Shenzhen. Today in China, anything good that happens in a flash is affectionately known as "Shenzhen speed." And there's no mistaking the city is built in our image. It has cutting-edge architecture, good shopping malls, a gadget-obsessed youth who own the latest iPhone, and it's building a Central Park. It also has chain stores such as Starbucks, McDonald's, and KFC, and Shenzhenites love flashy cars.

The southern China of my imagination was an alien factory world with a soulless focus on churning out the cheap clothes that I can't seem to resist. When I told friends I was going to garment factories in China, everyone assumed I was working on a sweatshop exposé, and I prepared myself for the worst. But during my trip I found it painfully obvious that China has blossomed while America's cities have withered. In 2010 America imported $364 billion worth of products from China, and according to the Economic Policy Institute, the trade deficit with China has cost the United States nearly 2.8 million jobs, or 2 percent of our domestic employment.[26]

I met Chinese young people whose job prospects weren't just on the factory line. Most of the youth who work in downtown Shenzhen seemed to have jobs in the service industry or in offices. Katy held a degree in horticulture from a university in the northern metropolis of Jilin City. She proudly showed me photos on her cell phone of her standing in several feet of snow on her college campus. The school cost her just $600 a year, and it gave her the chance to move to another city and get a job working with international clients. She lost her position at the garment factory a few months after I got back from China, and I asked her why. "It cost us a lot of money to move to this place," she wrote, referring to the brand-new factory and dorm that I visited. "And business this year is bad, less orders and higher cost for workers." I was nervous for her, imagining her wandering from factory to factory, begging for work. "Ha ha," she wrote back. "Don't worry. I have some money. I will find a new job, but this time, I will take more time to get a better job." She had a new job within weeks.

Infrastructure and technology are also moving at warp speeds. China now has a bullet train that covers the 819 miles from Shanghai to Beijing in five hours. Shenzhen's public transportation is so much more modern than New York's creaking public transit that one garment factory owner's only impression of my fair city was, "Your subway system is so old." Giardina told me that after traveling on China's high-speed rail, he finds train travel in the United States very frustrating. "It's embarrassing," he said. "It's like I'm on Thomas the Tank."

The first factory I visited in China was located in a drab yellow-tile complex on a shabby backstreet off of Humen Town's main drag. *Here we go,* I thought, as we pulled up and a guard let us into the ominous building that looked like fodder for a sweatshop investigator. But the inside was an oasis of modernity, with frosted-glass walls, track lighting, and Style Network–approved dusty lavender walls. A pretty woman flurried around me, serving me espresso, hard candy, and bottled water. This was the factory's head designer, who took a break from sewing a gorgeous Victorian-looking gown with a fitted bodice in brown plaid so she could show me around.

I was escorted to a third-floor showroom, which was set up like an atelier, with mannequins, display tables, and wall racks organized by style and color. It was shockingly swank and stocked with cropped wool jackets, linen shorts, and beautifully detailed silk dresses that were better made and more fashion-forward than anything I own. I had, on my first meeting, walked into the Rolls-Royce of Chinese apparel manufacturers.

Back in his office, the factory sales manager Harrison walked over to his desk, lit a cigarette, and pulled out a calculator. Harrison's office was oddly huge; his black leather couch and wraparound desk were lost in the space. I pointed to the Chanel posters on the wall. "I just like them," Harrison said sheepishly. I asked him to give me a price for a black shirred miniskirt that I brought from home, and he squished up his face. "Don't do it in polyester," he admonished. Harrison's factory is a branded manufacturer that mostly produces its own line of high-end women's fashion retailing in Japan, Singapore, and China. Polyester is not part of that vision. "In China there are thousands of suppliers; maybe some suppliers are cheaper," he said. "Quality is always our number one concern. The fabric quality and the sewing quality have to be good. Otherwise, we cannot survive."

A few days later I was at Katy's factory in a Shenzhen suburb named Longgang, standing outside in a cool drizzle on the concrete carport directly across from the company dorms. Downtown Shenzhen's manufacturing has long since given way to offices, corporate headquarters, luxury buildings, restaurants, and retail shops. But even this industrial suburb is becoming tony and expensive. This particular factory, a new building, was wedged between beautiful pink stucco condos on a street lined with freshly planted palms. It looked like a planned community in Florida for wealthy retirees.

However, this apparent wealth doesn't mean that China has attained America's labor standards or working conditions. Garment workers worldwide work long hours and don't make what they should. I didn't need to do any digging to find out this is still the case today in China.

Almost all Chinese factory workers live in dorms, no matter what product is being made, and often sleep six to eight to a room in bunk beds. This type of sardine living is often the subject of international scorn. Dorms are so prevalent at Chinese factories at least in part because the gap between the cost of living and factory worker wages is so huge. Providing a bed and a place to shower works to the factory's benefit because it means they can keep wages low. But dorms are also common because most of China's factory workers are migrants who have relocated for work. Katy from the Longgang factory lives at the dorms, but in her own ground-floor apartment. Some factories include room and board for the migrants; others take it out of the workers' wages. A 2006 study by the Chinese Labor Bureau found that about half of the 17 factories it surveyed charged for food and accommodations; a bed in the dorms cost anywhere from $1.50 to $12.50 a month and the monthly charges for meals ranged from $9 to $21.[27]

While I didn't go inside the dorms at any of the factories I visited in China, I was shown several factory kitchens and food stalls. Not surprisingly, factory food is nothing to write home about. At Lily's factory, the canteen was a dark hangar filled with long rows of metal picnic tables. Vegetables were being cooked in a huge cauldron near the floor behind a brick wall, a far cry from a proper kitchen. The rice was served uncovered out of a 30-gallon drum sitting on the floor about 15 feet from huge industrial washing machines and piles of children's jeans. Yet Lily was proud of her factory's facilities and took three meals a day here.

I asked Katy how many hours her workers put in: It's a 12-plus hour day, which starts at 7:45 a.m. and ends at 9:30 p.m., with an extra hour a day during the busy season. I asked why they work so much, and Katy responded, giggling, "Because we need the work. We have to get everything done." She viewed the long hours as a selling point and, in the era of cheap and fast fashion, a factory that's willing to do whatever it takes to get goods into stores is often the most successful.

At all of the factories I visited in China, the workers were putting in six days a week if not seven with one day off a month. Katy's factory had just changed its policy to one day off a week. The factories were working their employees almost 100 hours a month over the Chinese legal limit.

After I returned to New York, I e-mailed Katy and asked her to send me photographs of her factory's dorms. I told her that Fashion Forward Inc. was putting together ethical guidelines and we wanted to make sure the workers' housing followed our company's standards. Katy wrote me back that night. "I will take photos today for you. It's a piece of cake," she said. The next day, I received close to 20 photos from inside the four-story dorm. She apologized for the "arsy-varsy" condition of the dorms. She was trying to tell me the place was a mess, but it really wasn't.

In the first pictures two young women wearing jeans and V-necks sit in a small, bright room between bunk beds, pulling noodles up to their mouths with chopsticks while watching TV. The photos of the dorms were surprising, but not for the reasons I imagined. They looked at least a little like an American girl's college dorm room, cluttered with makeup, lotion, detergent, and pots and pans. The walls were decorated with flower decals and posters of tropical beaches. The beds were made up with brightly colored and feminine comforters. A small counter off to one side supported a slow cooker and a tiny sink. There were stretch denim jeans, lacy bras, and brightly colored T-shirts hung up to dry in the windows: everywhere, more signs of China's growing economic wealth and evolving consumer tastes. [28]

I traveled to China at a time when it was becoming evident that the world order was changing. We in the United States have lived with the assumption that each generation of Americans would have greater opportunities. Yet it seems now that our futures are uncertain. In 2011 unemployment was more than 9 percent in the United States and our economy was predicted to grow an anemic 2 percent. In 2009 China *gained* an estimated 11 million jobs. Not surprisingly, Western clothing companies that have built their businesses around cheap foreign production are in a state of hysterics over changing dynamics and rising prices in China. Factories are fleeing Guangdong and are predicted to disperse across the country to cheaper provinces.[29] Many others are scrambling to move production to lower-wage countries such as Cambodia, Vietnam, India, and Bangladesh.

I followed the flight of cheap labor out of China and into Bangladesh, landing in the capital of Dhaka around 10 p.m. The sleeping city was twinkling with colored Christmas lights in celebration of its cohosting duties of the Cricket World Cup. I had heard much about the traffic congestion in Dhaka, the largest city in the world's most densely populated country, but a nighttime trip from the airport to the hotel was quick. Out of the darkness darted past a few rickshaws and Dhaka's signature Dr. Seussian "baby green taxis," three-wheeled metal vehicles that look like beetles. I checked into my hotel, went to charge my laptop, and a blackout shut the electricity off just a few moments later. Out on the terrace I looked out over a collection of shanties built out of scrap metal and wood. I wasn't in China anymore.

Bangladesh may be a very poor country—its GDP is ranked 155 in the world—with a lot of labor unrest and infrastructure problems, but it is not a pitiable place. Dhaka is tidy, with swept sidewalks and pretty gardens; when I was there in the early spring, flowers were blooming everywhere. Bangladeshis are famously friendly, and the first thing they want to know is, *Do you love Bangladesh*? They seem to understand their position in the world order and appear to be trying, through an affable scrappiness, to change it.

As retailers move to Bangladesh to take advantage of its cheap workers, the garment industry is desperately trying to keep pace. The country's clothing factories now employ more than three million people, with apparel accounting for more than 80 percent of the country's total exports. Walmart, JCPenney, H&M, Zara, Lee, Esprit, VF, Umbro, Wrangler, Disney, and Nike all do business in Bangladesh, as do many Chinese apparel firms, which are now outsourcing their own cut-and-sew functions to sources of cheaper labor. Apparel factories are struggling to find enough workers to complete the ever-rising number of orders.[30]

Bangladesh's garment industry is a slipshod, fly-by-the-seat-of-your-pants affair. The people I'd reached on Alibaba turned out not to be factory owners but middlemen who wanted to place my order in a "portfolio of factories" that I would never actually see. Every garmento I met in Bangladesh seemed to have five different jobs, in as many different industries. Masud was the first one I met with; to my surprise he arrived at my hotel in a rickshaw. There are more than 400,000 rickshaws in Dhaka and it is the primary form of transportation, but more successful garmentos often run around in the local elite's favorite, road-clogging new toy—an automobile.

I squeezed into the very narrow seat next to Masud, a jittery businessman wearing pointy Italian dress shoes and a flashy watch. "How far away is the factory?" I asked. "Most buyers don't go to the factory; it's easier to take a meeting in the office," he said dismissively. I would not be seeing Masud's factory. Our ancient rickshaw driver stood and put the weight of his spindly legs on the pedals, pulling Masud and me through the diplomatic neighborhood of Baridhara. Maroon flowers were climbing up the gates of stucco villas. Dhaka is increasingly becoming a place for foreign investment, and you can see the wealth it's creating in the gated mansions on the private roads around the Gulshan District.

Masud has been in Bangladesh's garment industry for five years and has owned his own sweater factory for three. He was formerly working for a Korean-owned factory in an Export Processing Zone (EPZ), a special district that gives tax breaks to foreign investors who want to manufacture goods in Bangladesh. The factories in Bangladesh's EPZs, of which there are eight, are mostly owned by Japanese and Korean companies.

Masud's company now matches any number of factories in and around Dhaka to foreign clients, one of which is G-III Apparel Group, which handles the design and manufacture of select lines for huge brands like Calvin Klein, Ellen Tracy, Kenneth Cole, and Levi's. Another of his clients is the British fast-fashion retailer New Look, for which he handles huge volumes of knitwear, as much as 60,000 to 100,000 pieces at a time. "If an order is big, we use many different factories," he told me. "Sometimes one factory is not busy or one is busy, so we have to move orders around. We'll subcontract."

Despite his impressive roster of clients, Masud's business turned out to be a two-man operation run out of the third floor of a converted apartment building. There was a tiny sweater factory across the hall, but it wasn't his. We met in a wood-paneled room around a conference table sunlit by an open door overlooking a terrace. It's best always to be near a natural light source in Dhaka since the city is plagued by six or seven power outages a day. At one end of the table sat a good-looking Lebanese man, another garment buyer, smoking a cigarette; across from me was Masud's business partner, Shukur, a short man with poufy hair wearing a polo shirt and a tape measure around his neck. It was a boys' club.

The Lebanese buyer at the end of the table informed me that he was working out of Guangzhou in Guangdong Province until recently. He did business in China for so long that he's fluent in Mandarin. But he'd just moved his entire business to Bangladesh. "This time, I got an office here because I see that it's really better than the China market," he told me. "The price is higher in China. Prices are going up here, but it's still better." This handsome foreigner also said that he routinely buys canceled orders of H&M clothes and resells them in Europe. He tried to get me in on the action, but the practice is illegal in the United States.

Bangladesh has a very old and established textile industry, but the clothing it exports to the West consists of low-value basics such as T-shirts, sweatshirts, and plain sweaters. These types of garments are the domain of the world's least developed countries. Bangladesh's export industry originally flourished under the Multi Fibre Arrangement, while China suffered from stricter quotas. Bangladesh therefore established itself as the largest supplier of T-shirts to the European Union.[31] The industry is trying to diversify and offer more sophisticated, higher-value clothes, but the most fashionable thing I saw in Masud's sample room and perhaps in all of Bangladesh was a cotton knit top with those ubiquitous studs around the collar. Bangladesh is also largely a "CMT" country, capable only of cutting, making, and trimming garments, like China was in the early days.

I had the shirred polyester miniskirt with me. I pulled it out, laid it on the conference table, and asked Masud how much it would cost to order 3,000 pieces of it. "Most of the woven factories are booked through 2012," he told me, apologetically. Wovens are the non-stretchy type of fabrics that a lot of pants, jackets, dresses, skirts, and blouses are made of, and Masud was telling me I couldn't make my woven skirt in Bangladesh because other retailers had beat me to their overworked factories. Perhaps if I worked for Walmart or H&M, with huge order sizes, I would have found a factory. But Fashion Forward Inc. wasn't getting in.

I changed my strategy and said I was also interested in making a knit camisole, another item from my own closet. Bangladesh is a leader in knitwear, which employs more than 1.5 million people and contributes more than 40 percent of the country's exports.[32] From there, I ran into more problems. I chose a teal-colored 90 percent cotton, 3 percent spandex blend out of the fabric samples. "That can be done in a similar color, but not exactly tone for tone," Masud explained. For some reason I couldn't get the color I wanted unless I imported the fabric from India or China. My standards for my fake business were eroding by the second. Masud handed me the calculator: $4.80 for the knit shirt. "I want to offer you the best price," he said. "This is your first time in Bangladesh. Second time, you will be working with us because our quality is best." I left the camisole with them to make a sample from, and it arrived a month later smelling of smoke and made of a scratchy acrylic fabric unconvincingly called "cashmere-like."

As the fashion industry flees China, it is finding that other countries simply don't have the labor supply, infrastructure, pro-business policies, and technology.[33] Quality is another problem. Some garment producing countries, including Cambodia and Dominican Republic, have total populations similar to a single large Chinese metropolitan area like Shenzhen or Guangzhou. For larger brands that have built their companies around the big volumes Chinese factories can supply, smaller countries can only take on so much of the work.

In Bangladesh factories are being built where they shouldn't be and in a dangerously haphazard fashion, which has led to factory fires becoming all too common. The country is facing huge infrastructure problems, starting with the power outages. The sound of generators kicking in is the backdrop to life in the capital. The roadways also lag behind the goods they are expected to carry. A two-lane road with dirt shoulders is all that connects the capital to the major garment and textile producing areas around Dhaka. And car ownership is growing. It took me three hours to travel by car to the textile town of Narsingdi, less than 30 miles northeast of Dhaka. We spent most of the drive in a harrowing game of chicken, pulling out in front of and then maniacally passing rickshaws, mopeds, masochistic pedestrians, and handpainted trucks piled high with people and textiles. I can only imagine trying to keep production deadlines in the face of a Bangladeshi traffic jam. Though Bangladesh's garment industry is flourishing, it can't replace China's, and it will not be able to curb the inflationary prices in the fashion industry.

In the fall of 2010, back-to-school shoppers were met with something not seen in decades: higher prices for clothing. Wage increases in China, paired with soaring cotton and fiber prices, had backed retailers against the wall. According to *The Washington Post*, clothing prices were up an average of 10 percent from the year before. Lands' End had raised prices on its girls' corduroy pants by $7 in the face of almost double-digit increases in the price of fabric. Some retailers, including Lands' End, were adding extra features such as special stitching and nicer buttons to justify the price hike, while others opted to offset increasing costs by reducing the quality of their products. According to *The Washington Post*, retail analysts examined Abercrombie & Fitch's redesigned 2012 jeans, which cost about $10 more than usual, and thought the denim was thinner and of cheaper quality.[34]

H&M broke from the pack and dropped its already low prices even further, hoping that increased consumption would offset falling profits. The store raised not a few eyebrows when it introduced a $4.95 pinstriped dress in the fall of 2010.[35] The strategy backfired. By the following summer, H&M's profits had fallen 18 percent.[36] The changing conditions in the fashion industry and especially in China may mean that consumers will soon be forced to change their buying habits, whether they want to or not.

8

Make, Alter, and Mend

Sarah Kate Beaumont has been making everything she wears since the summer of 2008, not coincidentally around the time the global economy fell apart. It was an abrupt transition. A swift decision. "I could tell you where I was and what I was doing," the soft-spoken redhead told me from her sunny Brooklyn sewing studio. "It was a very clear moment. It was like if you were going to marry somebody, which I think is what has made it so enduring."

"What was the moment?" I asked. Was she standing amid the chaos of a sales rack? Was she holding a cheap-fashion find washed once that was already unraveling and fading? Or maybe facing down an overstuffed closet and still thinking the common refrain, *I have nothing to wear*? None of the above. "I was looking at my bank account statement, sitting on the floor of my living room," Beaumont says. "It started out as practical and economical." She wanted to make her own clothes because it was cheap.

Inside Beaumont's sewing studio, Very Sweet Life, a small room with a huge picture window located on a pretty side street in Boerum Hill, Brooklyn, there are pattern-making tables, several sewing machines, an ironing board, and a dress form wearing her latest creation— the first day I visited the studio, it was a pale-pink knit top with a gathered neckline. Beaumont herself was wearing a flowing floor-length navy cotton dress cinched with a black leather belt. A horizontal-striped bra strap was peeking out. She'd made every single thing she had on. I don't want to make Beaumont sound like a plain Jane walking around in everyone's worst vision of primitive, rough-hewn clothes. Her sewing is as good or better than what's found in most chain stores. And that's the point. When making her own clothes, Beaumont often chooses to use a high-end finish called a French seam, which encases the raw edge of the fabric within another fold of fabric. It's an expensive and labor-intensive detail missing on virtually all mass-market fashion. Beaumont also prefers materials like knit silk, velvet, and seersucker, which are often rejected by clothiers because even though they're beautiful and comfortable, they're expensive and more difficult to sew and maintain. By making her own wardrobe, Beaumont escapes the bottom-line logic of stores today, which dumbs down our clothes, and gets to wear nicer garments that she either wouldn't be able to find or afford in a store.

She took one look at what I had on and said, "I can tell the blouse you have on is made in China." It was. It was a polyester tank top from JCPenney and cost less than $3 on clearance. The construction technique of Chinese-made clothing is good, but Beaumont says the fabric is often poor quality and the stitching is basic and rushed. "China is all about producing things at the lowest cost and there's a speed to the way things are done," she says. Beaumont claims to be able to spot clothing from India or Italy and can tell at a glance if something is handmade. She says, "It's like when you're buying a car and you know about cars. The more you know, the more you can look under the hood and know what you're looking for. I can look under the hood in clothes."

Beaumont knew more about my clothes than I did. But only I could explain how I ended up wearing them. I was a thrift store shopper in high school and most of college. The clothes I wore were true finds, or cut and patched together until they were uniquely me. There's a photograph of me my first day of senior year in high school, in high-waisted flares that I cut off to sit on my hips. At 20, I went through a mod phase. There's a photo of me standing with my family, and I'm wearing a black beaded sweater vest with a short black skirt over pants, which was a look not found in any stores at the time. I started dabbling more in chain stores in college in Syracuse, in places like Aéropostale and Victoria's Secret. I don't think I looked good in anything I bought at the mall. It was generic; it was as if my entire personality had been erased when I had on those clothes.

On campus I spent most of my spare time lobbying the college administration to monitor the human rights conditions in the overseas factories where our college-logo apparel was being made. I got kicked out of a commencement ceremony for dropping a giant, hand-painted banner that read, "I graduated from Sweatshop University." My graduation culminated with the opening of H&M in the local mall. I knew I was against sweatshops, but evidently I was not against cheap. Ten years later, about three-quarters of my clothes were from H&M, thrift stores were in the rearview mirror, and cheap fashion had become an entrenched habit. I was stubborn to any clothing priced above $50, and I'd ended up with a closet full of hundreds upon hundreds of poorly made disposable trends.

By the time I met Beaumont, the sheen was off the fashion industry for me. It was clear that trends are industry-determined, created and destroyed arbitrarily in the interest of turning a profit. The fashion industry has gotten too large and is competing too fiercely on low price, and the only way it is able to run now is by creating new product cheaply and constantly. The quality of our clothing has been chipped away. The reason so many of us have no kinship with or respect for anything in our closets and why fashion can seem so self-indulgent and pretentious nowadays is because fashion has become a slick, industrialized, heavily marketed industry. Loving most clothes sold today would be like loving a fast-food sandwich.

What led me to Beaumont was her blog, *Very Sweet Life*. A post from September 13, 2009, reads: "There's a *slow food* movement; I will call the project to make the majority of clothing I wear *slow clothes*. Mass-produced clothing, like fast food, fills a hunger and need, yet is non-durable and wasteful. Home sewn garments, similar to home cooked foods, are made with care and sustenance. In a sense clothing can be nourishing." Beaumont is not the first to use the slow clothing moniker, but it's the best description I've found of a number of truly exciting new ways of thinking about fashion.

I set out to replace my chintzy blouses and tank tops with dazzlingly stylish clothes made of recycled plastic, organic cotton, or eco-friendly Modal sewn together by a designer who lived around the corner. That's not exactly what happened. Like many Americans, I have dealt with financial hardship since the recession started. I lost my job at a magazine in 2009 and went on unemployment. Then the real estate market in my neighborhood plummeted, and the value of my home fell along with it. Eventually I was able to sell at a loss. My financial situation placed new clothes far down on the list of priorities. Yet my taste for cheap fashion had completely soured, and I still swore off any store that drives down its prices by selling huge volumes of clothing, not to mention by underpaying the sewing-machine workers who actually make the clothing. Without much money to buy nicer things, this decision brought my consumption of clothing almost to a halt.

I'm not the first person to come to this closet crossroads. Many consumers feel that there is something missing in the way they approach clothing, and it leads them to shopping less. For the Uniform Project, a young woman named Sheena Matheiken wore the same dress (designed by Eliza Starbuck) every day for a year to raise money for charity and as a commentary on consumerism. A similar campaign, called Six Items or Less, challenges consumers to wear only six garments (excluding shoes, accessories, and underwear) for one month. The Great American Apparel Diet asks participants to pledge not to buy any new clothes for a year in order to answer: "Who are we without something hip and new in our closets?"

Most of us can't imagine clothing ourselves any other way than walking into a store and pulling something off the rack. With shopping cheap out of my life and my bank account hovering near zero, I had to totally rethink my wardrobe. Everyone has a different relationship to shopping, but I can tell you after a year of by-default nonshopping that I don't miss it. I used to always have some new piece of trendy fashion clogging up my closet; now I don't. But not shopping didn't make me *love* my clothes. I was still walking around in an unattractive hodgepodge of "good" deals. Not shopping was not a total solution.

I asked Beaumont how long she was going to go without buying anything new, and that's when my wheels started to turn in a different direction. "It wasn't that I even decided that I wasn't going to buy anything new," she said. "It was different. It was that I was going to make everything I needed." Unlike me, Beaumont is not a reformed fast-fashion junkie. She's never been one to consume a lot of anything. The change from store-bought to some other alternative for her was organic. For me, it was a revelation. I'm not sure if I'll ever make all or even most of what I wear—few will—but learning to sew promised to shift the way I thought about clothing. Human beings have been sewing for thousands of years; some peg it to the last Ice Age.[1] It's store-bought clothing, in its inflexible, prefab form, that is the recent invention. When we entirely gave up homemade and custom clothing, we lost a lot of variation, quality, and detail in our wardrobes, and the right fit along with it.

The invention of the sewing machine revolutionized society and fundamentally changed people's everyday lives. It offered women relief from the countless hours and tedium of hand-sewing. According to the Museum of American Heritage, it took about 14 hours to make a man's dress shirt and at least ten for a simple dress.[2] Sewing by hand could be enjoyable, but unless you had money to hire a dressmaker or a tailor, it was an obligation to sew and mend every single garment that you, your husband, and your children wore.

The earliest sewing machines were invented in the mid-1800s and were exorbitantly expensive. In the 1860s they cost about $125 at a time when the average yearly income was about $500.[3] But because of their miraculous timesaving powers, price didn't stop people from buying the newfangled machines. Many communities and organizations pooled their money to purchase a single machine for members to share. Companies such as Singer came up with leasing plans. Even though the expense was huge, sewing machines were an immediate best seller.

The sewing machine quickly led to factory-style garment production and store-bought clothing. But off-the-rack duds were initially very ill fitting, poorly made, and prohibitively expensive. Men's store-bought clothes—more uniform and less fashion-sensitive—were embraced almost immediately; by the 1920s women's wear had also taken off, with one leading department store in Indiana complaining that it sold only half as much fabric by the yard in 1924 as it had in 1890.[4] Yet home sewing, custom dressmaking, and tailoring persisted well into the twentieth century.

When cheap imports started to flow into America in the 1970s, sewing machine ownership and sewing skills started to wane. In recent decades, home sewing and custom clothing have almost gone extinct. It's generally accepted that cheap imported clothes did in home sewing and made obsolete the professions of dressmakers and tailors. Joyce Perhac, president of the Sewing & Craft Alliance, says, "You can go to a big-box store today and get a T-shirt for two or three dollars if you want. You could buy a dress today for ten or fifteen dollars. In the past you couldn't do that. When we started importing lesser goods from overseas, then it just changed the balance."

My mother learned how to sew from her mother and made an outfit from scratch in home economics class in high school. My grandmother on my father's side didn't make entire garments, but she was very skilled at taking her family's clothes in and letting them out. I never learned how to sew. In a single generation the skill was lost. I asked Perhac if it *really* mattered that we don't know how to sew anymore. After all, we can just go to a big-box store and buy that $2 shirt today. "Sewing is vitally important," Perhac countered. "People can't sew their own buttons back on, and that's such an easy thing to do. So they either wear the garment without a button, or they throw it away and buy a new one. It really is a skill that is being lost in a dramatic way and that's a shame."

I'm the lost generation, one of the first not only to lack sewing skills, but mending and altering skills as well. The clothes that I love the most get the most ragtag from constant wear, and yet it seems utterly foreign to repair them. I have a favorite corduroy jacket that I wear with a tear across the back and a beloved teal cardigan with a hole in the sleeve. Pants that are too long drag the ground, and shirts that fit in the shoulders but are baggy through the torso get worn that way.

Repairing our wardrobes, making sure they properly fit us, and buying the best quality we can for our money are all parts of clothing sustainability. Otherwise, our clothes go unworn or become garbage. On the Web site Brooklynbased.net, I tapped into a surprisingly vibrant tailoring and seamstress scene near me, where rates for a custom A-line skirt start at $80. I've had repairs and simple alterations done for as little as $25 an hour. A post on the site reads: "If you've ever loved a dress that fell apart after a single summer, held onto a too-long or too-small skirt in the hopes that it would magically fix itself in your closet, or imagined an outfit you're dying to rock but don't know how to make yourself, we've found four seamstresses who can re-create your favorite outfit or sew one from scratch." Once it occurred to me to actually fix my clothes and reimagine their design, I started hiring my friend Lesley Wolf, the sock designer and part-time seamstress, to patch up my jeans and take up my skirts. The French cleaners across the street from my apartment also offer alterations and are taking in my winter jacket.

Beaumont, in her early forties, grew up in Pittsburgh. Her grandmother showed her just a few sewing techniques when she was a kid, and from there she began to alter and embroider a lot of her own clothing. She spent eight years teaching in New York City's schools, including at an after-school program where she taught kids how to sew. Her class had a 100 percent attendance rate in a school otherwise plagued by high dropout rates. "Adults are just like kindergarteners when they learn to make something. They are proud of themselves," Beaumont says. "I'm not telling you should you learn to sew. I'm just saying it's *so* satisfying." She held in her breath in only slightly feigned ecstasy.

Sewing is tactile and visual. It's not something you just sit down and instantly pick up or can even easily learn about by reading. "That's why it was passed down from generation to generation and that's why it went away when somebody didn't pass it down," Beaumont says. There is nothing more frustrating that sitting at a sewing machine and not knowing how to properly set it up or getting the thread jammed after just a few pumps of the needle. Sewing takes memory, computation, attention to detail, and constant decision making, although patterns make it easy for those intimidated by dreaming up a design from scratch. If you really want to learn how to sew, have someone teach you.

The day I bought supplies for Beaumont's sewing class, I went to a quilting shop in Manhattan. There were hundreds upon hundreds of fabrics, from hazy watercolor-dyed fabrics to spider-covered prints. I had almost limitless choice. Fun, if not a little overwhelming. Clothing stores by comparison have a very narrow range of colors and style. I was no longer at the mercy of whatever a store wanted me to buy. I was in control of the quality of the thread and the fabric. I could use a French seam if I wanted to. I ended up choosing a quail-feather print fabric and a decent grade of contrasting burnt-orange thread. I, a lowly beginner seamstress, had all the decision making power of a fashion designer.

The other student in my class was named Harriet, and her goal was to learn to make clothes from patterns for her two kids, one of whom is a 16-year-old girl who Harriet swore was open to wearing her mother's homemade styles. Our first task, with me behind my smooth modern Kenmore machine and Harriet across the room behind hers, was to thread the machine. "It's like a wave," Beaumont told us, "and each part of the wave adds tension to the thread."

Each sewing machine is threaded slightly differently, but the general motion is the same. On my class machine, I pulled the thread around a metal hook, down and around a plastic finger, around another metal hook connected to the needle and then around yet another tiny hook next to the needle, and then finally pushed it through the needle's tiny eye. Next I removed the bobbin, the delicate, crablike object with a tiny, smooth rounded arm that holds thread inside the machine. I wound the bobbin with matching thread from my spool and reloaded it.

Much has been done to make sewing machines easy to use for novice sewers. Sewing machine companies have tried to reverse declining sales by reaching out to an entirely new market of sewers, the hobbyists. According to *Time* magazine, there were approximately 35 million sewing hobbyists in the United States in 2006, up from 30 million in 2000.[5] And the number is growing as more people tap into the pleasure of making something themselves.

To appeal to new hobbyists, sewing machines come automated, computerized, and jam-proof, with magnetic drop-in bobbin functions. Brother sells a Sew Advance Sew Affordable machine as well as a Simply Affordable one. Singer has machines called Simple and Confidence, advertised as "computerized, one-step, push-button fully automatic creative tools." Most newer machines have the threading functions numbered and a diagram next to the bobbin, so beginners don't put the thread around the plastic finger before looping it through the metal hook or wind the bobbin the wrong way. Our foremothers are probably rolling over in their graves at how much hand-holding we need to use a sewing machine, but I'd be lost without it.

Beaumont had Harriet and me leave open the hutch that conceals the bobbin so we could see how exactly the thread is looped and a stitch is made. She explained the purpose of the feed dogs, which grip fabric and move it along, and the flywheel, which manually controls the needle allowing it to be raised to remove fabric or turned by hand to form a stitch. The millimeter marks on the throat plate help in sewing a straight line and following patterns that call for a certain seam allowance. These are modern additions as well.

Sewing for the first time can be anxiety producing. There's partial dread of doing something wrong paired with the pressure you put on yourself to be a brilliant seamstress right out of the gate. But once the machine starts up and the tiny motor kicks into gear, the anxiety dissipates. In the course of three classes with Beaumont, I learned how to sew a basic pillowcase. Somehow, it was enough to make sewing part of my life.

I bought my first machine a few weeks later. When it came in the mail, I set it up on a little table in my bedroom, sat down and wound the bobbin and threaded the machine. I got out a pair of black jeans that had gone unworn for six months because of a tear. I took a square of black denim left over from a pair of cutoff jean shorts I'd made earlier in the summer and pulled the denim pieces together under the needle. I set the machine to a zigzag stitch to give it extra reinforcement and pressed the pedal. The thread snarled inside the machine immediately. But I simply took everything apart and set up the machine again, and then I patched my pants. Over the next few weeks, I patched more jeans, hemmed skirts, and took in the side seams on my baggy T-shirts. I somehow had gone 31 years without knowing how fulfilling it is to care for and personalize my clothes.

Most people are actually far more particular about their style than they realize, which is partly why we feel so frustrated with the clothes in our closets. There are so many things that we *would* wear if they were tweaked or just slightly altered. Dresses or skirts are rarely the perfect length, the color is wrong, shirts often hit us in not quite the right place, straps are too long or too short. We buy tops that we love *except* for that annoying ruffle or tie or bow. For me, learning to sew wasn't necessarily about making everything I wear. It taught me that clothes aren't static and unchanging. They can be altered, mended, and even totally rebuilt. Virtually everything in my closet suddenly had some potential to be something I'd get more use out of and maybe even love. Sewing also gave me the ability to recognize garments crafted with skill and care and made me crave quality clothing. I now see what a waste of money cheap fashion really is, because the materials and sewing often aren't even worth owning.

Beaumont's style is sort of romantic vintage meets prairie girl; floor-length dresses laced up the back and worn with petticoats. My personal style couldn't be more different. I love the boxy look of 1980s power dressing. I like short dresses with boat necks and shoulder pads and black paired with loud colors like hot pink. I like blouses with huge bows at the neck and capped sleeves on pretty much anything. Sewing also made me realize I could dress *exactly* how I wanted to, and then there was no going back. I plan to take pattern-making classes and intermediate sewing classes in the coming months. And I am saving up to order a custom blazer and a few tailored dresses.

When I shopped in cheap fashion stores, I owned garments that thousands, maybe tens of thousands, of other people owned. If they didn't own the same exact garment, they were wearing the same style or print as I was. At brunch a few years ago, I sat down and immediately noticed there were four people in the restaurant wearing nautical striped shirts, including me. Sure, we all had on a slightly different version of the shirt, but on the spectrum of what is possible to wear, we were dressed almost identically. These moments happen all the time in the age of mass fashion, making personalized and custom clothing all the more compelling. "If you make your own clothes, there is nobody else, *no one*, wearing what you're wearing. Think about that! It's incredible," Beaumont says.

"We're at a point of evolution and a point of transition. I think that's one reason there's been crisis in the fashion world," says Beaumont, referring to the skyrocketing clothing prices, cotton shortages, and high-profile designer breakdowns that are rocking the fashion world. "I'm certain that we are coming to the end of the two-tiered system." The prospect of people returning to custom and one-of-a-kind clothing makes life after "big fashion" exciting rather than scary. Though not everyone has the patience, time, or curiosity to sew, I hope more people sit down and learn basic mending skills and utilize the tailors and seamstresses around them. There are too few opportunities in modern life to actually produce the things we use and to determine the look and the function of the clothes we wear. Sewing gives back a feeling of agency and self-sufficiency. It allows you to look under the hood. Sewing gives you all the power of fashion and quality in your hands—and relinquishes nothing to the system. In my experience, it is just satisfying in a way that plucking clothes off a rack at a store never will be.

———

Jillian Owens, 29, is a Columbia, South Carolina, native and was a lifetime thrift-store shopper, until secondhand finds started to dry up. "I got burned out on thrifting because there wasn't that much there," Owens says. "A lot of stuff that you'll find at thrift stores is old H&M stuff, and it's completely worn-out." A few years ago she received a sewing machine as a Christmas gift and took it as a sign that she should try to sew her own clothes instead. She went to a local fabric store but was soon feeling defeated again. It was cheaper to buy clothes than it was to make them.

Sewing your own clothes can be very inexpensive. The cost depends on the quality of the fabric and the complexity of the garment. Sarah Beaumont's cute pink T-shirt that I saw on her dress form cost $3 in fabric to make. She usually chooses fabrics that are less than $10 a yard, and most garments typically take less than three yards of fabric. Beaumont also keeps her costs down by reusing sheets and the discarded "ends" of designer bolts of fabric, which she buys from fabric stores in New York's Garment District. She inspired me to make a cap-sleeve dress out of a sheet that I never used. Scraps from every project get reused for something else, like pillowcases, stuffed animals, and little bags.

But for Owens, it was important to not spend a penny more making clothes than she would to buy them new in a store. "Sewing used to be something women did to be thrifty," she says. "The fact that you could go buy an item of clothing new for less than what it would cost you to go to the trouble of making it seemed weird and wrong." So Owens returned to the thrift store, this time with the idea of buying used clothes and restyling them. She bought ill-fitting and out-of-date garments and lobbed off shoulder pads, cut off sleeves, and hiked up hems. For one project, Owens took a powder blue 1980s Liz Claiborne sack dress that overwhelmed her small frame and altered it into a cute, modern cocktail dress. She's made a ball gown out of men's dress shirts and a hip-hugging skirt out of a soccer jersey. "There's something so rewarding in making something yourself and fixing something yourself," Owens says. So rewarding in fact she's spun her restyling projects into a successful blog, *ReFashionista*, where she posts a photograph of a reformulated garment every single day.

With refashioning, there is always a risk of ruining a piece of clothing. "People are afraid to cut into their clothes. They're afraid to mess it up," she says. But for Owens the risk is part of the fun. It takes others longer to get used to the idea. A friend of hers complained for months about a ruffle on a new tank top she'd purchased. "Finally, she cut off the damn ruffle and then she liked the tank top," Owens told me, chuckling.

Refashioning is not a new concept. It's just a forgotten one. In eighteenth-century England, maids took their mistresses' castoff dresses and turned them into new outfits.[6] My grandmother, who grew up during the Depression, never threw her clothes away. They were patched up and reimagined until they were completely worn-out or passed down to siblings. When clothing and shoes were rationed during World War II and textile production was largely dedicated to military uniforms, fashionable women sewed old linens, scrap cloth, and their husband's suits into quite sophisticated styles. Refashioning was a way of life, as it provided novelty and allowed people to keep up with changing fashions. A new generation is reconnecting with the practice.

Several blogs and Internet communities dedicated to refashioning have cropped up. Owens assists in editing the Refashion Co-Op, an online community of refashioners from all over the world. Anyone can contribute to the site (refashionco-op.blogspot.com), with the stipulation that they post at least one new project a month. Owens is inspiring people in her community as well. Her ball gown of men's dress shirts was put on exhibit at a local museum. She's also collaborating with a local thrift store by taking damaged or out-of-style donations and refashioning them for resale. The proceeds go to a women's shelter. Owens says, "These clothes probably would have ended up thrown away if I hadn't done that. Everybody wins."

Vintage dealer Sara Bereket briefly toyed with the idea of starting a fashion line, but realizing the expense and the financial risk involved, she decided to build her business around refashioned vintage instead. The American vintage clothing market is one of the deepest in the world, but a lot of it is stained, torn, or too out-of-date to sell. Not everyone wants to or has the time to restyle or mend secondhand clothing themselves. Bereket offers these services for them.

Bereket is part of a growing number of secondhand clothing dealers who refashion and mend used clothes for retail. If something is perfect as is, such as the '80s Lanvin double-breasted jacket Bereket currently has for sale on her Web site, Saraz Closet, she'll leave it as is. But about three-fourths of the secondhand clothing she buys benefits from some kind of alteration. She's replaced broken buttons on an Yves Saint Laurent plaid jacket and removed the sleeves on jumpsuits. Since hemlines have gotten dramatically shorter over the years, most dresses and skirts get a lift. "I want to give my customer a finished product," says Bereket. "I want people to wear it straightaway."

Bereket strongly believes in consumer power and our ability to change the fashion industry through the way we shop. "If we decided we're not going to support H&M, for example, *oh my God*, that would change everything," she told me excitedly. "We blame companies. But at the end of the day we have to be responsible for our actions." Bereket also offers rentals of vintage dresses for special occasions through her Web site. "Part of eliminating waste is sharing what you have," she says. "I don't think we need to own anything anymore because we don't wear party dresses more than once."

For variety, and the thrill of something new to wear, clothing rentals and clothing swaps are resonating with many people. Swaps are community- or privately organized events where people bring clothing in good condition to trade for free or for a small donation. Clothing swaps are now being held around the country with more successful organizers like Boston's The Swapaholics hosting swaps attended by more than 400 people. *USA Today* commented on the phenomenon in an April 26, 2010, article: "When it comes to freshening their—and their kids' and husbands'—wardrobes, more women are exchanging shopping for swapping. Friends are gathering at homes to trade gently worn treasures (and gossip); strangers are exchanging stuff through online swap sites or at organized meet-ups." The article noted that women were gravitating toward swaps because of the interpersonal and social perks, of which shopping today is almost entirely devoid.

The first time I heard about clothing swaps, I had mixed feelings about the idea. It's impossible, without just showing up to a swap, to know that—even if you bring your expensive designer jeans and a good wool coat—everyone else is not going to bring their stretched-out and stained has-beens. Finding a well-organized swap where the style and quality are what you're after is all part of the process. When I found out on Facebook that a swap was happening a half mile from my house, it was time to check one out. I dragged all of the clothes I no longer wore out of my closet and selected a few things to trade, picking out a couple of H&M blouses that were still in decent condition, a never-worn sweater dress from Old Navy, a pair of well-made black corduroys from Gap, and a pair of white Diesel sneakers.

When I arrived at the swap, I handed my bag of clothes to a greeter, a policy intended to keep each person's donations anonymous. The swap, held in a large basement room at the local library, divided clothes into women's, men's, children's, dresses, outerwear, shoes, and miscellaneous. The selection wasn't exceptional, but I did find a few things that I liked—a high-quality long wool coat, a pair of red running shorts, and a baby blue corduroy skirt. After trying on everything at home, I decided to keep the shorts, and cast the rest back into the secondhand waste stream by donating them to a thrift store.

———

The first time I met Eliza Starbuck, I don't remember what she was wearing, only what I was wearing: a cheap tank top, cheap black boots, and a cheap knit skirt. I only paid $5 for the skirt. I was proud of my wardrobe of deals until I had to interview people who were well-dressed. Starbuck is absolutely striking; she's six feet tall and willowy, with clear blue eyes and a small cap of dark hair. Even though she's worked on the design staff of virtually every major clothing chain, as well as the luxury company Coach, Starbuck almost exclusively wears thrift-store finds such as tailored jackets and trousers and vintage pillbox hats. For the price, Starbuck says she can find items in thrift stores that are better made than almost anything in chain stores. "I can find a pair of really good trousers that are one hundred percent wool and they're twelve bucks," she says. "I know what to look for. I can find really good quality for nothing, for H&M's prices. Going into H&M or even Urban Outfitters, these stores torture me with the bad quality." Starbuck spends hours combing thrift stores for good finds, trying on what she claims is almost half the store.

Shopping in secondhand and vintage stores evokes a mixture of emotions for me now. While I love the hunt for 100 percent cotton sweaters, silk shells, and leather boots, the good stuff is getting bought up fast, and I'm reminded that the vast majority of clothes sold today are very poorly made. Quality is the missing link in the path back to valuing clothes and paying more for what we wear. We currently spend the most money on brand names and high-end designers. Instead of shopping for a name or label, our hard-earned money should be going toward good materials and garments with a strong and unique design vision. We need more designers making *good clothes*. And more consumers who are willing to buy them.

Starbuck believes that good fashion design means that consumers get more use out of what they wear. Instead of owning 34 tank tops and 21 skirts that all look shockingly similar, as I once did, her line Bright Young Things encourages people to own clothing that is both flexible and diminishes our need for more of the same. Bright Young Things is comprised of multifunctional and adjustable garments that can be worn in a number of ways. Her little black dress can be worn forward or backward or open as a jacket. Her Converter Pant is adjustable at the waist, transitioning from high-waisted to low-riding or to sitting right on the hip. She says her clothes have a message and a lifestyle ingrained in them: "Knowing how to style yourself and to be creative with your clothes trumps having a lot of them." Versatile clothing like this is becoming a more mainstream idea in fashion, with such retailers as American Apparel selling loose fabric along with styling pamphlets.

Starbuck's line was featured at the 2010 GreenShows, a runway show dedicated to sustainable fashion that is held in Manhattan at the same time as fall Fashion Week. By spring, Starbuck had four of her pieces from the GreenShows—the halter top in two colors, the pants, a coat-dress, and a cream wrap dress—in three Manhattan locations of Urban Outfitters. She and I met at the East Village location so I could test-drive her line, which we found hidden in a rack of tank tops in loud colors and the year's ubiquitous tiny floral prints. "These styles may not even be wearable in a season," Starbuck admonished, referring to the chain's trendy duds. "Because people will look at it and be able to date it very quickly and know exactly when you bought it. It'll be uncool." Starbuck made her own line in solids of maroon, black, and cream.

The Bright Young Things label reads, "How many ways can you wear it?" Luckily, I had the designer with me to help me answer that question. "The experience most customers should have," she said, laughing, as I trotted off. I tried on the adjustable halter first, deciding to twist it at the neck into a formfitting midriff. Starbuck said, "I've worn it sideways, which is even more scandalous." By flipping the halter around and putting one arm through, it creates an entirely different draped, asymmetrical look.

The clothing and lifestyles of women such as Sarah Kate Beaumont, Eliza Starbuck, Sara Bereket, and Jillian Owens have inspired me to make clothing my own and to become a part of and influence the entire process of clothing. Anything we wear can be altered and changed into something else, something more personalized and expressive. I take pride in wearing things that fit my frame. As I've gotten into the habit of having my clothes altered, I've developed this acute frustration whenever I am on the streets. No one's clothes fit them properly! And yet they could so easily. I also cut up my clothes with glee now, risking ruining things but usually ending up with clothes I like so much better. Here are just a few of my recent projects: I took a polyester blouse collecting dust in my closet, cut out a clammy synthetic lining and cut off a belt and ended up with a cool loose-fitting, sheer blouse that earns lots of compliments. I've sliced out the lining and taken up the hemline on a leather skirt from Salvation Army. Shirts with fun but sort of clownlike prints that I wouldn't wear in the light of day work just fine as tote bags and pillowcases. I've dyed black two pairs of brown leather boots bought at a thrift store, so they'd go with more of my wardrobe. I alter all of my T-shirts so they are the right length and fit.

Sarah Kate Beaumont projected my future and said that even years into making my own clothes, the effort would still feel satisfying. She said, "You will still be riding your bike thinking, *Oooooh, I made my top.*" She raised her eyebrows up and down and gripped some imaginary handlebars and we both laughed. Only time will tell. Maybe I'll realize sewing isn't for me, leaving me in the able hands of designers like Starbuck, refashioners like Bereket and Owens, seamstresses like Wolf, or any one of the other innovative slow fashion designers and retailers coming up the ranks.

9

The Future of Fashion

The Echo Park Independent Co-op looks like most edgy and slightly intimidating clothing boutiques. Located in the eponymous Los Angeles neighborhood, the window of the sleek storefront has an enigmatic logo of two black rabbits standing on their hind legs and crossing paws in the window. Inside the loftlike, museum-white space are racks of patchwork leotards, sequined jodhpurs, and short, flirty dresses in unusual prints. E.P.I.C. opened in March 2010 and by the time I randomly walked through the doors in August of that year, celebrity stylists were already swarming it to dress their clients. Fashion icon Lady Gaga's stylist had recently been in the store and pulled a dress for the pop star.

As I entered, a tall, boyish blond man in a red plaid shirt and snug jean shorts beamed and offered assistance. Within minutes, Tristan Scott and I had fallen into conversation, where I learned that this store is in no way what it seems: Almost all of the clothing in E.P.I.C. is both designed and produced locally, in Los Angeles, using environmentally friendly textiles and other ethical sourcing techniques.

I've often thought, *If only there were some utopian store where the clothes are really fashionable, environmentally friendly,* and *low priced all while supporting living-wage jobs (ideally jobs based in the United States).* Those stores don't really exist. Clothing that isn't produced at resource-draining quantities or by shortchanging the people making it is *not cheap*. Clothing that is well made is *not cheap*. There, I said it. I've had about two years to accept this. Perhaps it will take you less time. But all of these other ideals are now possible.

In recent years many Americans have started shopping at farmer's markets and dropping extra cash on organic eggs or locally grown produce in increasing numbers. More of us are patronizing farm-to-table restaurants that source their ingredients from nearby growers, all while swearing that the food tastes better and adds to our quality of life. Localism and a more thoughtful, slow approach to eating have a huge following, and slowly but surely the movement is spreading to fashion.

Ethical fashion of years past was associated with such style-blind, drab clothes as hemp shoes or plain organic cotton T-shirts that put the politics before good design. Not surprisingly, it had only a niche following. Organic and local food is popular because it *adds* to the experience of eating. Today's slow and local fashion movement is finally promising the same enhanced experience for pursuers of style.

When E.P.I.C. first opened, Scott and co-owner Rhianon Jones were mum about their ethics, wanting the fashion to take the spotlight. "We want it to be like when your mom sneaks brussels sprouts into your food," Scott told me playfully. "Surprise, it's organic! We just made you buy that," added Jones, a vintage-lover with a retro rocker style, and both of them pealed into laughter. Many of E.P.I.C.'s customers are completely unaware that when they shop in the store they're often buying things made of organic cotton, nontoxic vegetable-tanned leather, or recycled polyester. They come in for the 50 different edgy fashion lines including As Is, which uses recycled PET and organic cotton, and Gas'd, which uses the vegetable-tanned leather for its men's wear line. "It was really important to us—

because we're both so into fashion—to make sure people would still want to wear it," says Scott. The only way the slow fashion movement can succeed is if it produces clothes that surpass what's available from chain stores or hyped designer labels in terms of quality, creativity, and uniqueness, as well as in the experience of buying it and wearing it.

Kate McGregor, 31, has opened two stores in New York City behind the slow-fashion concept. Her boutiques, called Kaight, are understated, beautiful, and well put together; the clothing lines she sells are all either made domestically or produced from sustainable fabrics, often both. Among the designers Kaight carries is Feral Childe, the Brooklyn-based pair of artists who produce their own silk-screened textile prints. The store also carries Eviana Hartman's beautifully architectural Bodkin line and Prairie Underground, a Seattle line that sells high-quality, ultrafeminine hoodies and knit jackets. McGregor says she never once considered opening a store that touted its eco credentials above attractive fashion. "You should buy things because they're nice looking, amazing, well made, and you want to wear them," says McGregor. "That's the point."

Slow clothing differs in a number of other surprising ways from what we've been trained to expect from chain stores. Often the emphasis is on creating pieces that aren't trend driven and are instead unique enough not to really date. "If you're designing really cool, well-designed pieces, they're going to be relevant years from now," explains McGregor. E.P.I.C.'s Web site, for example, is selling a glittery dress with Marie Antoinette–style panniers and a gold lamé number with long streams of fringe dangling from the sleeves. We are long past the age where our manner of dress distinguishes us as either king or pauper. So why not take more risks with our clothes? In a way, personal style has become an imperative. Trends change so fast now that we are handed two choices: Change trends like you're manically flicking a light switch or have the courage to develop your own look.

"Fashion has become so much more about status than wearing a piece that's really interesting and artistically done, especially in the high-end fashion world," agrees Scott. He and Jones try to select clothes for E.P.I.C. that are truly unique, edgy, or artistic. Although Kaight favors slightly more wearable lines, the clothes are still quite creative. From Kaight, I own a pair of rainbow zebra-print flats by Melissa, a Brazilian company that makes its shoes from a patented, flexible recycled and recyclable plastic. The company runs on a closed-loop system, recycling its factory's water and waste; it also recycles overstocked shoes into the following year's collection.[1]

Slow fashion is also inherently more eco-friendly—no matter what materials are used—because it is produced in smaller quantities. Alicia Lawhon of Reclaimed in L.A., who sells through E.P.I.C., makes one-of-a-kind pieces made from reclaimed textiles, and the typical line in E.P.I.C. or Kaight is made in very small batches. The exclusivity of a slow fashion garment is not only better for the environment, it is a huge part of its appeal. It means owning something very few others have. By supporting local talent, slow clothing also has the potential to reestablish local and regional style lost over recent decades.

McGregor grew up in Springfield, Ohio, the daughter of a small business owner, and has been a fashion follower since childhood. "As a kid, I was raised on the mantra of always try to buy local first or source locally. It was about supporting small businesses. That was always part of my life," she says. McGregor developed an environmental consciousness as a college student in Boulder, Colorado, and started to think fashion was superficial and wasteful. "I kind of forced myself away from it unnaturally," she says, going in the extreme opposite direction, getting a job in financial journalism, before coming back to her passion. She opened her first store in 2006 on the Lower East Side with the idea of stocking designers who use sustainable textiles and expanded the vision from there. She says, "It has evolved to encompass every aspect of the process, including the production and how the garment is dyed and sourced."

At both E.P.I.C. and Kaight, the owners act as partners instead of gatekeepers, helping designers with strong aesthetic visions clean up their supply chains. The stores will connect the designers with the right eco-friendly textile resources or clue them into certain production techniques, such as vegetable-tanned leather or reclaimed materials. E.P.I.C.'s Scott and Jones have even gone on sustainable fabric shopping trips with their designers and have commissioned eco-friendly lines from designers who usually source from mainstream avenues. McGregor will likewise carry designers who work with a limited percentage of organic materials, with the caveat that they raise the percentage over time. And now that both stores have gained in popularity and designers are clamoring to get in, the ball is in their court. Jones says, "Now, we can actually ask for these things and a lot of times the designers will do it. And the more they do it, the more they understand it's not a big deal to use sustainable fabrics. It's not a huge shift."

Fashion schools are pushing sustainable design approaches, and E.P.I.C. is seeing more young designers sourcing ethically without any prompting. Roark Collective, a men's line that specializes in intricate and stylish leather jackets, was already using vegetable-tanned leather when it was approached to be in the store. "They're just out of fashion school, and this was already happening without us saying anything," recalls Scott. "We were really excited about it."

The price on sustainable fabrics is also coming down as more suppliers get into the field; the selection and quality also have improved dramatically in the past few years. "When I first started writing about eco-friendly clothing two years ago, hemp skirts were the only thing out there," remembers Jones, who was an ecofashion blogger before opening E.P.I.C. Now there are eco-friendly alternatives to virtually every kind of natural fiber. Wool and cotton are preferential, in my opinion, to polyester because they wear and feel better, are not oil-dependent, and are biodegradable. But I support recycled and repurposed fabrics of all kinds, and the overall goal should be to reduce the amount of toxins and chemicals used across the textile industry as a whole, as well as to reduce our consumption of fiber in general.

Cellulosic fabrics have also cleaned up their act in recent years. Starbuck's Bright Young Things collection uses a Tencel blend, a rayon trademarked by the Lenzing Corporation that feels like superfine cotton with a touch of silk. Tencel is derived by chemically processing eucalyptus pulp in an environmentally friendly closed-loop system, where the chemicals are recycled. I own a black sleeveless top made of Modal, a similar fiber by Lenzing, that is so amazingly soft I have to stop myself from running my hands across it in public. I've also fallen for silk, which I usually buy in thrift stores because it's more affordable and because it's so intensive to make. (It takes around 30,000 silkworms to produce 12 pounds of raw silk). Fabric is the foundation of a garment and perhaps its most important component. A good fabric should feel good next to your skin, wear and wash well over time, and have a certain texture and beauty that becomes recognizable once you start to look for it.

Local production is also growing again because designers are realizing it gives them far better quality control and speed to market. "If a line's rack gets really low, we can just call the designer and say, 'Hey guys, do you have anything you feel like whipping up this week?'" Scott explains. "It's just a lot more instantaneous. I'm surprised that more people don't try to operate that way." Similarly, Kaight's McGregor says, "You don't know if a style is going to be superpopular or not. If you have a good relationship with your factory here, you can get another run cut and get it to stores in two weeks, which is awesome." This just-in-time thinking is the legacy of the fast-fashion industry and the Internet age, but it's also how the industry ran when it was smaller and more independent. Being able to respond quickly to demand is giving domestically produced clothing lines a much-needed competitive advantage.

Against all odds, employment in the apparel manufacturing sector grew slightly in the first half of 2011. After reaching an all-time low of 155,000 jobs, employment climbed to 157,400 in May of that year.[2] As prices skyrocket in China, local manufacturing is not at the cost disadvantage it once was. And it's not just small designers who are turning to factories in the United States. There are major brands moving production back as well. According to California Fashion Association president Ilse Metchek, Target and Macy's are looking into domestic production to test new lines. "Macy's private label wants to make some high-end women's tops here," says Metchek, before it does its full runs overseas.

L.A. brand Karen Kane has moved as much of its production back to the United States as it can. Launched in 1979, Karen Kane moved more than half of its orders to China over the years to take advantage of lower costs, and also because the manufacturing resources in the United States became so limited. Two years ago, when prices started to climb overseas, the brand did an about-face and started moving work back to Los Angeles. It now makes all but 20 percent of its garments there. Likewise, the $15 million L.A. brand Single, which specializes in silk print dresses, moved more of its production back to the States from China in 2011 and now produces 90 percent domestically.[3]

Moving garment manufacturing onshore will not be an easy transition for bigger companies. A lot of larger, mass-market factories that can handle huge orders are gone and will have to be built back up. Many experienced factory managers and skilled workers have retired or gone into other lines of work. Machinery is aging or in some cases is nonexistent, sold to overseas manufacturers. The capacity to produce some kinds of clothing in the United States is all but lost. Sweaters are made on special knitting machines, and the machines have largely been sold to other countries. "If we wanted to get back into making sweaters, we'd have to buy the machinery back from China," explains Michael Kane, who says the company is figuring out how to make the best domestic products possible in the face of depleted resources. "We have to work much harder to find places that can make what we're trying to make," admits Kane. "And tapping back into our local resources has been interesting."

Erica Wolf from Manhattan's Save the Garment Center says that onshore manufacturing may be happening in New York as well, but the evidence is mostly anecdotal. "I think this is the year we make the switch with China," Wolf told me optimistically. Save the Garment Center is working with a number of groups in Manhattan and the city government to protect the manufacturing base there. "I would also like to see some of the more established designers here bring a little bit back," she says.

Wolf and many people I spoke to in the fashion industry supported tax incentives, equipment financing, training, and other types of government support to stimulate domestic apparel manufacturing. Wolf has been in Washington, D.C., lobbying to enact industrial development bonds for domestic manufacturers. Andy Ward's organization, the Garment Industry Development Corporation, uses state funding to train workers in higher sewing and pattern-making skills, and these sorts of efforts need to be expanded. Some type of resolution will need to be made regarding undocumented workers, as immigrants have historically been the backbone of the garment manufacturing industry.

Karen Kane partnered with department store Dillard's to launch a midpriced Made in USA collection in 179 stores around the country for the 2011 holiday season. For department stores, domestic production could be their saving grace because turnaround times are that much faster. Rather than ordering products five months out, Dillard's can wait to see what trends are taking off, work with Karen Kane to place reorders, and have them in stores within weeks instead of months. "They see it as a great way to build their business," says Kane. "By having so much more industry here, you can turn around and react to trends much faster. This might just be where the apparel industry is headed."

Local production also makes it easier for a designer to be watchful of factory conditions. Abuses and sweatshops still occur in the United States, but smaller production shops and a more locally minded industry focused on low-volume, better-made garments would improve accountability and correct some of fashion's labor problems. Increasing the price of fashion would also help correct the race to the bottom in garment worker wages. "It's a lot easier to keep an eye on what's going on by keeping things local," E.P.I.C.'s Tristan Scott says, although many of its designers produce in such small batches that the pieces are sewn in their own homes or personal studios. Some factory owners complain that state and federal labor laws are too strict, putting them at a competitive disadvantage. But the garment industry needs watchdogs, as history has shown, or conditions quickly erode.

Let's talk about price. I'm not going to make a big argument that everyone should go out and overhaul their sock, underwear, and T-shirt drawer and buy slow fashion basics and underthings, unless of course you can afford to and want to. Nor will I tell you to start putting your five-year-old in pricier, locally made fashion, only to have her outgrow it in a few months. One reason I think Alta Gracia is so promising is that it manufactures basics, not fashion. Living-wage and fair-trade factories in the developing world are a perfect solution to high-volume or more utilitarian clothing like T-shirts, which should be more affordable. I would love to see living-wage factories also producing other essentials, including socks, underwear, denim, and maybe even affordable winter coats and boots.

Slow fashion's strength is in, well, fashion, the clothes we wear to express ourselves. That's where we should be willing to own less and pay more. I always try to remember that the price we pay for things is connected to other people's paychecks, which ultimately comes back to fortify our own communities. A recent Moody's Analytics report noted that if consumers spent an extra 1 percent on U.S. goods, it would create 200,000 jobs.[4] I told McGregor that I used to not pay more than $30 for a shirt and all she could muster was, "Wow." Paying so little for clothing can't sustain good livelihoods for the people who sew or sell clothes. Unlike a salesgirl slogging away at a cheap fashion chain, McGregor has set her prices so that she's able to pay herself enough to be able to shop her own store, where things generally retail for between $50 and $300. And when clothes are viewed as investments instead of trendy throwaway items, these prices seem much less intimidating.

But how much is too much to pay for clothes? It depends on an individual's income and general financial situation and whether she's buying clothes for herself versus a partner or an entire family. After I stopped shopping cheap, I bought one or two items from independent designers who sold through local boutiques. And it hurt. The day I bought a $200 dress—a silk, sleeveless, midthigh shift—I had a lump in my throat as I walked up to the cash register. I had to ask myself in every possible way if it was something I really loved and thought I would wear. My clothing suddenly had financial implications.

I asked fashion industry people what a fair price for clothing might be, made at sustainable volumes, at a good quality level, and using responsibly paid labor. It's a tricky question, as the answer varies so much depending on what product we're talking about—a fair price for a winter coat is going to be very different from a fair price for a pair of boxer shorts. Not surprisingly, no one could give me a straight answer. The bottom line is that consumers have to educate themselves about quality construction and good fabrics, so they know when a garment is a rip-off or when they're actually getting their money's worth. If we could get to this collective place, retailers would have to be more responsible about pricing and sticker shock would more closely correspond to an exceptionally crafted garment.

A custom suit or dress is going to cost far more than anything in a mainstream store. If you're paying for the upper echelon of creativity and/or practically a one-of-a-kind design, I can tell you to expect prices much higher than a couple hundred dollars yet *much* lower than say, Prada. These are items to save and strive for. And if you're buying a line through a boutique, remember you're paying more to support both the designer *and* the store. And unlike in the luxury market, where prices are inflated, an honest retailer's prices are a better reflection of the actual worth of the garment and the labor and skill involved.

At E.P.I.C. the designers show the owners their wholesale and a suggested retail price and are questioned if the costs don't add up. There are no high markups in an attempt to make a product seem prestigious. "Our most expensive lines are the most time-consuming and intricate, so it makes sense," says Scott. Likewise, Kaight will sell pricier goods, but only when justified by the costs and intricacy of the item. And McGregor says her customers usually don't resist. "When people are familiar with a label and they know the quality is going to be amazing, it's not hard convincing them to pay a certain amount for a garment," she says. Consumers should ask for the story behind the prices. In order to close the gap between pricing and the actual products we're buying, the fashion industry as a whole simply must be more transparent.

If you currently shop cheap, you can shift your spending without paying more than you're used to paying overall by shopping less and with more intention. I don't spend more per year than I used to, and yet I own *much* nicer stuff that looks better on me. What a concept. I think it's smart to save up and put your biggest dollars into coats, shoes, and, for men, suits. Paying more in these categories almost always mean better fit and wear and a more classic, long-lasting style that doesn't have to be replaced as often.

In time, I've found that the urge to dress trendy and the desire to look good are often at odds. I don't look good in the billowy, loose-fitting shirts that are in right now. Before that, I didn't look good in the long, tunic style tops that were in. The further I move away from following trends, the more I am aware of what cuts and silhouettes work for me. This isn't to say that there aren't times when trends resonate with me. I like '90s minimalism in the form of a simple shell. The first place I look for trends is at a thrift store, since they're usually rehashed anyway or are so quickly discarded. I also don't have a hard and fast rule against chain stores, discounters, or even the occasional cheap fashion fix. If we just patronized these places at even half the pace that we do, it would put enormous pressure on the industry to clean up its act. No matter where our clothes are purchased, we should buy the best we can, make good use of them, and care for them.

Repairing our footwear also needs to be resurrected, not only because this means supporting local business but also because our shoes would have a long life span if only we'd replace the heels and soles. I replaced the heels on a pair of boots for the first time in the winter of 2010. Normally I would just bag them up with holes in the sole or sometimes practically unworn and take them to Goodwill or the Salvation Army and buy new ones. Instead, I looked up a shoe-repair shop in Brooklyn and called and asked plaintively, doubtfully, "Are you able to replace the heel on a boot?" I felt like I was asking something fantastical, like "Do you sell unicorn horns?" The man on the other end of the line responded gruffly, "What do you mean?" I clarified that the heels were worn down on my black, midcalf boots and were now at a knee-wrecking slant. He barked, "You probably need new heels. Goodbye." And he hung up on me.

The problem with repairing these boots was that they were cheap to begin with. I paid 50 bucks for them and the leather was shoddy, the soles were rubber, the stitching and glue were subpar. I'd owned these boots for all of six months, yet the leather was covered in mysterious silver spots and the soles were worn through. But I decided to get them fixed anyway. When I picked up my boots from the repair shop, I was astonished at how good they looked. The leather was moist, healthy-looking, and jet-black. The new soles and heels were sturdier and thicker than the original. My boots were literally better than new. I appreciated the repair even more when slouchy, pointy-toe boots went out of style the following season, and the stores were forcing me to switch my footwear to combat boots and round-toe boots and brown over black.

At the risk of sounding too earnest, we are all stewards of our clothing, responsible for seeing it through its different phases of life. Even if we don't have any use for a piece of clothing, it's up to us to make sure its next stop in the clothing life cycle isn't the landfill.

Clothing should be kept in good condition, able to be worn after us, which means caring for and maintaining it while we own it and cleaning it and repairing it before we donate it or sell it or give it away. When I pulled my winter coats out of storage this year, I spent a few days trying them on and asking myself, *Do the linings need sewing up? Would I wear this if it was taken in or altered somehow?* In some cases, the answer was that I simply didn't like them anymore and had in fact never liked them—with my new eyes I realized they were cheap and shoddy-looking. So I cleaned a handful of my coats, stitched the linings and sewed back on the dangling buttons, and donated them in the best condition possible.

Instead of driving to a mall and buying predetermined styles owned by thousands of other people, consumers are turning back to independent businesses and personalized fashion. More shops are opening where designers are combining their workshops and retail spaces so customers have input on the final garment. There's a shop in the Silver Lake neighborhood of Los Angeles called Matrushka Construction where everything is handmade on-site and items can be altered on the spot. I had a silk-screened top taken in on the sides, for example. The store also carries classic knit dresses that can be made-to-order based on print and sleeve length. Likewise, tailors and seamstresses who offer clients a choice of fit, color, and style are enjoying a small but significant resurgence. Slow fashion is about thinking and doing for yourself, and it's amazing to see those who feel inspired by it make it their own.

As for me, slowly but surely, my life and my wardrobe have changed. When people ask me about my clothes, I have a story to tell beyond, "I bought this at fill-in-the-blank" or "I only paid twenty bucks." If they've got a minute, I might tell them the story of the United States garment and textile trades and the high-quality, well-constructed clothes that are still being produced here. I get to share how I altered or made something myself, talk about the importance of fabrics, or introduce others to a local designer I like.

But what if more of us thought about clothing in the way people—until very recently—have always thought about it? Clothing is valuable. It should be valued. Cheap clothes not only undermine those who sew, sell, and design them, they're the pitiful result of decades of price pressure that has erased the craftsmanship and splendor of what we wear. Incessant deal hunting has also erased our collective knowledge of what clothing and style could be.

I know I will never go back to the way I dressed or shop in the stores where I used to shop. Because when I walk by an H&M or an Old Navy or a Target, I see what once looked like fashion meccas for what they really are: unsightly jumbles of cheap clothes dressed up as good deals. When we can recognize how clothing is put together, what it's made of, and can visualize the long journey it makes to our closets, it becomes harder to view it as worthless or disposable. Instead, we begin to want to own garments that are unique and made with a level of skill and good materials that cheap fashion simply can't provide us. If we could only give up our clothing deals and steals, we might just see that there are far more fortifying—not to mention more flattering—ways of getting dressed.

Afterword to the Paperback Edition

S ince the release of *Overdressed* in June 2012, I've found myself telling prospective readers that this isn't *really* a book about cheap fashion. It covers the entire apparel industry—all price points, all participants, from brand to factory to consumer—and describes how the whole thing went off the rails. It applies to every kind of shopper, from the office intern wearing head-to-toe Forever 21, to the label-obsessed fashionista paying $800 for a designer shoe, to those on a budget so tight that $7 shoes are the best they can afford.

Overdressed is not a book just for women, either. It's a book for everyone who wears clothes, even those who say they "don't care" about clothes. Americans spend nearly $360 billion on clothes and shoes every year,[1] and the apparel industry touches so many unexpected aspects of our existence.

As I've traveled and talked about the book over the past year, it has become increasingly evident just how closely cheap, trendy chain stores are tied to the outsourcing of American jobs, to human misery in garment factories around the world, and even to the growing economic inequality in the United States. Poverty and cheap, imported goods are two sides of the same coin. I believe we are shopping our way out of stable incomes and communities and into environmental despair, and clothing is at the center of it all.

Those same trendy chain stores are also the epitome of our disturbing consumer culture: We are buying and trashing electronics, furniture, home décor, and, above all, clothing at unprecedented and unsustainable rates, all in the name of what's "fashionable." Between 1991 and 2011, Americans doubled the items of clothing they purchased per year,[2] and textile waste has increased by 40 percent since 1999.[3]

Clothing is a microcosm of the challenges we face as a nation—the economic ones, the ecological ones, *and* the cultural ones. No, *Overdressed* isn't about just cheap fashion or even our clothing addiction—it's about our fast-fashion society.

Some of the book's darker predictions have already come true, and the fast-fashion system is starting to break down. In the chapter "China and the End of Cheap Fashion," I wrote about my travels to Dhaka, Bangladesh, in April 2011, noting that garment factories in the crowded capital city were "being built where they shouldn't be and in a dangerously haphazard fashion." The infrastructure problems and lapses in basic safety standards in Dhaka were apparent to me even then, and this recipe for disaster had already caused numerous fires and deaths. But even I was not prepared for what would happen on April 24, 2013, when an eight-story garment factory collapsed in an industrial suburb of Dhaka, killing at least 1,129 workers,[4] many of whom made clothes for Western brands. Six months earlier, a fire killed 112 people at Tazreen Fashions, also located in Bangladesh.

The collapse of the Rana Plaza building is believed to be the deadliest disaster in the history of the garment industry.[5] Around the world, it has galvanized a call to action for swift and fundamental changes to fashion's labor and safety standards. Major brands that operate in Bangladesh, including H&M, Walmart, Gap, Tommy Hilfiger, Calvin

Klein, Benetton, H&M, Abercrombie & Fitch, and Zara, were held in the crosshairs for not taking more responsibility for the working conditions in their factories. But Western consumers are far from innocent—our obsession with low prices puts downward pressure on companies, which is passed on to the factories and ultimately taken out on workers. Or, as *The Wall Street Journal* stated: "Americans' appetite for cheap clothes is one of the strongest of the economic forces that led to a boom in Bangladesh, with the resulting race to add manufacturing capacity setting the stage for the series of horrific accidents."[6] The 24/7 fast-fashion system demands that new trends be sewn and shipped day in and day out at the lowest possible price. When the name of the game is fast and cheap, clothes are often produced in the most treacherous factories with the worst working standards.

The factory collapse in Bangladesh struck a chord with American consumers for many reasons. I think, to put it bluntly, we'd already hit rock bottom with our cheap-fashion addiction. The wide public outrage to the Rana Plaza tragedy was a revelation (even to me), indicating that consumers are ready for a new fashion paradigm—one that is not built on exploitation, wastefulness, and greed. The tide turned, and it turned faster than I ever could have imagined.

In February 2013, *The New York Times* review of this book declared that "slow fashion" had reached "trend-worthy status." Of course, sustainability and ethical consumerism isn't just a trend—it's a crucial evolution and a deep-rooted movement. And major clothing companies have an important role to play in this movement. In Bangladesh, for example, retailers such as H&M, Gap, Walmart, Sears, JCPenney, and Zara are major employers to the country's four million garment workers,[7] and they have the power to elevate lives. Big companies must work to enforce labor standards in their supply chain, take responsibility when those standards are not met, and make those heightened standards part of their branding. Consumers are now demanding to know how and where their clothes are made, or, as *The New York Times* noted: "The revolution that has swept the food industry is expanding to retail: origins matter."[8]

What consumers are looking for is total transparency and feel-good stories when they shop for clothes. The online retailer Everlane, for example, provides photo slideshows and stories from inside the factories it uses. We also need to establish a credible, independent, and widely used fair-labor labeling system for fashion. Just as shoppers are able to walk into a grocery store and buy free-range eggs, organic produce, or fair-trade coffee, they should be able to walk into a chain store and buy a garment that they know with confidence is ethically produced and eco-friendly.

Should consumers be willing to pay more for such a product? Yes, but major clothing brands can dramatically improve workplace conditions and raise wages for factory workers in countries like Bangladesh—where the current hourly wage is 21 cents—without passing those costs on to consumers. In fact, the Worker Rights Consortium has found that it would take as little as ten cents per garment to make necessary improvements to Bangladesh's 4,500 factories.[9]

It sounds so obvious now, but innovation and technology are two of the most crucial components of ethical fashion. Big chain stores, million-dollar fashion labels, and major fashion schools have the resources and responsibility—just as much as individual consumers and eco-brands—to truly break ground in these areas. Sustainability is the buzzword in the industry, and we should acknowledge big companies that are taking steps in the right direction. Puma has developed the first Cradle-to-Cradle–certified line of shoes and apparel that are all either biodegradable or recyclable. Timberland has introduced Earth-keepers, a line that includes boots made of recycled rubber, organic cotton laces, and leather from an eco-friendly tannery. And, in response to a damning Greenpeace report that found hazardous chemicals in clothes sold by dozens of major brands, a bevy of companies have pledged to clean up their supply chains by 2020, including Levi's, H&M, Zara, UNIQLO, and Victoria's Secret.[10]

Celebrities are also helping to push ethical fashion into the limelight. Actress Helen Hunt wore a gown from H&M's Conscious Collection, made of recycled and organic materials, to the 2013 Oscars. Michelle Obama, whom I've criticized for wearing cheap, imported clothes from Target and H&M, wore a glamorous American-made Naeem Khan gown in her appearance on the 2013 Oscars. And actress Katie Holmes now runs a fashion line, Holmes & Yang, dedicated to heritage quality, domestic production, and close relationships with factories.[11]

Perhaps the most surprising change is that domestic garment production has experienced a small but significant uptick, and American-made goods are coveted once again. *The Atlantic* has heralded an "insourcing boom"[12] and *The New York Times* has observed that supporting local products "has acquired cachet."[13] We are buying American not out of patriotic duty, but because it's become synonymous with craftsmanship, heritage, and economic survival. Major brands like Brooks Brothers and Club Monaco have increased their U.S.-based production, and locally made lines like Pendleton's Portland Collection, Prairie Underground, and Raleigh Denim are big hits with consumers.

In a fascinating twist, many of the garment factories and independent clothing companies reopening in the United States are completely reinventing the apparel trade, focusing on quality, innovation, collaboration, and transparency. In Portland, Oregon, you can walk past the windows of Queen Bee Creations and watch a skilled sewing team cutting and stitching bags and wallets on industrial machines, and then you can buy a bag at the retail store next door. In Brooklyn, a groundbreaking hybrid of a garment factory and studio space for independent designers is scheduled to open before the release of this edition of *Overdressed*. Called Manufacture New York, the facility will house as many as 100 independent fashion designers under the same roof as sewing machine operators, lowering costs for all. Eileen Fisher, owner of the eponymous brand, is looking into owning a factory in the United States as well. Why? Because she wants to create a factory that represents her company's health, education, and profit-sharing values.[14]

We consume differently when we have intimate knowledge of where our stuff comes from. We don't need to make 100 percent of our clothes nearby, but we should aspire to make as much near home as we can. The main benefit is job creation, but the sense of connectedness and responsibility to one another, to our communities, and to our clothing is just as far-reaching.

S ince *Overdressed* was published, I've been thrilled to link up with a growing student movement that is fashionably and committedly green and is showing the rest of us how to do it on the cheap. Thrifting, shopping vintage, DIY fashion, and clothing swaps and sharing clothes are all the rage on campuses. A June 2012 *USA Today College* article described a "thrifting movement" among the university set built on five tenants: "old is new, mixing trumps matching, swapping beats shopping, the best things in life are free (or incredibly cheap), and social responsibility is the new black."[15] In the spring of 2013 I gave a presentation at The George Washington University's annual Trashion show, which features upcycled looks made of, yes, garbage. And while the YouTube shopping hauls I attack in the book are as popular as ever, the video site is now home to more than 245,000 DIY fashion tutorials as well.

Looking back, I probably overemphasized the sew-your-own-clothes approach to ethical fashion. Learning to sew was important for me to reconnect with the value and craftsmanship of clothing, but it is not for everybody and too time intensive for many. These days, I use my sewing machine to refashion and alter t-shirts and thrift-store finds and to customize off-the-rack garments. But I want to clarify that a sewing machine is not a requirement to be a slow-fashion follower.

There's another issue that I'd very much like to clear up. Some readers took away from "The Afterlife of Cheap Clothes" chapter that it's wrong to donate clothes to charities like Goodwill and the Salvation Army. What I had hoped to convey in that chapter is that consumers are too removed from the growing problem of textile waste and that donating clothes does not outweigh the ecological impact of overconsumption. But I should have gone on to say that if you are looking to discard an item of clothing that you aren't going to wear, donating it in good condition to a charity thrift shop is a responsible way to dispose of it.

The reality is that textiles are almost 100 percent reusable or recyclable, and charities are set up to direct even worn, torn, and stained clothes to recyclers or to secondhand clothing dealers—that's a good thing. And no matter what, consumers should not throw clothes away. Only 15 percent of textile waste is currently being recovered for reuse or recycling,[16] and the rest is going into landfills. The last thing I would want readers to think is they might as well just trash their clothes. When I downsized my 354-item wardrobe after writing *Overdressed*, I gave several trash bags of unwanted clothes to the Quincy Street Salvation Army location that I wrote about in the book. That wasn't a proud moment for me: I hope that will be the last time I donate more than an item or two at a time.

As our college trailblazers have figured out, reducing waste and reusing clothing and textiles is a major component of ethical fashion.

In addition to thrift store and consignment shopping, sharing, swapping, and renting clothes, consumers can also resell secondhand apparel on Web sites such as eBay, Etsy, Dresm, or Threadflip. And, increasingly, they can return used clothes to their point of purchase.

In early 2013, H&M joined Patagonia, North Face, and Eileen Fisher in introducing in-store recycling programs for used apparel. The H&M iCollect initiative is a step forward, as any brand of clothing is accepted, but Patagonia is really leading the pack by recycling donations into new collections.[17] The big chains that produce in vast volumes—such as Target, Forever 21, Walmart, Gap, Old Navy, Zara, and UNIQLO—should also rapidly incorporate recycled, recyclable, and biodegradable materials into their products. Levi's, for example, has introduced Waste<Less, a line of recycled polyester jeans. But such innovations need to be applied on a much larger scale and retailers must become more energy and resource efficient—from packaging and shipping to product development to the way stores are run.

S peaking personally, slowing down and changing the way I dressed felt forced at first, both as an idea and as a practice. I was, like so many consumers, addicted to the immediacy of cheap fashion, which offers a quick high with little to no long-term satisfaction. I liken my own transition from fast-fashion to slow-fashion consumer to dieting, as it initially felt a little depriving before it evolved into a fulfilling lifestyle change.

Over the past year I've received a lot of feedback from readers, but the question I get asked the most is: Where do I shop now? Ethical shopping choices expand and become more accessible with each passing day. As I mentioned in the final chapter, there are stores in New York City—such as Brooklyn's Kaight and now Bhoomki—where I'm able to walk in and shop without looking at a single label. Everything is first and foremost fashionable, in addition to being eco-friendly and fairly made or made in the USA. For consumers who don't have access to ethically minded stores, the Internet has quickly filled the void of brick-and-mortar shops. I've compiled a partial list of socially conscious brands under my Shopping Directory on Overdressedthebook.com.

FashioningChange and Modavanti are two online boutiques that are also changing the game. These sites are shoppable by style or cause (eco-friendly, organic, local, fair trade, etc.), but everything is fashion-forward, allowing socially responsible consumers to shop with principles without sacrificing style. On FashioningChange, you select your favorite brand—from Old Navy to Prada—and the site will generate ethical alternatives for you. Many of the offerings are quite affordable, with tops starting at just $28.

I often get asked how the average consumer can afford sustainable fashion. Many people have very tight clothing budgets (myself included), and there are three things I say to this: Buying less costs less. We need to relearn the art of delayed gratification and window-shopping. I try to abide by the give-it-a-week rule before buying new. Only if I'm still thinking about a pair of shoes seven days later will I go back and get them. This requires discipline, but it means saving money and spending money wisely on things I'm actually going to wear. As I've said, thrift stores and swapping with friends and family members are other affordable options.

Second, instead of buying three $20 shirts, I suggest buying one that is durable, beautiful, and carefully made. Most consumers don't realize how much of their money is going into disposable fashion, so they could spend less money over time on clothes by cutting out the cheap impulse buys all altogether and investing in pieces that can be worn season after season.

And finally, now that I've gotten the grandmotherly advice out of the way, I can also honestly say that the price of sustainable fashion is coming down and will continue to come down in the years to come.

The fashion industry is in the midst of a seismic transition. The price of labor in China is up, oil prices are up, and global dynamics are shifting. As sustainability and fair labor become widespread business practices, we'll see fewer retailers putting a premium on green and ethical products or marketing "eco" as a luxury category. As more factories open back up in the United States, garment-related resources will become more commonplace, and the price of production will go down. Ideally, with more middle-class jobs returning, many consumers will have more money in their pockets.

New business models are making quality clothes more affordable. Online-only brands like Everlane are emerging that, by cutting out the middleman (not selling through brick-and-mortar stores, and avoiding a retail markup), can price higher-quality, small-batch clothing more competitively. Designers who collaborate and share resources, such as a group of Brooklyn-based shoemakers who are sharing machinery, are also helping to lower their costs, passing the savings to the consumer.

In the 1960s, animal psychologist Glen Jensen discovered that when given the choice between an unlimited food supply and playing a game to earn their food, most animals chose to earn it.[18] Jensen's discovery seemed to indicate that effort is hardwired, and it revealed a strange truth that trying feels better than just taking what's right under our noses.

Jensen's experiments reveal the paradox of our fast-fashion society: We can keep chasing the fleeting high of new possessions, or we can see what happens if instead we slow down, get connected, share, and get creative with what we already own. I still believe our most rewarding experiences with clothes have nothing to do with walking into a store or spending money.

When I finished writing *Overdressed* in January 2012, I still owned and wore most of the same cheap, trendy duds that inspired me to write the book. I now possess about 90 items of clothing, down from the 354 I piled up in my living room in the Introduction. My closet is almost a third full of thrift store and vintage finds (an Italian wool blazer from Goodwill and a polka-dot silk blouse from a Lower East Side vintage shop are among my favorites), as well as nine garments from trades with friends or that were passed down to me from my family. I have a grand total of two shirts I made from scratch (I recently wore a home-sewn lavender knit top on a date). I've also held onto about two dozen items I already owned (yes, I even donned an eight-year-old H&M dress to a wedding this past summer).

My new, store-bought items are my statement pieces, the things I have to drool over before I'll open my wallet and take them home, such as a lipstick red silk dress by STATE and a canary yellow sleeveless top by Carrie Parry made of eco-friendly Tencel. I've also invested in three high-quality suiting pieces, including an American-made, silk-lined blazer that still has the tags on (lest I need to sell it to pay my rent).

My closet isn't perfect. It takes time to build a wardrobe and cultivate a personal style. It's a journey I'll be on for years to come. I feel so fortunate that through the process of writing the book I gained a passion for clothes and an interest in being well dressed. I spend a lot of time working with the pieces I own, trying them on and creating and planning outfits. Having the right thing to wear makes life easier and turns out to be a great self-confidence booster as well.

UK-based slow-fashion guru Kate Fletcher studies how consumers creatively use the clothing that they already own. She calls this habit the "craft of use," identifying it as a skill in and of itself. "Most of us are familiar with—and highly prize—the craft or expert skill of making things, like garments," writes Fletcher on her Web site.[19] But it also takes "skill, ingenuity and requires practice" to perfect using the clothes in our closet. This is such a wonderful and affirming description of building a wardrobe: Through constant and impassioned tinkering and customizing, you get it just the way you like it.

My grandmother and I recently went through her closet together. I said, "Grams, you don't wear your silk blouses from the '80s anymore; would you give them to me"? I love silk, shoulder pads, and boxy cuts—a pricey combination bought off the rack. We held an impromptu fashion show in her bedroom before I took home two tops, one blush-pink and the other hot pink, and went on to tweak them with a pair of scissors and my sewing machine. I wore the blush-pink one, sleeves tacked up, to do three different lectures this past winter. It's moments like these when I'm reminded how slow fashion is a mental and qualitative transformation as much as anything else.

The transformation is different for every consumer. There are so many different components of ethical fashion, which translates into just as many ways for people to personalize the movement and get involved. Maybe your thing is DIY style, clothing swaps, and vintage fashion, or maybe it's luxurious eco-textiles, buying American, and supporting indie designers. Maybe you want to own a factory or start a tailor shop or invent then next low-impact dyeing process. The point is, have fun with it and explore.

I think we're all headed in the right direction if we keep these simple principles in mind: Buy clothes you truly love. Don't buy too much. And get the most out of what you wear. In other words, it's become clearer to me that where you shop is less important than how you shop.

Elizabeth Cline
June 11, 2013

Acknowledgments

Thank you to my father, who gave me intellectual curiosity and confidence in my ideas, and to my mother, who showed me that the ultimate life experience is in seeing meaningful projects through to their completion. To my sister, Ginger, thank you for being my first fan—by telling me that you couldn't wait to read my book. I hope it satisfies. To my agent, Larry Weissman, thank you for making this opportunity possible and for helping me sharpen my thinking. A big thanks to everyone at Portfolio, including Adrian Zackheim, Amanda Pritzker, Christine D'Agostini, Eric Meyers, Brooke Carey, and especially my editor Courtney Young. To my former professors Donald Morton and Mas'ud Zavarzadeh, you convinced me that economics are at the root of all social phenomena. Fashion is no exception. To my entire family, you are smart, amazing, and showed me a life outside of tradition. Without you, I would not have courage. To my close friends Katrina and Keri and my bandmates Lesley and Caryn, thank you for your patience and support through this process. Eliza Starbuck, you were an invaluable resource, an inspiration, and a kindred spirit. Thank you to Jared Butler, George Gladstone at UNIS, Olean Kiker, Petra Langerova, Joann Lo, Michelle Mojica, Sally Rumble, Laura Severino, Judith Schwantes at the Fashion Institute of Technology, Kelsey Timmerman, and Jan Whitaker for your time, ideas, and resources. A big thanks to my readers Sascha Alper, Amos Barshad, William Johnson, Carolyn Murnick, and Megan Reid. A special thanks to the staff of

Alta Gracia and Sarah Adler-Milstein for opening their lives and their workplaces up to me and to Dalton Zahir for being such a gracious host in Bangladesh. Thank you to everyone else in the garment and textile industries who took the time to educate me and show me a piece of your essential and vibrant trade. I'm lucky to know you all.

Notes

Introduction: Seven Pairs of $7 Shoes

1. "Trends: An Annual Statistical Analysis of the U.S. Apparel & Footwear Industries," Annual 2008 Edition, American Apparel and Footwear Association.
2. Ibid.
3. "Outlet Stores: Where to Shop & How to Save Big Bucks." *Consumer Reports*, May 2006.
4. Stan Cox, "Dress for Excess: The Cost of Our Clothing Addiction," November 30, 2007, www.alternet.org/environment/69256.

Chapter 1: "I Have Enough Clothing to Open a Store"

1. Mark J. Perry, "Apparel Spending as a Share of Disposable Income: Lowest in U.S. History," March 21, 2010, http://seekingalpha.com/article/194764-apparel-spending-as-a-share-of-disposable-income-lowest-in-u-s-history.
2. Andrea Chang, "Teen 'Haulers' Become a Fashion Force," *The Los Angeles Times*, August 1, 2010.
3. William Meyers, "Retailers Buy Their Own Brands: A Trend Toward Private-Label Goods Leaves Vendors in the Cold," *Adweek*, December 15, 1986.
4. Isadore Barmash, "Gap Finds Middle Road to Success," *The New York Times*, June 24, 1991.
5. "The Gap Inc.: Company History" www.fundinguniverse.com/company-histories/the-gap-inc-history.html.
6. The First Thanksgiving, "Daily Life: Clothes," Scholastic.com, www.scholastic.com/scholastic_thanksgiving/daily_life/clothes.htm.
7. Jan Whitaker, *Service and Style: How the American Department Store Fashioned the Middle Class* (New York: St. Martin's Press, 2006), 55, 66.
8. Neil Reynolds, "Goodwill May be Stunting African Growth," *Globe and Mail* (Toronto), December 24, 2008.
9. Christopher Solomon, "The Swelling McMansion Backlash," MSN.com, http://realestate.msn.com/article.aspx?cp-documentid=13107733.

10. Bureau of Labor Statistics, *Consumer Expenditures 2010,* www.bls
    .gov/news.release/cesan.nr0.htm.
11. Eben Shapiro, "Few Riches in Rags These Days," *The New York
    Times,* January 5, 1991.
12. "Corporations: Jumpers at Jonathan Logan," *Time,* August 31, 1962.
13. Mark Miller, Jerry Adler, with Daniel McGinn, "Isaac Hits His Tar-
    get," *Newsweek,* October 27, 2003.
14. Teri Agins, *The End of Fashion: How Marketing Changed the Cloth-
    ing Business Forever* (NY: William Morrow and Company, 1999),
    187.
15. Isadore Barmash, "A Revolution in American Shopping," *The New
    York Times,* October 23, 1983.
16. Bruce Horovitz and Lorrie Grant, "Changes in Store for Depart-
    ment Stores?" *USA Today,* January 21, 2005.
17. Agins, *The End of Fashion,* 166.
18. Alice Z. Cuneo, "Gap Floats Lower-Priced Old Navy Stores," *Ad-
    vertising Age,* July 25, 1994.
19. Michael McCarthy and Stephen Levine, "Old Navy Pits 2 Shops
    Against Each Other," *Adweek,* March 17, 1997.
20. Mark Albright, "Dayton Hudson on Target with New Retail Strat-
    egy," *St. Petersburg Times* (Florida), June 23, 1991.
21. Eric Wilson, "Dress for Less and Less," *The New York Times,* May
    29, 2008.
22. Marina Strauss, "H&M Seeks High Profits from Low Prices," *The
    Globe and Mail* (Toronto), September 29, 2004.
23. Eric Wilson, "Is This the World's Cheapest Dress?" *The New York
    Times,* May 1, 2008.

Chapter 2: How America Lost Its Shirts

1. Toon Von Beeck, "Ten Key Industries that Will Decline, Even After
   the Economy Revives," *Commercial Insights,* IBISWorld, May 2011,
   www.ibisworld.com/Common/MediaCenter/Dying%20Industries
   .pdf.
2. Standard & Poor's Industry Surveys, *Apparel & Footwear: Retailers
   & Brands,* January 2011.
3. "Made in Midtown?" madeinmidtown.org, accessed November 11,
   2011.
4. "Struggling to Stitch," *The New York Times,* Video Library, March 21,
   2011, http://video.nytimes.com/video/2011/03/21/nyregion/1000000
   00735431/garmentlabor.html.
5. Anne D'Innocenzio, "Do the Math: Prices on Fall Clothes Up, Despite Gimmicks," *The Washington Post,* August 20, 2011.

6. Vikas Bajaj, "As Labor Costs Rise in China, Textile Jobs Shift Elsewhere," *The New York Times*, July 17, 2010.

7. Christina Binkley, "How Can Jeans Cost $300?: Shoppers Shell Out More for Designer Denim, Lured by Signature Details, 'Made in America,'" *The Wall Street Journal*, July 7, 2011.

8. Alana Semuels, "L.A.'s Garment Industry Goes from Riches to Rags," *The Los Angeles Times*, October 9, 2009.

9. Leslie Earnest, "Forever 21 Settles Dispute with Garment Workers," *The Los Angeles Times*, December 15, 2004.

10. Ari Paul, "Wolf in Sheep's Clothing: Sexist Antics and Union-busting Cast Doubt on American Apparel's Progressive Cred," *In These Times*, August 4, 2005, Web only feature, www.inthesetimes .com/article/2270.

11. Mark Mittelhuasuer, "Employment Trends in Textiles and Apparel, 1973–2005," *Monthly Labor Review*, August 1997.

12. United States Department of Labor, Bureau of Labor Statistics, Textile mills workforce statistics, www.bls.gov/iag/tgs/iag313.htm#workforce.

13. Stephen MacDonald and Thomas Vollrath, United States Department of Agriculture, "The Forces Shaping World Cotton Consumption After the Multifiber Arrangement," *Cotton and Wool Outlook*, Economic Research Service, online newsletter, April 2005.

14. Michelle Lee, *Fashion Victim: Our Love-Hate Relationship With Dressing, Shopping, and the Cost of Style* (New York: Broadway Books, 2003), 183.

15. Amy Kaslow, "The Price of Low-Cost Clothes: US Jobs," *Christian Science Monitor*, August 29, 1995.

16. T. A. Frank, "Confessions of a Sweatshop Inspector," *Washington Monthly*, April 2008.

17. Kaslow, "The Price of Low-Cost Clothes."

18. Edna Bonacich and Richard P. Appelbaum, *Behind the Label: Inequality in the Los Angeles Apparel Industry* (London: University of California Press, 2000), 262.

19. Ibid., 66.

20. Michael F. Martin, Congressional Research Service Report for Congress, "U.S. Clothing and Textile Trade with China and the World: Trends Since the End of Quotas," July 10, 2007.

21. Elizabeth Becker, "U.S. Puts Limits on Clothing from China," *The New York Times*, May 4, 2005.

22. Tiffany Hsu, "Trade Deficit with China Cost Nearly 2.8 Million U.S. Jobs Since 2001," *The Los Angeles Times*, Money & Company Blog, September 22, 2011, http://latimesblogs.latimes.com/money_co/2011 /09/trade-deficit-with-china-cost-nearly-28-million-us-jobs-since -2001.html.

23. Michael Lu, "New Job Means Lower Wages for Many, Studies Find," *The New York Times*, August 31, 2010.

24. Valli Herman, "With Robinsons-May Stores Closing, Few Midrange Department Stores Are Left. Is Shopping Becoming Polarized? Yes, and No." *The Los Angeles Times*, August 6, 2005.

Chapter 3: High and Low Fashion Make Friends

1. "Comments of Prof. Kal Raustiala (University of California at Los Angeles School of Law) and Prof. Christopher Sprigman (University of Virginia School of Law), Re: Innovative Design Protection and Piracy Prevention Act," Submitted July 13, 2011, to the Committee on the Judiciary, U.S. House of Representatives, Subcommittee on Intellectual Property, Competition and the Internet; data drawn from a table from data from the U.S. Bureau of Labor Statistics.

2. Agins, *The End of Fashion*, 214.

3. Hitha Prabhakar, "Price of Admission," *Forbes*, February 2, 2007.

4. Ibid.

5. Information about how Wall Street changed fashion in the 1990s is from Teri Agins's book *The End of Fashion*.

6. Dana Thomas, *Deluxe: How Luxury Lost Its Luster* (New York: The Penguin Press, 2007), 168.

7. Ibid., 51.

8. Ibid., 192.

9. CNN Live, September 14, 2011.

10. Stephen Todd, "Le Cheap, C'est Chic; Why Would the Designer of Chanel and Fendi Agree to Work for H&M?" *The Independent* (London); October 14, 2004.

11. Ibid.

12. Armorel Kenna, "H&M Looks to Lanvin to Bring Back Lagerfeld Effect," *Bloomberg Businessweek*, November 19, 2010.

13. Missoni Fashion Label Profile, 5 Min Media Life Videopedia, online video, www.5min.com/video/missoni-fashion-label-profile-284064055.

14. Adrienne Royer, "Missoni for Target: Is the Hype Worth the Quality," *BlogHer*, posted September 12, 2011, www.blogher.com/missoni-target-hype-worth-quality.

15. John Colapinto, "Just Have Less," *The New Yorker*, January 3, 2011.

16. John Duka, "A Farsighted Man of Fashion Steps Down," *The New York Times*, September 8, 1981.

17. Agins, *The End of Fashion*, 12.

18. "Shopping: The Rich and the Rest," *Time*, October 10, 2011.

19. Jeffrey D. Sachs, "Why America Must Revive Its Middle Class," *Time*, October 10, 2011.

20. Rachel Brown, Emili Vesilind, and Khanh T. L. Tran, "Price Insen-

sitivity: Contemporary Designers Continue to Buy, Regardless of Cost," *Women's Wear Daily*, March 8, 2007.

21. Ibid.
22. Whitaker, *Service and Style*, 66.
23. Lauren Sherman, "The Cult of Couture," *Forbes*, June 28, 2006.
24. For background on the history of early couture, see Gavin Waddell, *How Fashion Works* (Oxford: Blackwell Science Ltd, 2004), 94.
25. Whitaker, *Service and Style*, 55.
26. Ibid., 41.
27. Standard & Poor's Industry Survey, 1955.
28. Whitaker, *Service and Style*, 66.
29. Rachel Worth, *Fashion for the People: The History of Clothing at Marks & Spencer* (London: Berg, 2007), 50.
30. *The Fiber Year 2009/2010: A World Survey on Textile and Nonwovens Industry* (Oerlikon, May 2010), 92.
31. "Recycled Polyester," *Textile Exchange*, http://textileexchange.org/node/959.
32. John Luke, "A Polyester Saga Geography And All," *Textile World*, September 2004, www.textileworld.com/Articles/2004/September/Fiber_World/A_Polyester_Saga_Geography_And_All.html. Updated figures are from the Oerlikon Fiber Year report.
33. Agins, *The End of Fashion*, 12.
34. Teri Agins, "Why Cheap Clothes Are Getting Respect," *The Globe and Mail* (Toronto), November 9, 1995.
35. Leslie Kaufman with Laura Duncan Gatland and Adrian Maher, "Downscale Moves Up," *Newsweek*, July 27, 1998.
36. Whitaker, *Service and Style*, 70.
37. Todd, "Le Cheap, C'est Chic."

Chapter 4: Fast Fashion

1. Rachel Dodes, "Penney Weaves New Fast-Fashion Line," *The Wall Street Journal*, August 11, 2010.
2. Rana Foroohar, "A New Fashion Frontier: The Arrival of Fast Fashion European Giants Is Starting to Shake up the American Retail Scene," *Newsweek*, March 20, 2006.
3. Ibid.
4. Nancy M. Funk, "Retailers Keep Fingers Crossed On Leaner Holiday Inventories," *The Morning Call*, December 18, 1988.
5. Stryker McGuire with Anna Kuchment, Mar Roman, Leila Moseley, and Dana Thomas, "Fast Fashion," *Newsweek*, September 17, 2001.
6. Stephanie Strom, "U.S. Garment Makers Come Home," *The New York Times*, October 8, 1991.

7. Kasra Ferdows, Michael A. Lewis, and Jose A. D. Machuca, "Rapid-Fire Fulfillment," *Harvard Business Review* 82, no. 11, November 2004.

8. Ibid.

9. Ruth La Ferla, "Faster Fashion, Cheaper Chic," *The New York Times*, May 10, 2007.

10. Ferdows, Lewis, and Machuca, "Rapid-Fire Fulfillment."

11. Liz Barnes and Gaynor Lea-Greenwood, "Fast Fashioning the Supply Chain: Shaping the Research Agenda," *Journal of Fashion Marketing and Management* 10 (3): 259–71.

12. Håcan Andersson, H&M Press Officer, e-mail to author, April 19, 2011.

13. Maxine Firth, "M&S Used to Be the Biggest Initials on the High Street...Make Way for H&M," *The Independent*, November 18, 2004.

14. Graham Keeley, "Conquistador Who Took on the World of Fast Fashion and Won," *Times* (London), April 1, 2011.

15. "Fast-fashion Chains Thriving," *Nikkei Weekly* (Japan), November 16, 2009.

16. Lynn Yaeger, "Do I Get a Coffee? A Snack? Or Something to Wear? The H&M $4.95 Dress," *Vogue Daily*, vogue.com, last modified August 19, 2010.

17. Eva Wiseman, "The Gospel According to Forever 21," *The Observer*, July 16, 2011.

18. Leah Bourne, "H&M's Head of Design Ann-Sofie Johansson on Sustainable Fashion and Managing a Team of 140," *Thread New York*, www.nbcnewyork.com/blogs/threadny.

19. Julian Lee, "Buckle Up, Fast Fashion Is Here," *Sydney Morning Herald*, April 16, 2011.

20. Craig Lambert, "Real Fashion Police: Copyrighting Clothing," *Harvard Magazine*, July–August 2010.

21. La Ferla, "Faster Fashion, Cheaper Chic."

22. Wiseman, "The Gospel According to Forever 21."

23. Jenna Sauers, "How Forever 21 Keeps Getting Away with Designer Knockoffs," Jezebel.com, July 20, 2011.

24. Sarah Raper Larenaudie, "Inside the H&M Fashion Machine," *Time*, February 16, 2004.

25. Norman Lear, Laurie Racine, Tom Ford, and Guy Trebay, "The Ecology of Creativity in Fashion," Ready to Share: Fashion & the Ownership of Creativity, a Norman Lear Center conference, USC Annenberg School for Communication, January 29, 2005.

26. Agins, *The End of Fashion*, 24.

27. Izzy Grinspan, "Ever-Slippery Forever 21 Settles with Trovata,"

Racked.com, October 12, 2009, http://ny.racked.com/archives/2009/10/ 12/lawsuits_forever_21_keeps_perfect_record_settle_with_trovata.php.

28. Raustiala and Sprigman, "Innovative Design Protection."
29. Yaeger, "Do I Get a Coffee?"
30. Binkley, "How Can Jeans Cost $300?"
31. Suzy Menkes, "Galliano's Departure from Dior Ends a Wild Fashion Ride," *The New York Times*, March 1, 2011.
32. Barnes and Lea-Greenwood, "Fast Fashioning the Supply Chain."
33. Arianne Cohen, "A Clothing Store: H&M Flagship," *New York Magazine*, June 3, 2007.

Chapter 5: The Afterlife of Cheap Clothes

1. "Jeaneology: ShopSmart Poll Finds Women Own 7 Pairs of Jeans, Only Wear 4," PR Newswire, www.prnewswire.com/news-releases /jeaneology-shopsmart-poll-finds-women-own-7-pairs-of-jeans -only-wear-4-98274009.html.
2. "A Closet Obsession," *Time*, October 24, 2005.
3. Jana Hawley, "Sustainable Fashion: Why now? A Conversation Exploring Issues, Practices, and Possibilities," *Economic Impact of Textile and Clothing Recycling* (New York: Fairchild Books, 2008): 207–32.
4. "Avtex Fibers, Inc.," Mid-Atlanta Superfund, U.S. Environmental Protection Agency, www.epa.gov/reg3hwmd/npl/VAD070358684.htm.
5. Thomas Olson, "China Poised to Take Manufacturing Crown," *Pittsburgh Tribune-Review*, July 18, 2010.
6. Lucy Siegle, *To Die For: Is Fashion Wearing Out the World?* (London: Fourth Estate, 2011), 117.
7. Stan Cox, "Dress for Excess: The Cost of Our Clothing Addiction," November 30, 2007, altnernet.org.
8. For an exhaustive look at the environmental impact of textile production, see the chapter "Fashion's Footprint" in Siegle, *To Die For*, 103–22.
9. Ibid., 105. "To get that eighty billion kilograms of fabric into shape takes 1,074 billion kilowatt hours of electricity, for which we need 132 million tonnes of coal and somewhere between six and nine trillion litres of water." (Converted to U.S. imperial figures.)
10. Karen Tranberg Hansen, "Secondhand Clothing," *Berg Encyclopedia of World Dress and Fashion*, vol. 10 (London: Berg Publishers, 2010), www.bergfashionlibrary.com/view/bewdf/BEWDF-v10/ED ch10032.xml.
11. Hansen, "Secondhand Clothing."

12. "Your Donations and Purchases Change Lives," Goodwill Industries, www.meetgoodwill.org/about/statistics.

13. Randy Cohen, "His and Not Hers," *The New York Times*, June 10, 2007.

14. "Use of Shoddy Is Greatest in America," *The New York Times*, July 10, 1904.

15. For figures on the fiber and wiping rag market, see the SMART Media Kit, www.smartasn.org/about/SMART_PressKitOnline.pdf.

16. Siegle, *To Die For*, 222.

17. Jacqueline L. Salmon, "Goodwill Shutting Down Some Area Thrift Shops: Sinking Quality Hurting Bottom Line," *The Washington Post*, April 12, 2002.

18. Hansen, "Secondhand Clothing."

19. Ibid.

20. This statistic comes from an industry insider, 2004, told to Jana Hawley, "Economic Impact of Textile and Clothing Recycling," 225.

21. Siegle, *To Die For*, 217.

22. Hawley, "Economic Impact of Textile and Clothing Recyling," 228.

23. Siegle, *To Die For*, 226.

Chapter 6: Sewing Is a Good Job, a Great Job

1. For a broader understanding of how the Workers Rights Consortium calculates their living wage, see "WRC: Living Wage Analysis for the Dominican Republic," www.workersrights.org/linkeddocs/WRC%20Living%20Wage%20Analysis%20for%20the%20Dominican%20Republic.pdf.

2. Alexandra Harney, *The China Price: The True Cost of Chinese Competitive Advantage* (New York: Penguin Books, 2009), 40.

3. Bob Egelko, "Wal-Mart not responsible for factory conditions," *SF Gate*, July 11, 2009.

4. Siegle, *To Die For*, 68.

5. Nikki F. Bas, "Saipan Sweatshop Lawsuit Ends with Important Gains for Workers and Lessons for Activists," Clean Clothes Campaign, press release dated January 8, 2004, www.cleanclothes.org/newslist/617.

6. Barnes and Lea-Greenwood, "Fast Fashioning the Supply Chain."

7. T. A. Frank, "Confessions of a Sweatshop Inspector," *Washington Monthly*, April 2008.

8. Harney, *The China Price*, 53.

9. Anna McMullen and Sam Maher, "Let's Clean Up Fashion 2009" (Labour Behind the Label, April 2009).

10. For more information on subcontracting and Chinese "shadow factories," see *The China Price*, "The Five-Star Factory," 33–55.

11. Ibid.
12. Frank, "Confessions of a Sweatshop Monitor."
13. "Non-Poverty Wages for Countries Around the World," see the 2007/2008 table, www.sweatfree.org/nonpovertywages.
14. McMullen and Maher, "Let's Clean Up Fashion," 2009.
15. Labour Behind the Label interview with M. K. Shefali, executive director of Nari Uddug Kendra, www.labourbehindthelabel.org/news /item/523-how-low-can-you-go?-support-minimimum-wage -increase-in-bangladesh.
16. For a history of the BJ&B factory case, see the UK-based No Sweat campaign Web site: www.nosweat.org.uk/story/2007/03/20/bjb-gar ments-closure-threat.
17. Simon Clark, "A Furor over Fair Trade: An American Certifier of Fair-trade Goods Leaves the Mother Sship, and Purists are Appalled," *Bloomberg Businessweek*, November 3, 2011.
18. Peter Dreier, "NPR Debate Moderators All Wet On Sweatshop Labor," *Huffington Post*, December 6, 2007.
19. Dreier, "NPR Debate Moderators All Wet On Sweatshop Labor."

Chapter 7: China and the End of Cheap Fashion

1. Michael Wei and Luzi Ann Javier, "Gap, Wal-Mart Clothing Costs Rise on 'Terrifying' Cotton Prices," *Bloomberg News*, November 15, 2010.
2. Liu Shiying and Martha Avery, *Alibaba: The Inside Story Behind Jack Ma and the Creation of the World's Biggest Online Marketplace* (New York: CollinsBusiness, 2009).
3. "China Still Shines: Each Day, More Countries Are Trying to Replace Economic Powerhouse China as the Main Sourcing Point for Consumer Goods Companies," *National Post*, November 1, 2011.
4. Jon Hilsenrath, Laurie Burkitt, and Elizabeth Holmes, "Change in China Hits U.S. Purse," *The Wall Street Journal*, June 21, 2011.
5. Clay Boswell, "Garment Makers Feel the Heat: Textile Manufacturing Has Provided Much of the Thrust Behind China's Ascent as an Economic Powerhouse, but Changing Priorities Could Require Throttling Back," *ICIS Chemical Business*, October 31, 2011.
6. Keith Bradsher, "Wages Up in China as Young Workers Grow Scarce," *The New York Times*, August 29, 2007.
7. Harney, *The China Price*, 8.
8. Keith Bradsher, "Chinese Exports Surge, and Prices Rise; Trade Surplus Widens to $11.43 Billion, Raising Concerns in United States," *International Herald Tribune*, May 11, 2011.
9. Keith Bradsher, "As China's Workers Get a Raise, Companies Fret," *The New York Times*, May 31, 2011.

10. Harney, *The China Price*, 15.
11. Zhang Haizhou, "From Manufacturing Hub to Fashion Capital," Chinadaily.com.cn, September 21, 2011.
12. George Wehrfritz and Alexandra A. Seno, "Succeeding at Sewing," *Newsweek*, January 10, 2005.
13. Standard & Poor's January 2011 Industry Surveys, Apparel & Footwear: Retailers & Brands.
14. For a more in-depth discussion of China's manufacturing clusters, see Harney, *The China Price*, 9–10.
15. David Barboza, "In Roaring China, Sweaters Are West of Socks City," *The New York Times*, December 24, 2004.
16. Victoria de Grazia, *Irresistible Empire: America's Advance Through Twentieth-Century Fashion* (Cambridge, MA: The Belknap Press, 2006), 11, 131.
17. David Barboza, "China Turns into a Stage for Designer's Second Act," *International Herald Tribune*, December 18, 2010.
18. Caroline Wheeler, " 'Made in China' Labels Go Chic: Homegrown Firms Trying to Wean Wealthy Young Trend-setters off Hot Foreign Brands," *The Globe and Mail* (Toronto), June 7, 2011.
19. Jon Hilsenrath, Laurie Burkitt, and Elizabeth Holmes, "Change in China Hits U.S. Purse," *The Wall Street Journal*, June 21, 2011.
20. *The Fiber Year 2009/2010*, 37.
21. Wheeler, " 'Made in China' Labels Go Chic."
22. Leslie T. Chang, *Factory Girls: From Village to City in a Changing China* (New York: Spiegel & Grau, 2008), 19.
23. "Two Sides to the Boom in China Textile Towns," *South China Morning Post*, February 16, 2005. Converted from yuan.
24. Jim Boyd, "In record time, Economic Boom Hits Guangdong," *Minneapolis Star Tribune*, February 6, 1995.
25. Harney, *The China Price*, 157.
26. Tiffany Hsu, "Trade Deficit with China Cost Nearly 2.8 Million U.S. Jobs Since 2001," *The Los Angeles Times*, *Money & Company* blog, September 22, 2011, http://latimesblogs.latimes.com/money_co/20 11/09/trade-deficit-with-china-cost-nearly-28-million-us-jobs -since-2001.html.
27. "Falling Through the Floor: Women Workers' Quest For Decent Work in Dongguan, China," *China Labour Bulletin*, Hong Kong, September 2006. Converted at 2011 rates, 10 to 80 yuan is $1.50 to $12.50.
28. For a gripping and exhaustively researched look at the lives of China's factory workers, see Chang's *Factory Girls*.
29. Bradsher, "As China's Workers Get a Raise, Companies Fret."
30. Ibid.
31. Julian M. Allwood, Søren Ellebæk Laursen, Cecilia Malvido de

Rodríguez, and Nancy M. P. Bocken, *Well Dressed? The Present and Future Sustainability of Clothing and Textiles in the United Kingdom* (University of Cambridge Institute for Manufacturing, 2006), 59.

32. Syed Tashfin Chowdhury, "Bangladesh Gears Up for Knitwear Export Boom," *South Asia Times*, December 23, 2010.
33. Bradsher, "Chinese Exports Surge."
34. D'Innocenzio, "Do the Math."
35. Yaeger, "Do I Get a Coffee?"
36. "H&M Profits Fall Again on Higher Materials and Wages," BBC .com, June 22, 2011, www.bbc.co.uk/news/business-13872449.

Chapter 8: Make, Alter, and Mend

1. "History of the Sewing Machine," Museum of American Heritage, www.moah.org/exhibits/virtual/sewing.htm.
2. Ibid.
3. Ibid.
4. Whitaker, *Service and Style*, 56.
5. Anita Hamilton, "Circling Back to Sewing," *Time*, November 27, 2006.
6. Juliet Schor and Betsy Taylor, *Sustainable Planet: Solutions for the 21st Century* (Boston: Beacon Press, 2003).

Chapter 9: The Future of Fashion

1. Abigail Doan, "Sustainable Style: Plastic Fantastic 'Melissa Shoes,'" March 2, 2008, http://inhabitat.com/sustainable-style-plastic-fantastic -melissa-shoes.
2. Booth Moore, "Essential Elements; Keeping It Local: More Clothing Makers Are Producing in the U.S. Again, Finding the Investment Pays Off," *The Los Angeles Times*, June 19, 2011.
3. Ibid.
4. "'Made in America' series begins on ABC News," abc7.com, March 1, 2011, http://abclocal.go.com/kabc/story?section=news/national_ world&id=7988789, accessed November 12, 2011.

Afterword to the Paperback Edition

1. "We Wear Our Mission," A 2011 online report by the American Apparel & Footwear Association, accessed March 13, 2013, https://www .wewear.org/industry-resources/we-wear-our-mission/.
2. The 1991 figures are based on Juliet B. Schor's research in *Plenitude: The New Economics of True Wealth* (New York: The Penguin Press, 2010), 29, which says Americans "bought an average of thirty-four"

items of clothes; the 2011 figures are from the American Apparel & Footwear Association, which says "American spent more than $1,100 on 68 new garments and seven pairs of shoes" in 2011.

3. Council for Textile Recycling, "The Facts About Textile Waste," based on 2009 EPA figures, accessed March 13, 2013, www.weardo naterecycle.org/about/issue.html.

4. Krista Mahr, "Bangladesh Factory Collapse: Uncertain Future for Rana Plaza Survivors," *Time*, June 10, 2013, http://world.time .com/2013/06/10/bangladesh-factory-collapse-uncertain-future-for-rana-plaza-survivors/.

5. Keith Bradsher, "After Bangladesh, Seeking New Sources," *The New York Times*, May 15, 2013, www.nytimes.com/2013/05/16/ business/global/after-bangladesh-seeking-new-sources. html?pagewanted=all&_r=0.

6. Ann Zimmerman and Neil Shah, "American Taste for Cheap Clothes Fed Bangladesh Boom," *The Wall Street Journal*, May 12, 2013, http://online.wsj.com/article/SB100014241278873240597045784755 81983412950.html.

7. Four million garment workers is a 2010–2011 figure from "Number of Employment in Garment," Bangladesh Garment Manufacturers and Exporters Association, www.bgmea.com.bd/.

8. Stephanie Clifford, "Some Retailers Say More About Their Clothing's Origins," *The New York Times*, May 8, 2013, www .nytimes.com/2013/05/09/business/global/fair-trade-movement-extends-to-clothing.html?pagewanted=all.

9. Worker Rights Consortium press release, "Worker Rights Consortium Decries Latest Garment Factory Disaster in Bangladesh, Calls on Brands and Retailers to Sign Binding Building Safety Agreement and 'Put an End to this Parade of Horror,'" April 24, 2013.

10. For an updated list of brands who've signed onto Greenpeace's Detox Campaign, visit www.greenpeace.org/international/en/campaigns/toxics/water/detox/Detox-Timeline/.

11. Jessica Iredale, "Holmes & Yang: Away from the Circus," *Women's Wear Daily*, February 8, 2013.

12. Charles Fishman, "The Insourcing Boom," *The Atlantic*, December 2012, www.theatlantic.com/magazine/archive/2012/12/the-insourcing -boom/309166/.

13. Alex Williams, "A Label That Has Regained Its Luster," *The New York Times*, September 14, 2012, www.nytimes.com/2012/09/16/fash ion/made-in-the-usa-has-a-new-meaning.html.

14. Claire Whitcomb, "Conversations on China," &, Issue 2, Spring 2013, http://eileenfisherampersand.com/Conversations-on-China.

15. Dan Reimold, "Student clothing swaps, thrifting soar in popularity,"

USA Today College, June 11, 2012, www.usatodayeducate.com/stag ing/index.php/campus-beat/student-clothing-swaps-thrifting-soar -in-popularity.

16. Council for Textile Recycling, "The Facts About Textile Waste."
17. Patagonia's Common Threads Partnership allows consumers to return any Patagonia product for reuse or recycling into a new fabric or product. More information is available at www.patagonia.com/ us/common-threads/recycle?src=vty_recyc.
18. For more on Jensen's experiments, read Dan Ariely, *The Upside of Irrationality: The Unexpected Benefits of Defying Logic at Work and at Home* (New York: HarperCollins, 2010), 58–62.
19. Kate Fletcher, "Local Wisdom," accessed March 13, 2013, http://kate fletcher.com/projects/local-wisdom/.

Index

Abercrombie & Fitch, 18, 91, 146, 185
Adweek, 18
Aéropostale, 23–24, 189
Africa, 135–36
Agins, Teri, 28, 66, 67
Alibaba, 163–64, 168, 181
Alice + Olivia, 114
Alta Gracia, 138–42, 151, 153–59, 216
American Apparel, 13, 47–48, 205
American Eagle Outfitters, 18, 79, 141
American Gigolo, 65
American Journal of Sociology, 115
Ann Taylor, 149, 165
Appelbaum, Richard P., 54
Armani, Giorgio, 65
Arnault, Bernard, 67
As Is, 208

Babies "R" Us, 59
Ballinger, Jeff, 159–60
Banana Republic, 23, 52, 146
Bangladesh, 180–85
    garment factory fire in, 224
    textile industry in, 40–41, 43, 52, 123,
        145, 148–53, 165, 181–85
Barneys, 75
Baros, Dianna, 32, 34, 65–66
Basora, Gaby, 114
Beaumont, Sarah Kate, 187–91, 194–
        200, 206
bebe, 96
*Behind the Label: Inequality in the
        Los Angeles Apparel Industry*
        (Appelbaum and Bonacich), 54
Belk, 25

Bereket, Sara, 112–13, 134, 201–2, 206
Bergdorf Goodman, 62, 71–76, 109
Bernhard, Sandra, 19
BETC Luxe, 68
BJ&B, 154–55, 156
Blass, Bill, 39
Bobbie Brooks, 23, 29, 75
Bodkin, 114, 209
Bolton, Lisa, 24–25, 29
Bonacich, Edna, 54
Bonwit Teller, 93
Bottega Veneta, 72, 93–94
Bozich, Joseph, 157
Bright Young Things, 60–61, 89, 204–5,
        212
Brooks Brothers, 146
Bryant, Janie, 86
Budget Babe, The, 32, 34, 65–66
Budget Fashionista, The, 34

California Fashion Association, 17, 45,
        213
Calvin Klein, 17, 66, 112, 141, 146, 182
Cambodia, 165, 180, 184
Castro, Gemma, 141
Cato, 2, 92
*Celebration of Fools: An Inside Look at
        the Rise and Fall of JCPenney*
        (Hare), 95
Céline, 106, 110
Chanel, 63, 70, 71
Chanel, Gabrielle "Coco," 80
Chang, Do Won "Don," 104
Chang, Jin Sook, 104, 107
Chapman, Norman, 49, 50

charity thrift stores, 9–10, 119–21, 126–
    28, 130–32, 136–37, 188–89, 199, 204
Charlotte Russe, 2, 22, 96, 106
Chico's, 96–97
China, 3, 55, 125, 161–86, 213
    fashion in, 171–73
    garment factories in, 3, 6, 23, 43, 52,
        74, 91, 150, 161–67, 169–71, 173–80,
        213
    Guangdong Province, 123, 124, 167–
        70, 172–74, 180, 183
    labor pool in, 167
    Shenzhen, 123, 164, 168–69, 171, 174–
        77
    textile factories in, 123–24, 165
China Price, The (Harney), 168
Chinese Labor Bureau, 178
Christian Dior, 67, 103, 108, 115
Claiborne, Liz, 52
climate change, 124
closets, 121–22
clothing:
    custom and one-of-a-kind, 80, 192–
        93, 194, 206
    deficit myth, 127
    discarding of, 119–23, 126, 128, 130,
        132, 219, 229–30
    fabrics used in, see fabrics
    home sewn, 9, 80–81, 85–87, 187–88,
        190–200, 206
    local production of, 208, 212–15
    prices of, 1–3, 11–13, 17, 20–22, 31–
        32, 42–44, 58–61, 72–77, 80, 82, 88,
        114–16, 215–18
    quality and craftsmanship of, 81–82,
        85, 87–93, 116–18, 189–90
    quantities produced, 23–25
    recycling of, 122–23, 125, 128, 229–30
    repairing and altering, 132, 193–94,
        197, 201, 220
    secondhand, see secondhand clothing
    slow, 190, 208–10, 216, 220
    swaps, 202–3, 228
    versatile, 205
Coach, 89, 204
Cohen, Randy, 127

Consumer Reports, 75, 91
copyright laws, 105–7, 110
Cormier, Sean, 88, 89, 118
Costco effect, 99, 100
Councell, Lee, 11–16, 34, 103, 116
Council of Fashion Designers of
    America, 110
couture, 80
Couzens, Kimberly, 62–63, 76, 78–79
Cox, Stan, 125

Dalma Dress Manufacturing, 39–40,
    44, 57, 72
Darlene Knitwear, 86
de la Renta, Oscar, 72
Deluxe: How Luxury Lost Its Luster
    (Thomas), 67
department stores, 27–29, 80–81
    chain, 26, 28
    midcentury, 1, 20–23, 25–26
designer clothing, 62–79
designers, 9, 61, 89, 113–15, 204, 216, 220
    copying of, 105–11
Design Piracy Prohibition Act, 109–10
Dillard's, 215
Dior, Christian, 103, 108
DiPalma, Michael, 39–40, 42–43, 56,
    66, 72–73
Direct Sportswear Limited (DSL), 40–
    41, 148–49, 153
Disney, 181
Dockers, 22, 60
Dollar General, 2, 29
Dominican Republic, 43, 150–51, 184
    Alta Gracia factory in, 138–42, 151,
        153–59, 216
Donna Karan, 67, 141, 146
Donovan, Carrie, 30
Dress Barn, 146
Drexler, Mickey, 18
Duff, Hilary, 19
Dynotex, 57–58, 59

Echo, 40, 148
Echo Park Independent Co-op
    (E.P.I.C.), 207–12, 215, 217

Economic Policy Institute, 175
Eddie Bauer, 18
EliteGossipGirlStyle.com, 63
Ellen Tracy, 182
El Salvador, 53
End of Fashion, The: How Marketing Changed the Clothing Business Forever (Agins), 28
environment, 122–25
Environmental Protection Agency (EPA), 122, 123
Esprit, 181
Ethicist, The, 127, 129
Everlane.com, 232
Express, 18, 79

fabrics, 83–85, 89, 90, 92, 93, 212
  costs of, 42, 43
  polyester, 83–85, 123, 124, 165, 177
  see also textile manufacturing
Fair Trade International, 158
Fair Trade USA, 157–59
Family Dollar, 22
Fashion Institute of Technology (FIT), 74, 80, 84–85, 88, 103
fashion trends, 102–4, 106, 111, 209–10, 218
  coincidences in, 108
  copying of, 105–13
  prices and, 115–16
FashioningChange, 231
fast fashion, 2, 13, 17, 19, 33, 95–118, 122, 147, 166, 172, 178, 182, 191, 213
Fendi, 67, 68, 70, 78
Feral Childe, 111, 209
Filene's, 170
Finney, Kathryn, 34
Fletcher, Kate, 233–34
Forbes, 66
Ford, Tom, 67, 108, 110
Forever 21, 2, 12, 13, 15–16, 22, 29, 32, 46, 61, 69, 70, 77, 88, 93, 99–102, 104–5, 112–14, 122, 131, 162
  designs copied by, 105, 107, 108, 109, 111

Frank, T. A., 53, 148
Frugal Fashionista, 34

Galliano, John, 115
Gap, 17–19, 23, 24, 29, 30, 52, 53, 70, 79, 87–88, 91, 100–102, 106, 141, 145, 166, 167
  factories and, 146, 151
garment factories, 40, 50, 55, 138–60
  Alta Gracia, 138–42, 151, 153–59, 216
  in Bangladesh, 40–41, 43, 52, 145, 148–53, 165, 181–85, 224
  in China, 3, 6, 23, 43, 52, 74, 91, 150, 161–67, 169–71, 173–80, 213
  and consolidation of clothing industry, 144
  Fair Trade-certification of, 157–59
  full-package, 166
  import quotas and, 51–52, 54–55
  local, 208, 212–15
  in Los Angeles, 45–48, 54, 55, 56, 150, 162, 213
  move from domestic to overseas manufacturing, 41–42
  moving onshore, 213–14
  in New York City, 37–41, 44–45, 55–58, 61, 142–43, 144
  piece work in, 46–47, 48
  safety and working conditions in, 145–50, 156
  sweatshops, 44, 142, 143, 146–47, 159, 189, 215
  Triangle Shirtwaist, 44, 142–43
  unions and, 38, 44, 48, 51, 140–44, 154, 155, 163
  wages in, 42–48, 53, 56, 61, 141–44, 146, 150–53, 154, 156, 159–60
  Worker Rights Consortium and, 140–41, 142, 152, 158, 159
Garment Industry Development Corporation (GIDC), 36–38, 53, 214
Gas'd, 208
Gere, Richard, 65
Giardina, Sal, 84–85, 167, 171–72, 176
Gifford, Kathie Lee, 146

Gn, Andrew, 75
Goodwill, 119, 126, 127, 131, 132, 229
Goody's, 22
Gossip Girl, 63, 65, 79
Great American Apparel Diet, 191
Green Shows, 205
Grupo M, 141
Guess?, 15, 54, 67

HAE Now, 158
Hall, Jerry, 30
H&M, 2, 6, 11–16, 18–20, 23, 29, 32–34,
    58, 61, 69, 70, 77, 94, 96, 98–101,
    104, 106, 113, 114, 116–17, 131, 183,
    185–86, 189, 199, 202, 204, 221
  Conscious Collection of, 117, 227
  cost-cutting by, 113
  designs copied by, 107, 109, 112
  factories and, 145–46, 147, 151–52, 181
  Lagerfeld and, 70, 93
Hare, Bill, 95
Harney, Alexandra, 168
Hartman, Eviana, 114, 209
Harvard Business Review, 98, 99
Hasan, Mehedi, 152–53
Helmut Lang, 75
Hernandez, Lupe, 46–48
Hilfiger, Tommy, 18, 23, 24, 67, 91, 141,
    146
Hodge, Donnie, 155, 157, 159
Hong Kong, 41, 165

income inequality, 76–77, 79–80
Independent, The, 70, 93, 101
India, 41, 125, 180
Inditex, 145, 172
Inman Mills, 49
International Labor Rights Forum,
    151
International Ladies Garment Workers
    Union (ILGWU), 51
Internet, 15, 65, 103–4, 109, 115, 135,
    201, 213
  YouTube videos, 12, 13–15, 122
Isenberg, Alexandra, 64–65, 68, 73
It's Fashion, 92

Jacobs, Marc, 34, 62, 67, 68
Japan, 41, 51
J. Brand, 43
JCPenney, 22, 26, 52, 53, 95–96, 146,
    181
J.Crew, 18, 106, 146
jeans, 77, 114–15, 121
Jensen, Glen, 232
Jezebel.com, 107
Jimmy Choo, 76
J. McLaughlin, 57
JNBY, 172
Jonathan Logan, 22, 23, 26, 29, 98
Jones, Rhianon, 208, 211–12
Jones Apparel Group, 67, 146
Journal of Consumer Psychology, 69
*Journal of Fashion Marketing and
    Management,* 100, 147
Juicy Couture, 52

Kabir, Ashraful "Jewel," 40–41, 148–49
Kaight, 209, 210–12, 217–18
Kane, Michael, 90, 164–65, 166, 167,
    214
Karan, Donna, 67, 141, 146
Karen Kane, 90, 164–65, 166, 213, 215
Kenneth Cole, 182
Kiker, Olean, 49–51
Klein, Calvin, 17, 66, 112, 115, 141, 146,
    182
Kmart, 1, 12, 13, 26, 28, 31, 79, 131
Knights Apparel, 140, 155, 156–57
Kohl's, 2, 30
Korvettes, 26

labor unions, 38, 44, 48, 51, 140–44,
    154, 155, 163
Labour Behind the Label, 149
Lady Gaga, 207
Lagerfeld, Karl, 70, 93
Lands' End, 88–89, 185
Lane Bryant, 146
Langerova, Petra, 167
Lanvin, Jeanne, 80
Lauren, Ralph, 17, 22, 39, 40, 66, 91, 109
Lawhon, Alicia, 210

Lee, 181
Lee, Eunice, 60
Lepore, Nanette, 58, 114
Levi's, 17, 50, 54, 151, 182
Lilore, Anthony, 87
Limited, 18, 146
Lippes, Adam, 109
Lisicky, Michael, 26
Liz Claiborne, 146
localism, 208, 212–15
Lord & Taylor, 74
Los Angeles:
    Echo Park Independent Co-op in,
        207–12, 215, 217
    garment factories in, 45–48, 54, 55,
        56, 150, 162, 213
Louis Vuitton, 62, 68, 79
LVMH, 67

Ma, Jack, 163
Macy's, 6, 13, 22, 26, 28–29, 108, 213
Mademoiselle, 23
Mad Men, 45, 86
Maggie's Organics, 158
Maier, Tomas, 72, 94
Mango, 96, 100, 107
Manufacture New York, 228

Marie Claire, 34
malls, 26
Marc Jacobs, 34, 62, 67, 68
Matheiken, Sheena, 191
Matrushka Construction, 220
May Department Stores Company, 146
McCardell, Claire, 74
McGregor, Kate, 209, 210–12, 216, 218
McQueen, Alexander, 115
Melissa, 210
Menkes, Suzy, 115
Metchek, Ilse, 17, 19, 26, 27, 45, 47, 54,
    55, 213
Mexico, 54
Mexx, 52
*Michelle Obama: First Lady of Fashion
    and Style* (Swimmer), 19–20
Mid-West Textile, 128, 136

Miller, Nicole, 97, 110
Missoni, 6, 34, 70–71
    Target and, 69–71
Miu Miu, 62, 63
Mizrahi, Isaac, 24, 28, 33, 70
Modavanti, 231
Momolu, Korto, 158
Momsen, Taylor, 63
Montgomery Ward, 21
Mossimo, 22
Muhlke, Christine, 110
Multi Fibre Arrangement (MFA), 51–
    52, 54–55

Natsun, 167
Nautica, 91
New Look, 182
Newsweek, 93, 96
New York, 65, 116
New York City, 38
    Fashion Week in, 38, 65, 205
    Garment Center in, 36–41, 45, 56–58,
        87, 214
    garment factories in, 37–41, 44–45,
        55–58, 61, 142–43, 144
New York Sportswear Exchange, 41
The New York Times, 27, 30, 32, 33, 55,
    56, 74, 97, 110, 115, 127, 128–29
Ng, Alan, 57–59
Nicole Miller, 97, 110
Nike, 23, 40, 53, 100
    factories and, 146–48, 153, 154, 159–
        60, 181
Noneza, Michael "Maui," 120, 121, 126,
    137
Nordstrom, 146
North American Free Trade Agreement
    (NAFTA), 54

Obama, Michelle, 19–20
Observer, The, 107
Odlum, Hortense, 93
Old Navy, 2, 18, 23, 30–31, 33, 52, 90,
    92–93, 131, 141, 146, 221
Ortega, Amancio, 97
Owens, Jillian, 199–200, 201, 206

Paben, John, 128, 131, 133, 135–36
Pakistan, 41
Park, C. W., 69, 72, 76, 77–78, 100, 117
Parker, Sarah Jessica, 33, 64, 94
pattern makers, 38, 43, 58
Perhac, Joyce, 193
Perkins, Francis, 143
Phillips-Van Heusen, 146
Polo Ralph Lauren, 67, 146
polyester, 83–85, 123, 124, 165, 177
Posen, Zac, 110
Prada, 68, 106
　　Miu Miu, 62, 63
Prairie Underground, 209
Project Runway, 65, 113, 158

Quan, Katie, 48, 55, 143–44
Quant, Mary, 86
Queen Bee Creations, 227

Ralph Lauren, 17, 22, 39, 40, 66, 91, 109
　　Polo, 67, 146
Raustiala, Kal, 110
Recessionista, The, 34
Reclaimed in L.A., 210
recycling:
　　of clothing, 122–23, 125, 128
　　of textiles, 128–31, 133, 135–37, 212
Reebok, 154
Refashion Co-Op, 201
refashioning, 134, 200–202, 206
ReFashionista, 200
Reference, 46
Reid, Sally, 44, 149–50, 165
Reilly, Joan, 75
repair:
　　of clothing, 132, 193–94, 197, 201, 220
　　of shoes, 132–33, 218–19
Rice, Paul, 159
Richford, Rhonda, 31
Riley, Robert, 74–75
Rinaldi, Don, 132–33
Roark Collective, 211
Rock & Republic, 66
Ross, Robert, 144
Rucci, Ralph, 71–72, 75

Rudes, Jeff, 43
Rue 21, 2
Rykiel, Sonia, 68, 73

Saipan, 146
Salvation Army, 10, 119–20, 126–27,
　　130, 136–37, 229
Sanchez, Julio Cesar, 138–39, 140
Sarazcloset.com, 202
Save the Garment Center, 87, 214
Scafidi, Susan, 105–9, 111, 112
Schenkenberg, Marcus, 30
Schrader, Abe, 39, 66, 85
Schullström, Ingrid, 145
Schultz, Lisa, 18
Schwartz, David, 98
Scott, Tristan, 207–12, 215, 217
Ship 'n Shore, 87
shopping malls, 26
ShopSmart, 121
seamstresses and tailors, 9, 10, 42, 58,
　　80–81, 87, 194
Searching for Style, 65
Sears, 21, 53, 81
Secondary Materials and Recycled
　　Textiles (SMART), 130
secondhand clothing, 201–2
　　exporting of, 135–36, 137
　　refashioning of, 134, 200–202, 206
　　thrift stores, 9–10, 119–21, 126–28,
　　　130–32, 136–37, 188–89, 199, 204,
　　　229
　　see also vintage clothing
*Service and Style: How Department
　　Stores Fashioned the Middle Class*
　　(Whitaker), 20, 80–81, 93
Seventeen, 23, 85–86
Sex and the City, 33, 64, 65, 76
sewing machines, 42, 138–39, 192–96
　　sergers, 82
sewing your own clothes, 9, 80–81, 85–
　　87, 187–88, 190–200, 206, 229
　　refashioning used items, 134, 200–
　　　201, 206, 229
Sheen, Charlie, 19
shoedazzle.com, 122

shoes, 122, 132
  repairing of, 132–33, 218–19
shopping hauls, 13–15, 122
Siegle, Lucy, 125, 135, 136
Simmel, Georg, 115
Single, 213
Six Items or Less, 191
slow fashion, 190, 208–10, 216, 220,
  225–28, 227, 229, 233–34
slow food, 190, 208
Sonia Rykiel, 68, 73
South China Morning Post, 173
sportswear, 45
Sprigman, Chris, 110
Starbuck, Eliza, 60–61, 73, 89–90, 191,
  203–6, 212
Starr, Malcolm, 39
Steele, Valerie, 80, 86, 103–4
Stone, Sharon, 19
Stubin, Eric, 129–31, 133
Sussman, Nadia, 55–56
Swapaholics, The, 202
sweaters, 214
Swimmer, Susan, 19–20
Syracuse University, 146–47

tailors and seamstresses, 9, 10, 42, 58,
  80–81, 87, 194
Talbots, 146
Target, 2, 6, 15, 19, 22–24, 30–34, 69, 70,
  77, 78, 91, 113, 131, 146, 213, 221
  Isaac Mizrahi and, 24, 28, 33, 70
  Missoni and, 69–71
Tech Talk, 71
textile manufacturing:
  in China, 123–24, 165
  environmental impact of, 123–25
  factories, 48–51, 123–24
  with man-made fibers, 83–85, 124–25
textile recycling, 128–31, 133, 135–37, 212
Textile World, 84
Theory, 114
Thomas, Dana, 67, 68
thrift stores, 9–10, 119–21, 126–28,
  130–32, 136–37, 188–89, 199, 204
Time, 22, 76, 98, 196

Times (London), 101
T.J. Maxx, 2, 8, 13, 30
TNS Mills, 50
Today show, the, 19
Tommy Hilfiger, 18, 23, 24, 67, 91, 141,
  146
Topshop, 100
Trans-Americas Trading Co., 129–30,
  133
Trebay, Guy, 110
Triangle Shirtwaist Factory, 44, 142–43
Trovata, 109
Tucker, 114

Ullman, Myron, 95–96
Umbro, 40, 148, 181
Uniform Project, 191
unions, 38, 44, 48, 51, 140–44, 154, 155,
  163
UNIQLO, 2, 33, 70
UNIS, 60
UNITE HERE, 48
Universal Studios, 40
Urban Outfitters, 13, 43, 60–61, 73,
  204, 205
USA Today, 202
Usigan, Ysolt, 71

Valentino, 62, 63
Van Meter, Jonathan, 17, 19
Variety, 31
Varsity, 148
Veblen goods, 77
Versace, 6
Very Sweet Life, 187–88
Very Sweet Life, 190
VF, 181
Victoria's Secret, 189
videos, YouTube, 12, 13–15, 122
Vietnam, 165, 180
vintage clothing, 133–34, 135, 201–2,
  204
  designs copied from, 112–13, 120
  refashioning of, 134, 200–202, 206
Vogue, 17, 22, 30, 31, 34, 64, 65, 114,
  171

Vogue.com, 113
von Furstenberg, Diane, 62, 110, 171

Wagner, Robert, 143
Wagner, Stacy, 158
The Wall Street Journal, 43, 92, 93, 95
Walmart, 2, 12, 13, 15, 18, 23, 24, 26–27,
     30, 31, 70, 95, 96, 100, 131, 144, 181
     factories and, 144–48, 151, 159
Walton, Sam, 95
Wanamaker's, 1
Ward, Andy, 36–38, 41, 43, 45, 52, 53,
     142, 214
Warner Brothers, 148
Washington Monthly, 53, 148
The Washington Post, 132, 185
well-spent.com, 60
What's in a Dress?, 143

Whitaker, Jan, 20, 22, 23, 80–81, 82, 93
Wintour, Anna, 64
Wolf, Erica, 58, 214
Wolf, Lesley, 168, 194
Women's Wear Daily, 77
Worker Rights Consortium (WRC),
     140–41, 142, 152, 158, 159
World Trade Organization, 54
Wrangler, 181

Yves Saint Laurent, 66, 67, 71

Zara, 2, 13, 96–101, 104, 106, 145, 172,
     181
     designs copied by, 106–7, 110–11